New Insights into Audiovisual
Translation and Media Accessibility

APPROACHES TO TRANSLATION STUDIES
Founded by James S. Holmes

Edited by   Henri Bloemen
                   Dirk Delabastita
                   Cees Koster
                   Ton Naaijkens

Volume 33

New Insights into Audiovisual Translation and Media Accessibility
Media for All 2

Edited by
Jorge Díaz Cintas
Anna Matamala
Josélia Neves

Amsterdam - New York, NY 2010

Cover image: Carlos Neves, IDEA, Leiria – Portugal

Cover design: Studio Pollmann

The paper on which this book is printed meets the requirements of "ISO 9706:1994, Information and documentation - Paper for documents - Requirements for permanence".

ISBN: 978-90-420-3180-7
E-Book ISBN: 978-90-420-3181-4
©Editions Rodopi B.V., Amsterdam – New York, NY 2010
Printed in The Netherlands

Table of contents

Acknowledgements

We would like to express our most heartfelt thanks to all those who have worked hard and diligently in the production of this book. First of all, our thanks go to the contributors for sharing their work and knowledge with us. Special thanks should be extended to our TransMedia colleagues Mary Carroll, Pilar Orero, Aline Remael and Diana Sánchez for always being supportive, encouraging and willing to peer review contributions. It is always a pleasure to work with them and our collaboration has born fruit in the organisation and running of three international conferences in Barcelona (2005), Leiria (2007) and Antwerp (2009).

This book has its origin in the second *Media for All* conference that took place in Leiria, Portugal, and was entitled *Text On Screen, Text On Air*. We are extremely grateful to the local team for organising a memorable conference, for their warm welcome and friendliness, and for creating an atmosphere that was the perfect setting for both academic and social interchange.

Our special thanks to the editorial staff at Rodopi, in particular to Esther Roth for her support in bringing this book to publication, and to the series editors of Approaches to Translation Studies Henri Bloemen, Dirk Delabastita, Cees Koster and Ton Naaijkens, who received our proposal enthusiastically. We also owe thanks to Caroline Rees and Andrés García García for helping with proofreading, revising and formatting the manuscript.

Last but not least, we are also very grateful to our friends, colleagues and families, for their support, understanding and patience. Neves and Pedro, Xavi, Núria and little Farners (who was born while the book was being prepared), and Ian have been all part of this endeavour. It is thanks to their unstinting support and human generosity that we have been able to come forward with a new work that we sincerely hope will go some way to making audiovisual translation and media accessibility better known to all.

Media for All: new developments

Jorge Díaz Cintas

Imperial College, London, UK

Anna Matamala

Universitat Autònoma de Barcelona, Spain

Josélia Neves

Instituto Politécnico de Leiria, Portugal

Gone are the days when audiovisual translation (AVT) was seen as a minor area within the broader domain of translation. It has now grown to be considered a discipline in its own right thanks to the numerous publications, conferences, courses, and research projects of recent years that have focussed on it as the main object of study.

The initial interest of professionals, who saw AVT as a source for profitable work on a global scale, soon gave way to academics' attention who found reason enough for developing training programmes and research projects in the area. In many ways, this new scholarly field has developed a character of its own probably deriving from the fact that its very foundations were built upon very strong interaction between the industry and academia. In what could be seen as a response to Wagner's appeal (in Chesterman and Wagner, 2002:133) for "a different kind of theory that we [professionals] could help to create: practice-oriented theory – a theory rooted in best practice, directed at improved practice, and attentive to practitioners throughout the profession", much has been written about 'doing' audiovisual translation, i.e. about the actual process. Volumes centred on the intricacies of the main AVT modes are reasonably common if not plentiful, with a significant number of works on dubbing (Hesse-Quack, 1969; Pommier, 1988; Ávila, 1997; Maier, 1997; Chaves García, 2000; Chaume, 2004; Paolinelli and Di Fortunato, 2005), subtitling (Ivarsson and Carroll, 1998; Díaz Cintas, 2003; Díaz Cintas and Remael, 2007; Bogucki, 2004), and subtitling for the deaf and the hard-of-hearing (de Linde and Kay, 1999; Neves, 2005; Matamala and Orero, 2009). The remaining modes have been discussed to a lesser extent in academic exchanges, but readers can still find interesting works on voiceover (Franco, 2000; Pageon, 2007; Franco *et al.*, in press), audio description (Fix, 2005; Jiménez Hurtado, 2007), and even marginal activities like fansubbing (Díaz Cintas and Muñoz Sánchez, 2006; O'Hagan, 2006).

This list is by no means exhaustive but it amply demonstrates that there is a body of practice-based theoretical work that is quickly gaining recognition, contributing to what might soon be labelled as Audiovisual Translation Studies. Numerous other writings could be added to this nucleus, creating the potential for an interdisciplinary approach to this field.

In this sense, the scope of research topics has been widened, and a steady development can be perceived in the fact that most works have departed from the pioneering technical and linguistic approaches to encompass the sociocultural dimension of AVT. There is no doubt that the ubiquitous presence of audiovisual media in our society has had a positive effect on the visibility of AVT and has attracted enormous academic interest in this form of communication. As clear evidence of the fruitful marriage between Translation Studies and Cultural Studies, today's AVT authors tend to show an increased awareness of the cultural embeddedness of translation. This awakening has led to the discussion in academic circles of a myriad of new issues connected with AVT, which are pushing the boundaries of AVT studies further away from canonical theoretical frameworks, for example some of the contributions that form part of this volume.

Traditional attitudes to our field meant that in the beginning the the bulk of analysis and research was devoted to fiction films. Thankfully, the situation has changed considerably and the breadth of our scholarly analysis has expanded to include sitcoms, animation films, cartoons, documentaries, corporate videos and commercials to name but a few. From programmes primarily targeted at adult audiences, studies have now branched out to include productions designed with other audiences in mind, children and teenagers, for instance.

Despite all these developments, it may be too soon to speak of AVT as a discipline in its own right when Translation Studies (TS) itself is still not accepted as such within the broader scholarly community. While TS is still addressed by some as a subsidiary of linguistics and comparative literature, Audiovisual Translation Studies will have to work towards making TS worthy of an independent existence. In many ways, AVT could potentially elevate the status of Translation Studies thanks to the polymorphic nature of its research object and the fact that it makes use of knowledge from diverse fields, at the same time as feeding into fields of research that are equally diverse.

Research projects in AVT draw both from fields in the social and in the so-called exact sciences. Even though linguistics continues to be the focus of most such projects, and contact with the arts and social sciences comes naturally, others are reaching out to areas as diverse as medical sciences, informatics, statistics and engineering, domains which do not normally interact with mainstream research in the arts. Furthermore, the close connection that AVT presently has with technology, with global economy and with industry at large makes it a field with endless applications and approaches and a strong candidate for testing continual change and development.

In principle, audiovisual translation is innate to humankind; people have been translating the audio/visual world which they live in from time immemorial. Every expression in art is, in its own way, a form of AVT. However, AVT can be connected to the advent of the moving image and of the talkie in particular. What might seem to be little more than a philosophical discussion, serves to justify a few of the underlying premises of AVT studies today. Focus no longer seems to be placed solely on the intricacies of linguistic transfer, but has broadened to include the other 'transferables' that Jakobson (1959) enclosed in the all encompassing 'intersemiotic translation'. His tri-partite view of translation – i.e. interlingual, intralingual and intersemiotic –, has come to be seen as a springboard for the systematic growth of the field. The verbal and/or the technical dimensions no longer seem to be the only ground on which AVT is differentiated from other translation practices; it continues to challenge research methodologies and to question existing theories. New trends in studies in AVT are now to be found in a close focus on the multi-functional, multi-layered polymorphic nature of audiovisual texts in general and in the complexities that derive both from context and reception. More and more often, studies are taking AVT outside its own parameters. Long gone are the days when it was associated exclusively with the screen. AVT is now making information and leisure available to everyone in contexts as diverse as to sports events, on public transports, green spaces, funfairs, public functions, museums, and as many places as those in which communication is to take place.

It is now clear that the "new dynamic umbrella" that Orero (2004) wrote about in her introduction to *Topics in Audiovisual Translation* is rapidly growing and re-shaping itself to cover an ever-changing reality. Just as it is true that AVT is now to be found in every conceivable context, it is equally true to say that the challenges that each new context poses share common ground with the more traditional ones and paves the way to new avenues of research. As Gambier (2003:179) puts it in regard to screen translation, the keyword in the all-encompassing domain of AVT as it stands today is that of accessibility. In many ways, AVT has basically crept both into old and new contexts to make information, knowledge and leisure available to each and everyone of us.

At present both information and entertainment are closer to the end-user than ever before and are available in multiple platforms and formats. However, there are still a few barriers to be broken before the content can be considered fully accessible. This is of course one of the crucial objectives of AVT and media accessibility.

On the one hand, language is undoubtedly a barrier. By means of various transfer modes that have been traditionally described and analysed within AVT studies (e.g. subtitling, dubbing, voiceover, interpreting, etc.), content is made accessible to those who do not understand the original language. Sensorial barriers are another hindrance, which are being overcome thanks to subtitling, audio description and sign language, just to name some of the main modalities which are at the core of media accessibility, a new research line which has been perfectly accommodated under the umbrella of AVT studies.

This innovative line of research is nowadays the focus of TransMedia, an international research group made up of academics and practitioners from different universities and companies with a common interest in audiovisual media transfer. Since 2004, the group has been concentrating on media accessibility and has organised three conferences, with a fourth one to be forthcoming in London.

Media for All I was held at the Universitat Autònoma de Barcelona in 2005 and showed the state of the art in media accessibility. Professional experience and incipient research were presented, and initiatives and training models were proposed. It became clear that media accessibility could not just be the result of voluntary work and that measures had to be taken to make audiovisual media accessible to all, as accessibility is a human right. The result of this first conference was that a book of selected papers which dealt with subtitling for the deaf and the hard-of-hearing, audio description, and sign language, sampled their use in Europe, and gathered relevant contributions by practitioners and academics (Díaz Cintas, Orero and Remael, 2007).

A conference held at the Instituto Politécnico de Leiria in Portugal in November 2007 followed. *Media for All II: Text on Air, Text on Screen* brought together professionals, scholars, practitioners and other interested parties to explore AVT in theory and practice, discuss its linguistic and cultural dimensions, and investigate the relevance of translation theory to this very specific quickly expanding translational genre. It also promoted cooperation in AVT between the business and the educational worlds, and special attention was devoted to accessibility issues.

The present book is the result of this second conference: it includes not only selected papers from the conference but also contributions by other authors who have been invited to take part in this volume in order to offer a wide overview of the current state of AVT studies. Apart from updated research on media accessibility, an extremely active field in AVT, the changing landscape in the audiovisual world has given a boost to new fascinating practices such as respeaking and has opened new markets and applications to long established transfer modes, such as dubbing in Poland.

The book has been divided into three distinctive sections pivoting around the main areas of subtitling and dubbing, media accessibility covering SDH and AD, and different didactic applications of AVT.

The first section of the book includes eight chapters on subtitling and dubbing and opens with an article written by Patrick Zabalbeascoa, entitled *Translation in constrained communication and entertainment*, in which the author puts forward several new concepts for dealing with translation in a fast-changing world which requires rethinking certain approaches to translation and to communication. The first concept is that of constrained communication, which encompasses practically all communicative situations, as opposed to a more ideal one that exploits complex combinations of messages sent in such a way as to be perceived by four or even five senses at the same time. Such an approach finds interesting common ground between constraints, regardless of whether they are due to individuals – personal limitations or disabilities – or to the communicative environment.

As mentioned before, AVT has seen one of the greatest and fastest evolutions in the field of Translation Studies over the last few years, and although most works have focussed on audiovisual materials that share a similar function – entertainment and/or instruction – the translation of audiovisual advertising texts has received hardly any scholarly attention. As argued by Adrián Fuentes Luque in his article, *Audiovisual advertising: 'Don't adapt to the text, be the text'*, these texts are very different in many ways: from the length of the message and its function (mainly persuasive) to the purpose (to sell a given product or service). In addition, they are designed in numerous, new forms, distributed in several media, like TV, cinema and the internet, and are dubbed or subtitled. Illustrating his article with concrete translation examples from commercials, he offers a thorough analysis of the main characteristics that define audiovisual advertising texts and delves into their evolution in the media in terms of format, mode, and constraints.

Due to the time and space constraints on subtitling, one of its traditional characteristics has been the omission of many linguistic and paralinguistic features that are present in the original soundtrack. One such feature that is often considered redundant, and therefore frequently not translated, is discourse particles. In *But that's like, it's not all that I am, you know. The Swedish subtitling of discourse particle* you know *in ten US films*, Jenny Mattsson focusses on the two main meanings, textual and interpersonal, of the English particle 'you know' and analyses how these functions are conveyed – or lost – in the Swedish subtitled version. The study shows evidence of a clear tendency for the textual function to be translated more often than the interpersonal one.

Jan Pedersen, in his paper *When do you go for benevolent intervention? How subtitlers determine the need for cultural mediation*, deals with the problems involved in transferring cultural references in subtitling. The importance of appraising the transculturality level (i.e. how well known a reference is in the target culture) of these references is stressed, and also how such an appraisal can be carried out. This is done in order to answer the crucial question of when it may be legitimate for a subtitler to go for benevolent intervention in order to help the viewers understand a cultural reference, and thus make sense of the text. According to the findings of the author, there are indications that benevolent intervention is not always carried out anymore, and viewers are thus sometimes left in the dark.

In *Towards a creative approach in subtitling: a case study*, Anna Foerster explores creative new trends in subtitling. She first offers an overview of conventional subtitling practices and points to the invisibility paradox in the field of subtitling. She then explores the aesthetic dimensions provided by subtitles. The English subtitles of the Russian film *Night Watch* (2004) are analysed and compared with the way conventional subtitling practice is carried out. The author discusses whether aesthetic subtitling has the potential to become a professionally recognised approach and concludes that although a more inventive approach to subtitling may be needed, traditional practices should not be forgotten altogether.

In the last article on the field of subtitling, a professional overview is offered by Kristijan Nikolić in *The subtitling profession in Croatia*. Based on personal experience, a survey amongst subtitlers and an interview with the Head of the Translation and Subtitling Department of the Croatian public television *Hrvatska Televizija*, the main goal of this contribution is to find out the kind of professional training that practising subtitlers have received and, if none, whether they would be interested in any potential form of professional training. It also aims to gauge their opinion as to whether research is important and relevant for their daily work.

The article by Irene Ranzato, entitled *Localising Cockney: translating dialect into Italian*, marks the transition to dubbing. According to this author, one of the most fertile, lively and creative objects of research today can be found in the marriage between sociolinguistics and dialectology with translation in general, and AVT in particular, thanks to the varied and exhaustive number of examples of linguistic variation at phonological, syntactical, and lexical levels offered by audiovisual texts. In the case of Italian, the translators' attitude towards linguistic variations is still markedly influenced by the strong emphasis placed during their formative years on the study of Standard English and Received Pronunciation. Examples taken from films of various genres and dubbed in different periods help the author illustrate some of the strategies which have been used to dub the Cockney variant of English into Italian. She also tries to detect the most appropriate solutions that help achieve a pleasant exotic effect without falling into any of the two potential extremes, i.e. of an incoherent localisation or banal neutralisation.

The last article in the first section of this volume is written by Agnieszka Chmiel. Screen translation in Poland has long focussed on voiceover and its market position seems to be strengthened by rather unsuccessful dubbing attempts. However, in her paper *Translating postmodern networks of cultural associations in the Polish dubbed version of Shrek*, she argues that the audience's generally negative approach to dubbed films in Poland has changed thanks to *Shrek*. After presenting a general overview of AVT in Poland and describing the polysystem of films in the country, the author analyses the main strategies applied in the dubbing of *Shrek*, a highly intertextual original work. She emphasises the fact that the dialogue exchanges and US cultural referents were domesticated when dubbed into Polish, and this is one of the reasons why they appealed to Polish viewers since jocular allusions to Polish reality and culture abounded. In the author's view, this domesticating approach seems to have changed the perception of many Polish viewers towards dubbing.

The second section of this book is made up of six chapters dealing with one of today's most thriving translation areas: media accessibility. The first three contributions focus mainly on subtitling for the deaf and the hard-of-hearing, whilst the remaining three are devoted to the practice of audio description for the blind and the partially sighted. Agnieszka Szarkowska's article, *Accessibility to the media by hearing impaired audiences in Poland: problems, paradoxes, perspectives*, examines the accessibility situation for hearing impaired viewers in Poland. After offering an overview of subtitles for the deaf and hard of hearing (SDH) and sign language interpreting (SLI) in Poland, the article explores the availability of these two AVT modes on television, DVDs and in cinemas. Although SDH has been available to the Polish public on TV since 1994, it is the author's contention that its provision is still inadequate. Similarly to other countries, SDH is also subject to debate on whether edited or verbatim subtitles are better for the hearing impaired audience. Unlike other countries, SLI available on public TV does not use Polish Sign Language, a natural means of communication among Deaf Poles, but Signed Polish, a system of signing based on the Polish oral language. This has also fuelled controversy within the Deaf community since not only is Signed Polish incomprehensible to many viewers, but it is also ideologically unacceptable. The article ends with a discussion of legal regulations on media accessibility and some suggestions for improving accessibility to AVT programmes for hearing impaired viewers.

Soledad Zárate, in *Bridging the gap between Deaf Studies and AVT for Deaf children*, also deals with subtitling for the deaf and the hard-of-hearing, concentrating on the special needs of children. Now that the main British national channels have reached a SDH target of 80% to 100% of all their programmes broadcast, the author claims that very little research has been conducted on subtitling for deaf children, and the guidelines and standards relied on, which resulted from research carried out in the early 1980s, are clearly outdated and do not take into consideration the full potential of digital technology. She takes an interdisciplinary approach in order to bridge the gap between AVT and Deaf Studies, two fields that have so far developed independently. Focussing on the reading comprehension abilities of hearing impaired children, and looking at dimensions such as syntax and vocabulary, the author proposes ways on how this knowledge can be extrapolated to improve current SDH practices.

The last contribution on the topic of SDH, *Standing on quicksand: hearing viewers' comprehension and reading patterns of respoken subtitles for the news*, is written by Pablo Romero-Fresco and deals with respeaking. Although the interest regarding live subtitles is shifting from quantity to quality, given that broadcasters such as the BBC already subtitle 100% of their programmes, hardly any research has been carried out on how viewers receive this type of subtitle. The author's aim is to cast some light on this issue by means of two empirical experiments focussing on comprehension and viewing patterns of subtitled news. The results obtained in the first experiment suggest that some of the current subtitles provided for the news in the UK prevent viewers from being able to focus on both the images and the subtitles, which results in an overall poor comprehension of the programme. In order to ascertain whether this is due to the speed of the subtitles or to other factors, a second experiment is also included. In this case, an eye-tracker has been used to record the participants' viewing patterns. The results show that the word-for-word display mode of live subtitles results in viewers spending 90% of their time looking at the subtitles and only 10% looking at the images, affecting overall comprehension.

The next three articles in the book turn to audio description for the blind and the partially sighted. The phases of audio describing a film are explained by Gala Rodríguez Posadas in *Audio description as a complex translation process: a protocol*. The film chosen is *Memoirs of a Geisha*

(2004), of which the Spanish AD was commissioned to the author of the article. Each stage is described in detail, from the first contact with the client to the recording of the final script, and the author places particular emphasis on stages in production, trying to ascertain the issue of problem-solving from a functional perspective and basing her approach on a theoretical framework inspired by Risku (1998).

In her article *The benefits of audio description for blind children*, Alicia Palomo López focusses on AD for children, with its own particular features and requirements. She presents a contrasting analysis of an empirical corpus formed by two audio descriptions, one in English and one in Spanish, of the same Disney film: *Lady and the Tramp* (1955). The study focusses on the amount of description provided, the type of language used, the tone and delivery of the narration, and the treatment of songs, music, and sound effects. The researcher also discusses to what extent official guidelines and recommendations by British and Spanish bodies are followed. She claims that visually impaired and blind children have different needs from the general public, as they are more likely to have delayed language than other children because of the gaps in their experience, and defends the view that these children can acquire and develop language skills through the use of audio described films.

Finally, Cristóbal Cabeza i Cáceres, in his article *Opera audio description at Barcelona's Liceu theatre*, starts describing AD practices in Catalonia and the UK and then moves on to propose a new method of AD implemented in Barcelona's opera house by researchers from the Universitat Autònoma de Barcelona which includes audio introductions and a comprehensive AD that does not overlap with the lyrics. With Giordano's *Andrea Chénier* as his case study, he describes the process of audio describing an opera – documentation, attending the dress rehearsals, writing the AD and live testing the AD – and summarises the main challenges found in this particular production.

The third and final section of this volume consists of four articles discussing some didactic applications of AVT. The first contribution, by Elena Zagar Galvão and Isabel Galhano Rodrigues, deals with simultaneous interpreting in *The importance of listening with one's eyes: a case study of multimodality in simultaneous interpreting*. The authors concentrate on nonverbal communication in simultaneous interpreting and address the main functions of gestures in the booth. Their main objective is to compare the relationship between nonverbal communication (especially hand gestures) and speech in speakers, trainee simultaneous interpreters and professional simultaneous interpreters using a multimedia corpus. The first part of the article explains how the multimedia corpus was collected and prepared for analysis; the second part provides a multimodal microanalysis of various short clips extracted from one of the speeches and their parallel interpretations, and the third and final part focusses on the preliminary conclusions that can be drawn at this stage of their project.

Designing an AVT module requires the development of both practical and theoretical approaches. Reflection on translation has taken place throughout the centuries, thus contributing to the shaping of a contemporary theoretical framework, and it is only natural that students should be made aware of these issues. In *Translation goes to the movies: a didactic approach*, Maria José Veiga acknowledges that it can be hard for translation teachers in general, and more particularly AVT teachers, to approach translation issues with their students from a theoretical standpoint, particularly when the technical component of AVT courses seems so appealing when compared to reading texts. She then suggests some avenues for exploring scenes in films that relate directly to the discussion of some seminal texts on translation matters. The methodological approach that she posits places emphasis on the use of films directly related to questions posed by the topic of translation: its aims, practices, limits, and so forth. The main focus is on feature films, namely *Lost in Translation* (2003), *The Interpreter* (2005) and *Babel* (2006), so as to underline their potential ground for theoretical reflection on translational dynamics, and to shed light on some methodological questions raised when approaching the complexity of (audiovisual) translation as subject matter.

From a pedagogical perspective, Conceição Bravo, in *Text on screen and text on air: a useful tool for foreign language teachers and learners*, describes an experiment carried out in Portugal to test the effect of subtitling exposure on the understanding of English, hence on the validity of AVT as a language learning tool. Two groups of Portuguese state school students aged 13-14 were chosen: whilst one was exposed to interlingual subtitles (English-audio and Portuguese-subtitles), the other one was exposed to intralingual subtitles (English-audio and English-subtitles). Besides raising learners' awareness of this learning resource, some of the issues analysed by means of tests – several weeks after the experiment and again three months after its conclusion – included the vocabulary acquired, their understanding of idiomatic expressions and phrasal verbs. The author concludes that AVT can promote autonomous language learning as a life-long process, as well as mediating linguistic, social and cultural issues between source and target communities.

The last of the contributions in this volume is by Noa Talaván and considers *Subtitling as a task and subtitles as support: Pedagogical applications*. The author analyses the role of reading subtitles and producing subtitles as functional activities and didactic tools in foreign language education. Firstly, it examines the need for the educational use of both subtitles and subtitling in the classroom. Then, it provides a sample activity that exploits both tools with the aim of improving oral comprehension skills. All in all, the didactic application of an activity based on the use of subtitles as learning support and of subtitling as the active production of subtitles by students in front of the computer, entails a series of benefits outlined by the author; namely it assists students in the development of oral comprehension skills, provides them with different types of support (visual, textual, and technological) for language development, encourages learners to face authentic input, and produces tangible output (the subtitles produced by students) that can be shared with their peers (or even on the web).

This selective compilation of 18 studies constitutes a rounded vision of the many ways in which media accessibility and audiovisual translation can be approached from an academic point of view. Not only do these contributions highlight present interests and developments in AVT, but they also offer a prospective outlook by opening up new avenues and new routes of research in audiovisual translation. It is hoped that the articles compiled here will provide food for thought and trigger reflection on the rapidly changing times and changing attitudes to translation.

Bibliography

Ávila, Alejandro (1997) *El doblaje*. Madrid: Cátedra

Bogucki, Łukasz (2004) *A Relevance Framework for Constraints on Cinema Subtitling*. Łódź: University of Łódź.

Chaves García, María José (2000) *La traducción cinematográfica: el doblaje*. Huelva: Universidad de Huelva.

Chaume, Frederic (2004) *Cine y traducción*. Madrid: Cátedra.

Chesterman, Andrew and Emma Wagner (2002) *Can Theory Help Translators? A Dialogue Between the Ivory Tower and the Wordface*. Manchester: St. Jerome.

Díaz Cintas, Jorge (2003) *Teoría y práctica de la subtitulación: inglés / español*. Barcelona: Ariel.

Díaz Cintas, Jorge and Aline Remael (2007) *Audiovisual Translation: Subtitling*. Manchester: St Jerome.

Díaz Cintas, Jorge and Pablo Muñoz Sánchez (2006) "Fansubs: audiovisual translation in an amateur environment". *The Journal of Specialised Translation* 6: 37-52.
www.jostrans.org/issue06/art_diaz_munoz.pdf

Díaz Cintas, Jorge, Pilar Orero and Aline Remael (2007) *Media for All: Subtitling for the Deaf, Audio Description and Sign Language*. Amsterdam: Rodopi.

Fix, Ulla (ed.) (2005) *Hörfilm. Bildkompensation durch Sprache*. Berlin: Erich Schmidt Verlag.

Franco, Eliana (2000) *Revoicing the Alien in Documentaries: Cultural Agency, Norms and the Translation of Audiovisual Reality*. Leuven: Katholieke Universiteit Leuven. PhD Thesis.

Franco, Eliana, Anna Matamala and Pilar Orero (In press) *Voice-over Translation: An Overview*. Bern: Peter Lang.

Gambier, Yves (2003) "Introduction. screen transadaptation: perception and reception". *The Translator* 9(2): 171-190.

Hesse-Quack, Otto (1969) *Der Übertragunsprozeß bei der Synchronisation von Filmen. Eine interkulturelle Untersuchung*. Munich and Basel: Reinhardt.

Ivarsson, Jan and Mary Carroll (1998) *Subtitling*. Simrishamn: TransEdit.

Jakobson, Roman (1959) "On linguistic aspects of translation", in Reuben Brower (ed.) *On Translation*. Cambridge: Harvard University Press, 232-9.

Jiménez Hurtado, Catalina (ed.) (2007) *Traducción y accesibilidad*. Frankfurt am Main: Peter Lang.

de Linde, Zoé and Neil Kay (1999) *The Semiotics of Subtitling*. Manchester: St. Jerome.

Maier, Wolfgang (1997) *Spielfilmsynchronisation*. Frankfurt am Main: Peter Lang.

Matamala, Anna and Pilar Orero (eds) (2010) *Listening to Subtitles. Subtitles for the Deaf and Hard of Hearing*. Bern: Peter Lang.

Neves, Josélia (2005) *Audiovisual Translation: Subtitling for the Deaf and Hard-of-Hearing*. London: Rohampton University. PhD Thesis: http://roehampton.openrepository.com/roehampton/handle/10142/12580

O'Hagan, Minako (ed.) (2006) *Special Issue on Anime, Manga and Video Games. Perspectives: Studies in Translatology* 14(4).

Orero, Pilar (ed.) (2004) *Topics in Audiovisual Translation*. Amsterdam and Philadelphia: John Benjamins.

Pageon, Daniel (2007) *The World of the Voice-over*. London: Actors World Production.

Paolinelli, Mario and Eleonora Di Fortunato (2005) *Tradurre per il doppiaggio*. Milan: Hoepli.

Pommier, Christophe (1988) *Doublage et postsynchronisation*. Paris: Editions Dujarric.

Risku, Hanna (1998) *Translatorische Kompetenz. Kognitive Grundlagen des Übersetzens als Expertentätigkeit*. Tübingen: Stauffenburg.

Section 1

Subtitling and dubbing

Translation in constrained communication and entertainment

Patrick Zabalbeascoa

Universitat Pompeu Fabra, Barcelona, Spain

Abstract
This chapter proposes several new concepts for dealing with translation in a fast-changing world which requires rethinking certain approaches to translation and to the broader dimension it belongs to, i.e. communication. The first concept is that of constrained communication, which encompasses practically all communicative situations, as opposed to a more ideal one that exploits complex combinations of messages sent in such a way as to be perceived by four or even five senses at the same time. Such an approach finds interesting common ground between constraints regardless of whether they are due to individuals, particular limitations or disabilities, or constraints of a different more environmental nature.

1. Evolution towards prehistoric communication

Today, we have enough evidence to convince everybody that we are living in an audiovisual, screen-dominated era. There are CCTV recordings in more and more places, private and public; virtual online environments with the computer screen as interface; there are interactive whiteboards in schools; writers are only really socially visible when they go on strike as script producers for Hollywood film and television; 3D television is on the way, while reading and writing are banned from TV reality shows like *Big Brother*. Certain news items, if not most, are selected not so much for their social interest (depending on how you define that, of course) as for their visual impact, or at least some visual support for the story. These are just a few examples; there are many more. But how did we get to this point? Let us rewind.

History is defined as the period that starts with the advent of writing. Prehistoric communication, then, is carried out through natural language, i.e. oral speech, and different forms of signing and miming. We can imagine the people of prehistoric times making use of strategies that are complementary to the oral mode (as proposed in the frequent binary distinction made in linguistics between oral and written modes to the exclusion of other alternatives, such as a plausible audiovisual mode); when people engaged in communication are close enough to chat, then smell and touch can easily come into play, in addition to sight, of course, and resorting to these senses can develop alternative modes to 'pure' orality (e.g. speaking on the radio, audio speech computer files, audio description of films for the blind, talking to someone who cannot be seen, in the dark for instance). Communication acts of the prehistoric period involve only a small number of people, ranging from pairs to groups who might sit around a fire for a tribal get-together; at most, speakers can spread what they have to say by roaming nomadically, preaching or telling stories. Recording and dissemination systems are limited (constrained, as we shall see below) to the use of memory, mostly, collective and individual, or semiotic renderings in such 'media' as cave walls or pottery, or other such crafts. The dependence on learning things by heart probably explains in part the popularity of rhyme and repetition, and certain figures of speech. Rituals also help in this respect. So, human communication in its 'natural' state, involves the oral verbal language of interlocutors, who are present, and because they are present they can exploit other ways of retrieving information through other signs and senses (eyesight mainly), as in the case of body language (including distance, as studied by proxemics, and touching) and certain signs made with the hands or face. Translation already existed in this period, either as oral interpreting or semiotic translation of stories and experiences in the form of cave wall paintings or visual arts and crafts.

An interesting (and important) complement to communication is entertainment, as an aspect of the human need for pleasure. Stage productions, theatrical and ritualistic events, do not only have a communicative function, but are also a part of entertainment, they help to pass the time and they are a source of enjoyment, just as literature, art forms in general, cuisine, perfume, the feel on our skin of certain cloths and materials of our clothes, and games (which nearly always involve some verbal and some non-verbal components). So, communication can be a component of entertainment just as some forms of entertainment and pleasure may include communication components through either verbal or nonverbal sign systems, or both. The important point to be made here is that full effective communication may or may not involve all the senses, whereas I would say that fully comprehensive entertainment may aspire to satisfy the largest number of senses possible. Thus, one can imagine sitting around a camp fire with a group of friends eating something tasty while watching a spectacle of music, dance and song or poetry, feeling a cool summer-night breeze, as well as touching in various forms, such as holding hands, and also becoming involved in the show in some way or other (interactivity). Audiovisual texts (and audiovisual translation) are basically, when not exclusively, aimed at the senses of sight and hearing, whereas audiovisual, multimodal entertainment has no interest in discarding the exploration of ways to stimulate and satisfy other senses as well, and thus, provide new forms of entertainment. Steps in this direction are touch-screen technology as interface and alternative to the keyboard, or surround sound systems for cinemas devised in the seventies to make us feel the vibrations of, for instance, earthquakes in films.

From this point of view, anything that is in the way of total communication to (or stimulation of) all of the senses is a constraint. I would say the same not only of any of the five senses, but also of human competences of perception through cognitive processes such as recognising, remembering, understanding, and reasoning. Also from this point of view, (self-construed) multimodality may involve watching an art exhibition while listening to instrumental music and the recital of a poem, and sipping a glass of wine. I say wine because, for thousands of years, wine has been an obvious alternative to water for stimulating the senses (taste, smell, sight, feel). It may be no coincidence that people like to eat and drink at cinemas and sports stadiums, and even on the couch in front of the television. However, no-one, to my knowledge, has yet proposed specific menus for watching certain films. Food for thought, though.

Constraints regarding the senses may be *internal*, due to personal difficulties in sensory perception (as in the case of the hard-of-hearing, the short-sighted, the tone deaf, or the colour-blind, etc.), just as constraints to enjoyment (or appreciation) may be due to personal intellectual shortcomings (e.g. lack of intertextual knowledge due to insufficient input of or exposure to the 'necessary' texts, lack of wits). But these constraints may also be due to *external* factors, which may be social, technological, or financial. The conclusion we can draw from this reasoning is that we may talk about constrained communication, and accessibility, without having to divide people into special needs groups. A constraint may be operative, and a valid alternative mode of communication found, regardless of whether the source of the constraint is internal (personal) or external (contextual, environmental). Thus, lessons learnt from devising special forms of communication, and greater accessibility, for certain social groups may find useful applications of their systems for a wider population, just as certain types of sensory impairment may find useful alternative applications to communication systems developed for extreme environmental conditions, including space travel, underwater exploration, or poverty (money is always a constraint). Thus, for example, subtitles, in different ways, are a useful alternative to people with and without perfect hearing.

To return to the historical account, the arrival of writing made it possible to introduce certain features in communication that had been impossible until then, namely, the invariability of the message, durability, and dissemination, among others (or, as we have just outlined above, people with certain speech or hearing impediments, for example, used to carry a notepad and pencil around their necks, applying the invention of writing to their specific needs and communicative constraints). Furthermore, the written message became meaningful in itself, i.e. it meant something to put words into writing rather than merely to utter them in speech. Examples of this include written contracts, and words etched on buildings. These acts of writing might be considered a complement to the theory of speech acts. Too often we forget that a message comprises not only the content of what it says but that the choice of medium and mode of expression is also meaningful. Poetry, for example, in some ways, shifted from being an oral, musical-rhetorical art to a visual art form from the moment layout on the page became an essential part of certain verse forms, and other graphic or graphemic features, such as acrostics. Writing, as an invention evolved and developed over many centuries according to the progress of the technology involved in producing new and better writing, recording, formatting, publishing, and communication systems. Thinking about translation did not take off until this period of written communication (i.e. History), especially as writing gained prestige over oral and natural communication. So much so, that translation equates to the written translation of written texts.

The presence, prestige and excellence of writing cannot do away with people's yearning for 'natural' communication and for a fuller experience of the senses in communication (and entertainment), and writing hardly satisfies any of the senses, other than evocatively, by connotation, or through suggestion and imagination, i.e. the mind's eye, which is never to be disdained. Although writing is visual, it is not a pleasant visual experience (our eyes were made for hunting and other such 'natural' prehistoric activities, whereas reading strains the eyes, especially in constrained environments such as poorly lit rooms, small print, bad handwriting, etc.). The pleasure of reading words is in its intellectual dimension, not sensorial, unless there is a strong presence of paralinguistic and nonverbal features, including calligraphy, and layout, colours, illustrations, etc. The senses appreciate the feeling, smell and look of the paper, or leather binding; just as some people have also seen fit to perfume their writing-paper.

Audiovisual technology heralds yet another period, beginning with photography and film, the gramophone, radio and the telegraph. Cinematography owes some of its roots to traditional visual and performing arts, music and oratory. It is most probably also propelled by this need to communicate, entertain (and teach and carry out research) through the senses as well as in a purely intellectual verbal manner. Reading the printed word, or manuscript, is very demanding in terms of concentration and literacy skills; and rewarding, in terms of the intellectual gain and stimulation of the imagination. But the written verbal message communicates nothing to the senses directly, although indirectly it is capable of appealing to all the senses through memory, association and suggestion, demonstrating that the senses are ultimately dependent on the brain just as reading and writing are, and that is where they all meet up, in the mind's eye, so to speak.

Audiovisual technology displays most of the features that justified the existence of writing, as stated above: durability, invariability, dissemination, etc., and it introduces a more direct appeal to the senses, visually and acoustically (the nonverbal elements of photography, moving pictures and music). Cinematography communicates with two of our senses, but that does not mean that attempts have not been made to introduce features such as smells and vibrations in the theatre. From the point of view of translation theory, film translation has been ignored, when not actually derided or excluded, even when it had been around for seventy, eighty, ninety years and more. Only in the past decade or two has it been taken seriously, although it has mostly been regarded as constrained translation, i.e. a lesser, non-canonical, non-prototypical form of translation. It is one thing to pay limited attention to it but another very different matter to allow it to challenge long-standing tenets regarding translation practice and theory. The important aspect of film-making is that it produces the illusion of 'natural' oral communication (along with other illusions, such as 'being' in a different time and place), and the point I wish to make is that this is so because there is a yearning for technological advances that will take us back to 'natural' communication, or some kind of ideal communication (and entertainment) in touch with the senses, or otherwise lends itself better to certain senses when a particular sense is not readily available due to either internal (personal) or external (technical or social) reasons, or a combination of both internal and external reasons. From this point of view, it is not the translation that becomes constrained in the first instance, but communication, since unconstrained communication, as defined here, is either impossible or very difficult to imagine.

Beyond audiovisual technology, or as part of its progress, opening a new historical period in this brief account of centuries of human, social and technological communication, computer science aspires to simulate reality in practically every aspect, the goal being to stimulate all our senses (or our brain, which is where we gain awareness of our senses) and to create the illusion of 'living' in a virtual reality (i.e. to trick our brain into processing certain stimuli as first-hand experience through holograms or some other technology). We all know that inside a cinema the speakers are not necessarily located right behind the screen, yet our brain provides us with the illusion that the sounds are coming from the lips of the characters on screen (or off-screen but in any case within the audiovisual text), through analogy to previous experience, just as the suspension of disbelief allows us to forget that there is even a screen to enable us to believe that we are temporarily at a different place and time, sometimes even within a different dimension. Examples of this abound, of course, from Second Life to virtual reality motor racing or medical education simulators, not to mention cutting-edge wireless videogames, operated by pushing buttons, joysticks, or even body movement. We are now moving beyond mere two-dimensional screens towards tactile interactive and 3D, or 360° screens, or helmets and gloves that provide a spectacular substitute to a screen. On the other hand, work is also being carried out to produce computer screens that have paper-like qualities to reduce stress when reading e-books.

The popularity of the term localization (for a certain type of translation) is symptomatic of a resistance to acknowledge the broader nature of translation, i.e. of a restricted view of what translation is all about. Fully interactive virtual and simulated realities may cancel out practically all the constraints of more traditional communication systems, except, of course, the element of 'primitive' naturalness. The result is *displaced* communication that creates the illusion of not being displaced but 'live' and real. There is a huge difference between reading the written version of *The Lord of the Rings*, and witnessing, or even participating in, the adventure story in a virtual simulated environment. From the point of view of promoting literacy, some might find this sort of development a step in the wrong direction, whereas from the point of view of medical – or other professional – training, or communicating with people with various different sorts of personal disabilities or limitations, the idea that we can use technology together with greater communicative awareness (better theory) opens up all sorts of possibilities.

I think translation theory should indeed shift its main ground from asking about how to translate (written) texts to asking the question how translation fits in with the issue of effective communication according to the means at our disposal (adapting and responding to ever-changing communication constraints, improving accessibility and broadening its scope). After all, defining the limits of translation matters less than understanding how people communicate, how they seem to want to communicate, how they respond to different forms of communication, and what can be done (theoretically, technologically and otherwise) to improve communication, education, entertainment, and our understanding of art. 'Media for all' is a brilliant way of putting it in a nutshell.

2. Defective textual and communication modes as part of constrained communication

The evolution of communication devices and systems seems to show a pattern of what the underlying yearning is. If we consider telephones, intercoms to get into buildings, email, television, and how they have changed, we can see the ways in which they were regarded as defective or constrained, and how these problems were solved somehow. The telephone, for example, was constrained because you could not see your interlocutor, so videoconferencing was invented. This was similar for the intercom. Television, likewise, was constrained because it was not interactive, and because it had no colour. Colour was then introduced followed by various forms of interactivity. Firstly these were primitive, involving viewers sending in postcards, then making phone calls, and becoming ever more sophisticated through the use of computer technology and the internet. Even classroom blackboards have turned into interactive whiteboards.

The hypothesis of 'natural' and constrained communication can find further evidence in the short life of modes and media which are clearly defective and then exchanged for newer technologies, in the quest for an 'ideal' mode of communication. This can be illustrated by examples such as telegrams, Morse code, telex, fax, etc. The advantages they had were counterbalanced by the difficulty of reading or producing them, by their cost, or by not appealing enough to our senses, or because they did not imitate or reproduce 'natural' oral communication satisfactorily enough. People send short text messages over the phone because it is cheaper than a phone call, but one can imagine how popular video messages are going to be as soon as they become cheap enough, since text messages are tedious to produce.

Written communication has the advantage of durability, possession and re-readability over natural speech. It is also a highly effective means of education. The fact that it is not as lively as other forms of communication could be numbered among its defects or constraints. It is often de-contextualized, requires training in reading skills, and it does not appeal to the senses unless it is accompanied by paralinguistic and nonverbal features. It was invented when recording, disseminating and studying oral communication were impossible. It is not available to people who find it difficult or impossible to see (here, of course I am referring more to traditional book forms, rather than forms of technology that enhance accessibility). Natural oral communication can be lively and interactive, the interlocutors being present, although it is limited because it is ephemeral and can never be repeated in the way a film can be replayed. Rhyme, rhythm, and repetition were born to cope with the defects of spontaneous oral communication. The defects of cell-phone writing (text messaging) are that they are difficult to produce, and to read, but they are useful because they are cheap, and might even be recommended in (internal or external) conditions where hearing is difficult or impaired. Photography is defective because it is static; just as traditional telephone and radio are by definition constrained by having no visual component. Going to the cinema is more ephemeral than owning a recording, and less interactive than a live stage performance, but can be re-viewed as exactly the same AV text, unlike natural – unscripted – conversation. The advantage of a DVD, when compared with the cinema, for instance, is that it is a portable, durable, audiovisual, personal object. The disadvantage is that it requires a playing device, recorder, etc. and is not interactive. Internet chatting, its name and the difference between it and regular verbal messages such as email also serve to illustrate this point. Email began as a system that could only send alpha-numerical characters. It evolved to support formatting and attachments. Internet search engines have changed from searching for written text pages to pictures and eventually to include video.

Video games are audiovisual and interactive; and often simulate and even compete with real social interaction. The irony in the case of successful simulation video games is that they pose a threat to a person's 'real' social life, possibly even fostering social autism, or at least detracting from real face-to-face social and family intercourse. Users can go and sit in front of a screen and interact with other people (real or otherwise) through cyberspace. The defect, or constraint, then here is one of replacing real 'natural' communication and social intercourse, which is ironically due to the perfection of the simulation, or virtual reality. Of course, users and players who are socially inclined end up organising conferences and face-to-face meetings (even if they carry their PCs with them!).

Bookshops and libraries can no longer afford not to include audiovisual material, which begs the question as to whether or not to implement new literacy standards that would include a degree of audiovisual literacy. We need to ask the question to what extent are people 'educated' if they have not seen 'essential' filmography, and if they are incapable of 'reading' an audiovisual text, in the sense of interpreting its symbolism, connotations, its intertextual relations, and so on. And to what extent are other people to be regarded as uneducated if they do not read books but have acquired considerable knowledge and (simulated) experience through audiovisual means and virtual reality educational materials and simulations? Familiarity with vast amounts of literature and education may be gained through audio-books and, as pointed out above, the motivation or the need to resort to audio-books rather than to graphemic representation may be disregarded in internal cases such as when vision is impaired, or external, for instance when driving, or indeed somewhere in between these, such as a passenger in a car who finds it more comfortable to listen to a text than to read it. Can one call oneself an expert on Shakespeare through books alone, without having seen any stage productions or a number of film versions?

3. Constrained communication and natural ideal communication

From what has been outlined above, we can glean that writing is 'defective', constrained, communication, since it is not necessarily interactive; and audiovisual texts seem somewhat less defective because they represent some elements of natural, if not ideal, communication, and convey speech and paralinguistic and nonverbal elements that often support speech. *Unconstrained communication* might be defined as a scenario whereby all the senses are called upon and the interlocutors may also resort to an array of communication and sign systems to complement each other in view of providing a full 'picture' of the message or act of communication. This is probably the ideal scenario within multimedia systems.

I think the ingredients of *an ideal natural communication act* should include at least the following: the oral communication of a small number of interlocutors who are physically present, thus enabling the full vision of all of the participants, and a required degree of proximity. In other words, the importance of 'being there' (so that videoconferencing will probably never dispense with personal meetings entirely). If this is the basis for establishing a *prototype of human communication*, audiovisual texts come closer to it than do written texts. However, this does not yet seem to have convinced translation scholars of the need to bring audiovisual translation closer to centre stage when it comes to theoretical thinking, and to revise the idea that audiovisual translation is constrained translation, or is not really translation proper.

Constraints in communication, then, can come from various areas, namely, technology, financing, socio-cultural factors (social practices and norms, cultural heritage), general human limitations (regarding memory, attention span, sensory perception, etc.) and personal profiles ([dis]likes, [dis]abilities), and, of course, different codes systems (e.g. the language barrier). In audiovisual translation, for example, producing a DVD with dubbed versions and an array of different subtitles (according to different audience profiles) is a question of technology, money, and socio-political interest in varying degrees. For example, it would be possible to produce different versions of subtitles for different reading speeds or levels of education, or simply different types of familiarity with subtitling practices and possibilities. Obviously, the question of money and policy go hand in hand. There must be a profit (motivation, incentive) and if it is not financial then it must be social or political. From the public's point of view, they may choose to watch a dubbed version together with the subtitles although these may have been produced as mutually exclusive alternatives. Some television commercials are redundant in regard to what we can hear and what we can read, and even see, on screen. This is because the advertiser may not know exactly who is watching and with what senses; so, rather than lose part of the audience the message is sent across in various overlapping (mutually redundant) forms.

What is at stake, then, is not how we translate but how we communicate and interact with each other and, related to this question, how we communicate and interact most effectively when certain constraints are operative. What is crucial seems to be the pursuit of effective, satisfactory communication/interaction, and ease of communication/interaction according to the circumstances of each situation. Different forms and systems of constrained and defective communication can be justified by circumstance or purpose, or indeed by efficiency criteria. Let us take the example of subtitles. Subtitles tend to be related somehow to telegrams in that they are close to purely verbal messages (if we consider for a moment only what is included in the caption area). They are produced on the basis of displaying very few paralinguistic and nonverbal elements. But lately, there have been some calls for subtitles to introduce symbols (icons) as well as letters and punctuation marks (Neves, 2005; Neves and Lorenzo, 2007). Symbols like smileys, for example. A frequent feature of film is its multilingual nature, especially in recent times. To deal with these different languages, inserting a little national flag in the caption box of the subtitles might be suggested, indicating which language is being translated, if there is no other way that the audience can be made aware of this, and too often no other clue is provided. Other alternatives would (hypothetically) be to use different coloured lettering for each language, or font, or to use an abbreviation or initial to signal each language. The flag seems the clearest of them all, but the main point is that there are different options that have to be weighed up: some verbal, some paralinguistic, some nonverbal, some a hybrid of these.

If there is difficulty in hearing, for example, it may be *internal* due to a hearing problem (personal profile), or an *external* environmental factor such as noise or distance. In any case, if communication systems, such as speech, that depend on hearing, cannot be used effectively, then presumably we resort to other means of communication that involve other senses, e.g. writing, signing, and icons. The same would be the case for difficulty in seeing, either a personal (*internal*) impairment of sight (e.g. blindness) or an (*external*) environmental factor such as poor lighting, or distance. In this case, too, we would expect communication to be sought through alternative means, such as speech or audio description, acoustic signalling (hearing), or Braille (touching). If the audience is assumed to be one of mixed abilities or the constraints are unforeseeable, then there may be a greater degree of redundancy in the message (as stated above in the case of some television commercials); or different semiotic systems, means and modes of communication may be simultaneously present, just as there are multilingual texts (e.g. instruction booklets) when the addressees cannot all be expected to know the same language. If, thanks to technological progress, we now have a greater range of communication systems, and if the written mode of communication is constrained and defective in some way, it should come as no surprise that we may be witnessing a change from a writing-based society (and so too translation theory) to an audiovisual, multimodal, multi-semiotic and multilingual society. Then, hopefully, more notice will be taken of audiovisual translation, both as a research topic and as a contribution to a general theory of translation.

4. Audiovisual communication and translation

Audiovisual texts tend to be projected onto a screen (TV, PC, DVD, cinema, and handheld devices), and are *displaced* (i.e. the author or text producer is communicating by recording or transmitting through a device such as a camera, rather than communicating directly to the text user). However, audiovisual texts may include stage productions, where there is no screen, or even combinations of *displaced* screen communication with *direct* personal communication (see *displaced* versus *direct* below).

    Audiovisual communication may be interactive to a greater or lesser degree. So, too, is its semiotic nature, regarding the presence and importance of verbal (oral and written) and nonverbal items. Thus, audiovisual translation has a semiotic dimension, being semiotic rather than inter-semiotic. It does not fit in well within the idea of inter-semiotic translation, as proposed by Jakobson (1959). It is also important to remember that audiovisual is more of a multimodal parameter (textual mode) than multimedia (which involves transmitting simultaneously through different media), if we bear in mind that it can combine writing and speech along with other sign systems, and in turn it can be viewed in many different formats and be sent through many different media.

    If we can use the term *direct* to refer to communication where the interlocutors are present, as distinct from *displaced* communication, which is defined by first recording the text onto paper or film for instance, or by transmitting it through a device such as the telephone even without recording it – then we can see that oral, written, signed, mimed, and audiovisual forms of communication may be either *direct* or *displaced*. In the early days of cinematography, sound could not be recorded onto the film, so only the visual component was *displaced*, although these films were not usually viewed in silence so that the audio component was *direct*, with the presence of musicians and/or narrators, or performers in the cinema. An academic lecture may be seen as a *direct* audiovisual act of communication, with teacher and students present, as opposed to *displaced* if the teacher has recorded the lecture and the student is watching it over the internet, or a hybrid version, if the teacher is present, but uses a DVD or PC projection as part of the lecture. The same might be said of many modern stage productions that may use screens as props.

This shows that audiovisual/multimodal translation can occupy a more central position in theoretical thinking about translation since audiovisual communication seems to be more frequent and desirable than others, and is more influential among people. I would say that there are two types of audiovisual translation study. In the first, the specific nature of AVT is examined, a study which often involves applying general theories of translation to AVT, combined with descriptive and case studies. In the second, AVT is studied in order to know more about the nature of translation, and maybe even communication, involving the testing, questioning and development of general theories. Probably, most of what has been done so far in audiovisual translation studies fits in better with the first type. Holmes (1972) proposed the idea of partial studies and general theories, but there is an important difference between partial and marginal. Audiovisual and multimodal translation studies should shake off their marginal theoretical status and aspire to influence the general theory from their status as partial studies, not marginal ones. An interesting starting point would be the most obvious common ground between general translation and audiovisual translation. I would say there are six points that stand out particularly, although there may be many more: (1) team work versus translator as a loner; (2) the social impact of translation (including norm theory, media studies, etc.); (3) language variation (and the usefulness of conversation analysis, and studies in multilingualism); (4) textuality (text linguistics, communication acts); (5) verbal and nonverbal interaction (semiotics); and (6) technology as a principal player in (almost any) translation. We should ask ourselves how general translation studies benefit from AVT.

1. AVT points very clearly to the variability of factors involved in translation. I myself devised a model of general translation by combining these factors as Priorities or Restrictions, based on my studies of AVT, and the difficulties involved in accounting for certain translational phenomena by using traditional theories of translation (Zabalbeascoa, 1993, 1997).

2. AVT provides a greater awareness of the verbal / nonverbal semiotics of human (verbal) communication and interaction (Delabastita, 1989; Zabalbeascoa, 2004a).
3. We can learn how to deal with problems that are more frequently found in AVT, but which also exist in other modes of translation (e.g. language variation, multilingualism), or problems that present different characteristics (e.g. metaphor, humour, irony) (Zabalbeascoa, 1996, 2003a).
4. AVT studies help us to open up a wider range of possible target-text solutions in approaching source-text and equivalence problems from a different angle, taking us beyond traditional proposals of translation techniques (Zabalbeascoa, 2003b, 2004b, 2005a).

Polysystem (Even Zohar, 1979) and norm theory (Toury, 1981) are steps towards broadening the scope of translation studies. Importantly, they take into account the social, literary and professional dimensions of translation, but probably not enough has yet been done. Although they are not linguistically based, they mainly focus on the verbal dimension of texts. The common ground they share with AVT is their interest in film censorship, and language policies. One of the most important contributions comes from Delabastita (1989). A similar case can be found in text linguistics. Features and conditions of textuality (cohesion, coherence, intentionality, informativity, acceptability, situationality, intertextuality) do not entail the verbal dimension exclusively. None of them are solely dependent upon words for their definition or their manifestation. From the paradigm of text linguistics, nonverbal, paralinguistic, contextual, pragmatic factors may come in. The parameters of text linguistics are not restricted to verbal elements alone. Coherence, cohesion, intentionality, intertextuality, acceptability, informativity, situationality can be obtained through combinations of verbal or nonverbal elements, or a mixture of both. Just as there is *filmic language*, we can also speak of *audiovisual grammar* (syntax, morphology, textuality...) and just as there is verbal grammar, we might wish to explore the nature of AV grammar, and other semiotic grammars. The existence of such grammars implies new standards of grammatical competence (e.g. in education), new types of literacy, and the need to explore the nature of translating not only from one language to another, but also the nature of transcoding between sign systems.

      One of the most important contributions of AVT is that it reveals the limitations of most traditional dichotomies in traditional thinking about translation. We can no longer afford to think in terms of one-to-one relationships. There are multiple variables: the language is not 1 to 1, the textual mode is not 1 to 1, and the semiotic system is not 1 to 1. We need to adapt our thinking to human interaction, and textual communication, which is increasingly multicultural, multilingual, multimedia, multimodal, multisemiotic, multisensory, multipurpose, multiauthoring, affecting not only translation but linguistics, literature, education, media, special needs, sociology and so on. Table 1 (adapted from Zabalbeascoa 2005b) illustrates how the source-text and target-text relationship can no longer be seen as one-to-one: there are multiple source texts and multiple target texts. The shaded area pinpoints AV translation:

Table 1 – The ST-TT relationship is not one-to-one

Source Culture	Source texts	Target texts	Target Culture
literary tradition	ST-1 'book': basis for the script	TT-1 book-translation: basis for the script (ST 2,3,4)	tradition for literature and translation
culture of scripts and screen writing	ST-2 script pre-production	TT-2 script: adjusted and synchronized	scripts and screen writing
film traditions, conventions, styles, genres	ST-3 AV text	TT-3 translated AV text (dubbed, captioned, etc.)	film traditions, conventions, styles, genres
other references	ST-4 script postproduction	TT-4 transcription	other references
society, history	ST-5 versions / remakes	TT-5 versions / remakes	society, history

What we have seen in this brief account of the position of AVT within translation studies is a result of the development of ideas expressed in previous publications (most notably Zabalbeascoa, 2003a/b, 2004a/b, 2005a/b) to which the idea of *displaced* versus *direct* communication has been added with, in addition, *external* versus *internal* communication constraints, as well as the idea of *constrained communication* as being more relevant to the theory than that of constrained translation. For each translation, AV or otherwise, indeed for each act of communication, we need to understand the relationships between all their constituent parts (e.g. complementarity, redundancy, and separability as proposed in Zabalbeascoa 2003a and 2005b), including verbal and nonverbal elements. We also need to understand the reasons behind the choice of communication modes, and the various ways of exploiting each mode or type, real or hypothetical. There is still a long way to go before we can effectively exploit and control all the effects and possibilities involved in a whole array of different communication possibilities, both within the paradigms of accessibility and communication at large.

References

Delabastita, Dirk (1989) "Translation and mass communication: film and T.V. translation as evidence of cultural dynamics". *Babel* 35(4), 193-218.

Even-Zohar, Itamar (1979) "Polysystem theory". *Poetics Today* 1-2, 287-310.

Holmes, James (1972/1988) "The name and nature of Translation Studies". In *Translated! Papers on Literary Translation and Translation Studies.* Amsterdam: Rodopi.

Jakobson, Roman (1959) "On linguistic aspects of translation", in Reuben Brower (ed.) *On Translation.* Cambridge: Harvard University Press, 232-9.

Neves, Josélia (2005) *Audiovisual Translation: Subtitling for the Deaf and Hard-of-Hearing.* London: University of Surrey-Roehampton. PhD Thesis.
http://roehampton.openrepository.com/roehampton/handle/10142/12580

Neves, Josélia and Lourdes Lorenzo (2007) "La subtitulación para s/Sordos, panorama global prenormativo en el marco ibérico". *Trans* 12, 95-114.

Toury, Gideon (1981) "Translated literature. System, norm, performance: toward a TT-oriented approach to literary translation". *Poetics Today* 2(4), 9-27.

Zabalbeascoa, Patrick (1993) *Developing Translation Studies to Better Account for Audiovisual Texts and Other New Forms of Text Production.* Lérida: Universidad de Lérida. PhD Thesis.

Zabalbeascoa, Patrick (1996) "Translating jokes for dubbed television situation comedies". *The Translator* 2(2), 235-57.

Zabalbeascoa, Patrick (1997) "Dubbing and the nonverbal dimension of translation", in Fernando Poyatos (ed.) *Nonverbal Communication and Translation: New Perspectives and Challenges in Literature, Interpretation and the Media.* Amsterdam and Philadelphia: John Benjamins, 327-42.

Zabalbeascoa, Patrick (2003a) "Translating audiovisual screen irony", in Luis Pérez González (ed.) *Speaking in Tongues: Languages across Contexts and Users.* Valencia: Universidad de Valencia, 303-22.

Zabalbeascoa, Patrick (2003b) "From techniques to types of solutions", in Allison Beeby, Doris Ensinger and Marisa Presas (eds) *Investigating Translation.* Amsterdam and Philadelphia: John Benjamins, 117-27.

Zabalbeascoa, Patrick (2004a) "El texto audiovisual: factores semióticos y traducción", in John Sanderson (ed.) *¡Doble o Nada!* Alicante: Universidad de Alicante, 113-26.

Zabalbeascoa, Patrick (2004b) "Translating non-segmental features of textual communication", in Gyde Hansen, Kirsten Malmkjær and Daniel Gile (eds) *Claims, Changes and Challenges in Translation Studies.* Amsterdam and Philadelphia: John Benjamins, 99-111.

Zabalbeascoa, Patrick (2005a) "Humor and translation: an interdiscipline". *Humor* 18(2), 185-207.

Zabalbeascoa, Patrick (2005b) "Prototipismo textual, audiovisual y traductológico", in Raquel Merino, J.M. Santamaría and Eterio Pajares (eds) *Trasvases culturales: literatura, cine, traducción 4.* Vitoria: Universidad del País Vasco, 177-94.

Audiovisual advertising: "Don't adapt to the text, be the text"

Adrián Fuentes Luque

Universidad Pablo de Olavide, Sevilla, Spain

Abstract
Audiovisual translation has certainly seen one of the greatest and fastest evolutions in the field of Translation Studies over the last few years. Most studies have focussed on audiovisual materials that share a similar function – entertainment and/or instruction – and audiovisual advertising texts have hardly been studied to date. These texts differ in many ways, from the length of the message and its function (mainly persuasive) to the purpose (to sell a given product or service). They are also distinct in that audiences are constantly exposed to them, and most of the time viewers are forced to watch them even if they do not want to. In addidition, they are designed in numerous, new forms and distributed in several media, like TV, cinema and the internet. As audiovisual texts they are subject to many of the media constraints and yet they also have their own characteristics. In this paper, some of the main characteristics of audiovisual advertising texts and their evolution in the media in terms of format, mode, and constraints are analysed. Examples are used to illustrate some of the current translation procedures used for commercials.

1. Introduction

Audiovisual translation (AVT) has certainly witnessed one of the greatest and fastest evolutions in the field of Translation Studies over the last few years and has seen the publication of numerous studies on various aspects and modes of translation. So far, most studies have focussed on specific genres and text types – films, TV series, documentaries – but very little has been written on audiovisual advertising texts, with the exception of a few studies (de Pedro, 1996; Valdés, 2001). Major works in this field, like those published by Adab (2000), Bueno (2000), Guidère (2000, 2001) and Valdés (2004), have mainly dealt with graphic, static advertising texts.

Commercials, or spots, are short films broadcast mainly between television programmes, or during advertising breaks. Their length is not fixed and varies from country to country. Thus, TV ads can last for 10, 20, 30, 40, 60 seconds, or even more, although 20 and 30-second spots are, by and large, the most frequent option. In Spain, for instance, most television commercials normally last 20 seconds. In the UK, however, until recently, and following a unique British tradition, spots used to be 7, 14, 30, 45, and 60 seconds long. At present, most television ads in Britain last 30 seconds. In India, over 70% of television commercials last between 5 and 15 seconds, whereas China's TVBS-E usually airs 30-second commercials. In other countries, like the United States, commercials are much longer and often last over a minute.

However, not all audiovisual advertising is designed for TV. Increasingly, brands are opting for the internet not only as support back-up for their TV/cinema advertising, but also as a platform to include audiovisual advertising on their websites. The trend, however, includes extended versions with some of them being short films lasting as long as 10 minutes, as is the case of Shell's *Eureka* and *Clearing the Air* campaigns, with multilingual, dubbed and subtitled versions (Web 1), or those carefully crafted ads for Stella Artois beer (Web 2). The internet is rapidly replacing television as a mass media and, in this sense, there seems to be a trend to use TV commercials as a taster, often including a final line on the spot inviting viewers to click on the brand's website and watch the entire film.

In this paper, some of the main characteristics of audiovisual advertising texts and their evolution in the media in terms of format, mode, and constraints are analysed. Examples are used to demonstrate some of the current translation procedures for spots.

2. The presence of audiovisual advertising texts

One of the main differences between a 'normal' audiovisual text (such as a feature film or a TV series) and audiovisual advertising texts is that viewers are exposed to the latter continuously and most of the time they are forced to watch them even if they do not want to, a technique known in the industry as 'push advertising'. According to a study mentioned in the Spanish newspaper *ABC* (2006), Spain has the third highest number of viewers who watch commercials in the world, averaging about 642 TV commercials a week (about 92 ads a day and 33,384 per year), while US viewers watch 789 spots per week, and Indonesian viewers 728. In contrast, the Lebanese only watch an annual average of 102 commercials, i.e. 79% less than the global average (Publicidad y marketing en la red, 2006). In the case of Spain, the reasons for these rates are a high consumption of television productions, long advertising breaks, and the length of commercials, well below the world average, which means that viewers watch more commercials per advertising slot.

Online advertising is also on the rise, and the internet was the medium with the highest and fastest growth in 2007, with a 55.4% increase (Corral, 2008). Together with traditional online advertising, there is a dramatic transfer of dynamic – including audiovisual – advertising to other online platforms, such as Second Life community and online gaming (also known as 'advergaming'). Formats range from two-dimensional objects (billboards on a football pitch) to 3-D dynamic objects (different car models which change with every new game) or streamed media (movie trailers). Brands, marketers and advertisers have realised that social networking over the internet holds a tremendous market for advertising and potential consumption. In fact, some internet giants like Google and MySpace are entering into combat with competitors like Myface and Facebook. All this expansion of audiovisual advertising implies an increase in professional translation activities and a need for further translation research.

Interactive advertising is now available to digital television viewers in many European countries, and technology also allows for the possibility of including online interactivity so that players and internet users can also become buyers. The scope of these new technologies, such as PVR (programming video recorder), and forms of advertising is still to be determined. In this sense, a European Commission study (2002: online) argues that PVR "can be as much a constraint for advertisers (by the possible elimination of advertising) as an advantage (fine selection of the target envisaged by the campaign)".

As a result of the development of mass media and information technologies, a new phenomenon is arising: although, as discussed earlier, most advertising is 'imposed', a new trend for audiovisual advertising aficionados is developing and building a distinct market, a sort of alternative launching pad for television ads at an international level. This is similar to what happens with films or TV series. Traditionally, these have been released and then perhaps rerun years later. Today, such films and TV series are being translated, retranslated and sold by the season, as a response to the demands of new audiences. In the case of audiovisual advertising, there is certainly a new market too, a new audience for spots, appreciating and even collecting these audiovisual texts as a sort of variation to the seventh art. Thus, some TV channels (ITV in the UK, Canal+ in Spain and France, CTV in Canada) have recently included programmes devoted to analysing advertising, with a special emphasis on spots.

3. Dimensions and functions of audiovisual advertising texts

The language of television is perhaps the most complex of all mass media languages as it works simultaneously in time and space, allowing the integration of visual elements (both static and dynamic) as well as aural ones (linguistic and non-linguistic). The combination of all aural and visual elements produces a unique, distinctive reading of the advertising message, in which meanings are nuanced by combining language with tone, gestures and a myriad of other contextual elements. As a form of communication discourse defined by conventional forms and styles, advertising, and audiovisual advertising in particular, has a uniqueness derived from its capacity to combine language with music, pictures and substance or medium (Cook, 2001).

Basically, the elements of audiovisual advertising language are: image, text (graphic or verbal), music and sound effects, and special visual effects (digital postproduction). I would also include here the aural and/or visual silence element (in the form of a black or blank screen for a few seconds during the spot, for example), which plays a key role in audiovisual advertising, in terms of, for example, inviting the viewer to reflect on a particular issue. The connotative and phatic load of a pause or silence in a spot can be very powerful both in terms of reflection about a given idea, concept, situation, product, service or cause, as the audiovisual message aims at triggering a reaction in the viewer. Culturally speaking, silence can be a tricky tool in global audiovisual advertising since, like other paralinguistic devices, it is subject to different interpretations depending on the country in question. Thus, while English speakers avoid silence and emphasise simultaneous speech during conversation, using overlapping and competing for their turn to speak, in Japan silence is considered a virtue, and Japanese people tend to use longer pauses and avoid overlapping in conversation to show respect for other people (Bohn, 2004:25-6). In the event of an international advertising campaign, translational challenges could be solved by shifting from the oral to the written code, exploiting the fact that in Japanese society the cultural value of silence enhances the sense of importance of written over spoken words (Noda, 2002:36). This strategy may not be appropriate in countries with low literacy rates but similar consumption levels, such as Thailand, where TV ads tend to rely on visuals and spoken language over written text.

As far as intention is concerned, advertising texts are usually described as purely persuasive. However, not all (audiovisual) ads are devised to sell a given product or service, and even if they all share the same root function, i.e. to persuade, each of them carries a different intention: to sell a product or service, to warn or prevent (as in institutional or governmental advertising), to provide information, or to raise awareness (as in the case of NGOs). Whatever the intention, their primary goal is to trigger the desired reaction in the viewers and get them to react and respond.

4. Cr3aTVty in the translation of audiovisual advertising

Translating audiovisual advertising into other languages and cultures is a very difficult task. It is not only a question of putting a given message into a different language. The constraints of the medium will determine, among other things, the length of the written or spoken message. Languages behave differently when it comes to expressing ideas. English, for example, is much more synthetic than Spanish, which tends to use longer, more complex sentences to convey a given idea. Providing a more or less literal translation of the text and asking the dubbing actor to speak faster is just not a solution.

Translation is often considered one of the main hurdles in international advertising. In the case of printed advertising, the replacement of the visual elements is usually required since visuals are as strongly culture-bound as language. As claimed by de Mooij (2005:27): "advertising themes and concepts are based on buying motives and only adjusting the execution won't do. The motives used in advertising, the form, the communication style are all culture-bound". With this is mind, global audiovisual advertising campaigns such as those shown on international television channels could be interpreted as samples of creative brand advertising that transcend cultural borders, rather than "triumphs of cross-cultural communication" (Hackley, 2005:172).

Dubbing has always been the preferred translation mode for advertising campaigns in many European (Spain, France, Germany or Italy) and Latin American countries (Argentina, Mexico or Colombia). Nevertheless, as Jones (2000:35) confirms: "in sophisticated advertising markets [...] it is regarded by consumers as an insult if a commercial is dubbed: you must film in several languages [...] or limit yourself to voice-over". However, subtitling seems to be getting more and more popular in audiovisual advertising in countries like Spain.

It appears that BMW's campaign for its X3 SUV, launched in Spain in October 2006, has been a landmark as far as the use of subtitling in audiovisual advertising in this country is concerned. The spot consisted of an excerpt of a black and white interview with martial arts actor Bruce Lee, who utters with great emphasis the following sequence, in English, with subtitles in Spanish (Web 3):

English soundtrack	Spanish subtitles
Empty your mind.	Vacía tu mente.
Be formless. Shapeless.	Libérate de las formas.
Like water.	Como el agua.
If you put water into a bottle, it becomes the bottle.	Pon agua en una botella y serás la botella.
If you put it in a teapot, it becomes the teapot.	Ponla en una tetera y será la tetera.

Water can flow...	El agua puede fluir...
or it can crash.	...o puede golpear.
Be water, my friend.	Sé agua, amigo.

His words then fade into music, taken from the fantasy film *The Chronicles of Narnia*, and an image appears of the advertised car on an extremely long, straight road. The following voicedover slogan can be heard: *¿Te gusta conducir?* [Do you like driving?], as the ad's motto *No te adaptes a la carretera. Sé la carretera* [Do not adapt to the road. Be the road] can be read on the screen.

Although there have been some previous attempts at subtitling commercials in Spain, the BMW spot is certainly the most successful one to date, not only in terms of the popularity of the campaign, but also in the choice of the translation mode used. Longer than usual for Spanish standards, the BMW spot lasts 30 seconds, with the first two thirds concentrating on Bruce Lee's speech. Two different translation modes are used: subtitling for Bruce Lee's words (English audio, Spanish subtitles) and voiceover in Spanish for the spot's strapline.

The combined use of these two translation modes is new to Spanish audiovisual advertising, and seems to have succeeded in capturing the audience's attention. Far from rejecting the spot for its use of subtitling, the Spanish audience, more familiar with dubbing, welcomed it to such an extent that people have been imitating both the Asian actor's words and the slogan for quite some time, and the spot has become a viral. The juxtaposition of different semiotic systems – visual, textual, and iconic – and different translation modes seem to be masterfully intertwined, creating a cohesive product. In terms of both the ad's inner structure and the storyline, there does not seem to be any mismatch or incoherence between the translation mode used and the audience's expectations, as proven by its commercial success: BMW increased the sales of its X3 model by 73% (Cano, 2007). It is worth mentioning that this BMW campaign was not the result of a careful strategic plan. Rather, its success happened by chance: the campaign was launched at the end of the year, and the client had almost run out of production budget, so the advertising agency did a lot of thinking and decided to look for some canned material that they could use as a starting point. The gambit was successful.

In response to BMW's success, another car manufacturer, Mitsubishi, used the BMW spot to produce its own spin-off for the new Montero model, using a similar structure and making a clear reference to Bruce Lee's words. In this particular commercial, a substitution strategy was employed producing an example of intra-translation. The Mitsubishi 2006 ad is based on a former, very successful Mitsubishi spot from 1994 (Web 4). The same 1994 visual text is used unaltered, but the original soundtrack, which included references to some cultural events that took place in Spain at that particular time, was replaced by a new one that includes the reference to Bruce Lee's water and bottle metaphor. The slogan 'Don't be like water. Be water, my friend' has become *No te adaptes al campo. Sé de campo* [Don't adapt to the countryside. Be the countryside] (Web 5). The Spanish audience would expect to hear the 1994 soundtrack. Instead, the new dialogue makes a clear reference to the Bruce Lee spot. Thus, this substitution strategy would theoretically be set against a basic coherence pattern, so that the audience is unable to relate what they hear to what they see on screen. However, they can establish a relationship between the text in the Mitsubishi commercial and that of the BMW, since the chain of semiotic codes is purposely expanded to trigger the association with both the company's former spot and the competitor's spot. The film setting of the Mitsubishi 2006 commercial is immediately associated with Spanish rural areas and a typical Spanish farmer. He asks about a Chinese man talking on television and becoming a bottle if he drinks water, making a clear reference to the 1994 Mitsubishi Montero ad on the one hand, and to the spot with Bruce Lee on the other. This double intertext enhances the coherence between the textual components and between the text and the context, which is reinforced in the slogan of the spot *No te adaptes al campo. Sé de campo*, which is written on the screen while the ringing sounds of sheep bells can be heard.

Finally, another good example of creativity in audiovisual advertising is the Eurolingo campaign (Web 6) run by Inlingua Language Schools, which won, among others, the Gold Lion at the 2003 Cannes International Advertising Festival for Best Commercial Public Services ad. The plot of the ad is simple: what would happen if you took nine European languages and mixed them together into one that nearly everyone could understand? Here it is: Eurolingo! The spot concentrates on a text running onscreen from right to left, in which readers find themselves in a surprising Eurolingo story composed of easily recognisable words from nine different languages. Apart from being very original, the spot is in itself a unique example of a ready-made advertising copy, where translation is the motif that holds the entire concept of the spot. Although the commercial is one minute and thirteen seconds long, which greatly exceeds the usual European standards, the pace and the onscreen running text make it seem shorter. The important thing is the text, the message. As viewers read the onscreen text, they can develop an idea about the advertised product or service, but it is not until the final pack-shot that they realise that it is about learning languages and cultures. Although it includes words in several languages, the text essentially follows an English grammatical structure. This is a good example of international, translinguistic / transcultural advertising, where translation was not needed. Should it be used, for example, in an Asian-speaking market, the motif and momentum-building structure of the commercial could stay the same, and it would only require adaptation of the text to the 'local' grammatical structure, although certain ungrammatical structures might be permitted.

5. Conclusion

The translation of audiovisual advertising plays an increasingly prominent role in international advertising and intercultural communication. Different translation modes are increasingly being used in audiovisual advertising in many countries, both Western and Eastern. As has been illustrated, the growing diversity within the media results in exponential creativity, in combination with different semiotic systems and translation modes. This is also the case in Spain, where two perspectives are established: interlingual translation (subtitled or dubbed) and intralingual translation (in the form of open captions for accessibility purposes).

There is a clear need for further collaborative research in the fields of international promotion, advertising and translation. The latter plays a key role in promoting and developing advertising procedures, namely, in devising a dynamic advertising strategy in the creative stage and during the pre- and post-launch testing.

Empirical social sciences have proved to be extremely useful for advertising practitioners. Translation practice and theory have not, so far, sufficiently exploited the huge benefits of empirical studies. In this sense, translation and advertising have many features, functions and goals in common. For example, research into professional advertising has to be justified in terms of outcome or practical implications in a way that academic research does not. Academic research has, apparently, to be justified in theoretical terms. Hackley's claim (2005:212) that much academic research into advertising is entirely self-referential because it makes sense only in terms of its connection to other academic theories would seem applicable to much of the academic research into translation which is being carried out today. Drawing on literary theory, applied linguistics, critical theory, or cognitive studies, to name but a few, is an acceptable and positive criterion. In such a practical discipline as translation, and especially the translation of audiovisual texts of genres such as audiovisual advertising, research based on empirical studies (observation, professional and user/consumer practices, experience of both users and practitioners, etc.) and interdisciplinarity would surely yield extremely interesting and valuable findings.

References

ABC (2006) "España, tercer país del mundo en consumo de anuncios de televisión". *ABC*, 30 September.

Adab, Beverly (2000) "Towards a more systematic approach to the translation of advertising texts", in Allison Beeby (ed.), *Investigating Translation*. Amsterdam and Philadelphia: John Benjamins, 225-37.

Bohn, Mariko T. (2004) "Japanese classroom behavior: a micro-analysis of self-reports versus classroom observations – with implications for language teachers". *Applied Language Learning* 14(1): 1-35.

Bueno García, Antonio (2000) *Publicidad y traducción. Vertere*, Monográficos de la Revista *Hermeneus* 2. Soria: Diputación Provincial de Soria.

Cano, N. (2007) "Bruce Lee elevó un 73% las ventas del BMW X3". *El País*, 19 October.
www.elpais.com/articulo/economia/Bruce/Lee/elevo/73/ventas/BMW/X3/elpepueco/20071019elpepueco_9/Tes

Cook, Guy (2001) *The Discourse of Advertising*. London: Routledge.

Corral, David (2008) "La publicidad 'online' crece un 55,4% durante 2007". *El País*, 5 March.
www.elpais.com/articulo/internet/publicidad/online/crece/554/durante/2007/elpeputec/20080305elpepunet_4/Tes

European Commission (2002) *Study on the Development of New Advertising Techniques*:
http://ec.europa.eu/avpolicy/docs/library/studies/finalised/bird_bird/pub_rapportfinal_en.pdf

Guidère, Mathieu (2000) *Publicité et traduction*. Paris: Editions l'Harmattan.

Guidère, Mathieu (2001) "Translation practices in international advertising". *Translation Journal* 5(1).
http://accurapid.com/journal/15advert.htm

Hackley, Chris (2005) *Advertising and Promotion. Communicating Brands.* London: Sage.

Jones, John Philip (ed.) (2000) *International Advertising. Realities and Myths*. London: Sage.

de Mooij, Marieke (2005) *Global Marketing and Advertising: Understanding Cultural Paradoxes*. London: Sage.

Noda, Mari (2002) "Reading as a social activity", in Hiroshi Nada and Mari Noda (eds) *Acts of Reading: Exploring Connections in Pedagogy of Japanese*. Honolulu: University of Hawaii Press, 24-37.

de Pedro, Raquel (1996) "Beyond the words: the translation of television adverts". *Babel* 42(1) 27-45.

Publicidad y marketing en la red (2006) "La saturación publicitaria toca techo en España". 29 September. http://ifreemarketing.blog.com/1103767

Valdés, Cristina (2001) "Extranjerización y adaptación en la traducción de espots publicitarios", in Frederic Chaume and Rosa Agost (eds) *La traducción audiovisual en España*. Castellón: Universitat Jaume I, 183-92.

Valdés, Cristina (2004) *La traducción publicitaria: comunicación y cultura*. Castellón: Universitat Jaume I.

Valdés, Cristina and Adrián Fuentes Luque (2008) "Coherence in translated television commercials". *European Journal of English Studies* 12(2): 133-48.

Web 1: http://realenergy.shell.com/?lang=en&page=homeFlash

Web 2: www.stellaartois.com

Web 3: www.youtube.com/watch?v=OW-cnizLDEE

Web 4: www.losmejoresanunciosdetelevision.com/2006/11/17/%C2%BFy-franco-que-opina-de-esto

Web 5: www.youtube.com/watch?v=51QARhaQLzA

Web 6: http://youtube.com/watch?v=xtsoWEnaETQ

But That's Like, It's not All that I Am, You Know.
The Swedish subtitling of discourse particle *You Know* in ten US films

Jenny Mattsson

University of Gothenburg, Sweden

Abstract
Due to the time and space constraints on subtitling, many features in the original soundtrack of a film have to be omitted. One feature that is often considered redundant, and therefore frequently not translated, is discourse particles. These words express different functions in discourse depending on the type of context they are in. The present study investigates further the discourse particle *you know* and its Swedish translations in ten US films. Focus is on the textual and interpersonal functions of *you know* and on the different treatment of these in the subtitles. The study demonstrates a tendency for the textual function to be translated more often than the interpersonal one.

1. Introduction

The subtitling of films or TV programmes for a foreign language audience is of interest not only to translation studies but also to the study of language learning (Commission of the European Communities, 2007:12). Sweden is part of the 'bastion of subtitling' (Ivarsson and Carroll, 1998:5) which is Scandinavia. According to a study initiated by the Swedish Ministry of Culture (Kulturdepartementet, 2002:238), the language of subtitling, because of its quantity and ubiquitous character, has a significant influence on its Swedish readers, which is reason enough to investigate subtitling.

A typical characteristic of subtitling is the time and space constraints which are, of course, a prerequisite for all kinds of subtitling. A two-line TV subtitle is allowed a maximum of six seconds on the screen, and the lines can only accommodate approximately forty letters each, including the blank spaces (Ivarsson and Carroll, 1998:53 and 65). These constraints vary according to different media. DVD and cinema subtitles, for example, are usually given more space on the screen and a higher reading speed than TV subtitles. As a consequence of these constraints, the exclusion of some source text features has become a necessity in subtitling. The question is not whether or not omissions take place in subtitling, but rather which items are translated and which are not.

One feature frequently omitted in subtitling is discourse particles (DPs). This feature is elusive and difficult to define, hence the vast array of labels used in the literature referring to them. Another reason for the many names used is the different theoretical frameworks in which DPs are incorporated. A few examples of labels that have been used or are still in current use are *pragmatic particles* (Östman, 1981); *pragmatic expressions* (Erman, 1987); *discourse markers* (Schiffrin, 1987; Blakemore, 1987; Lenk, 1998); *discourse particles* (Aijmer, 2002); and *pragmatic markers* (Brinton, 1996; Andersen, 1999; Erman, 2001). For a more extensive list, see for instance Brinton (1996:29).

In the present study, the term *discourse particle* (Aijmer, 2002) is used instead of the more common *discourse marker* or *pragmatic marker* because it is frequently used in the literature on pragmatics. The term *discourse marker* is often associated with purely textual functions and features of written language (e.g. conjunctions). As understood in these pages, the label DP includes words or expressions that are more common in spoken than in written language, and which show both textual and interpersonal functions, such as *well, you know, I mean* and *like.* Most DPs have gone through the process of pragmaticalisation (Erman and Kotsinas, 1993; Watts, 2003) and have lost most of their referential meaning. Consequently, they are often stigmatised and viewed as redundant features of language. Even though DPs may not carry any meaning in themselves, they influence the proposition which they precede or follow.

The aim of this study is to explore the subtitling into Swedish of the DP *you know* in ten contemporary US films. Taking as its starting point professional advice on how best to deal with DPs in subtitling, this paper will focus on the two possible main functions of *you know* – textual and interpersonal – and on how these functions are dealt with in the translations. The number of occurrences of *you know* in the source texts (STs) and target texts (TTs) will also be discussed. I am fully aware of the constraints on subtitling as well as the difficult working conditions for subtitlers in Sweden today and it is not the aim of this paper to criticise subtitlers or subtitling in any way. The objective is to empirically observe the subtitling of one feature which is often omitted in subtitles, in order to see what type of meaning is most likely to be omitted and what effects this omission may have.

2. Material and methodology

The material consists of a corpus of the fully transcribed soundtrack and subtitles of ten US films, which was originally compiled for a study of the subtitling of DPs in general, not only *you know.* The films were selected according to a variety of internal and external criteria such as production, broadcasting, and language type. All the films in the corpus are from the USA and make use of an American English accent. To find as many DPs as possible in the film soundtracks, the American English in the films had to be contemporary and thus all the films in the corpus are set in the 1990s or at the beginning of the 21st century and all were produced between 1994 and 2001.

In order to be able to observe whether the different constraints on different media influence the subtitling of DPs, a variety of TTs were chosen. All ten films in the corpus were released for cinema and DVD as well as broadcast on the Swedish public television channel SVT and on either of the two Swedish commercial television channels, TV3 or TV4.

Because the main objective behind compiling the corpus was to focus on DPs, which usually occur in informal spoken dialogue, there was a need to include a great deal of dialogue within the corpus. To facilitate a comparison of how the different discourse types in the films influence the treatment of DPs in the originals and the translations, a division of film genres was needed. As the genre division is not the main focus of this paper, it will not be discussed in great detail, but because it is an important criterion for the choice of material it needs to be mentioned. The ten films have been classified into five genres, loosely based on the genre division made by the Internet Movie Database (IMDb, www.imdb.com). This division of genres overlaps at times and often there is not a clear-cut boundary between film genres. For example, the film *Nurse Betty* is categorised in the IMDb as a comedy/crime/drama/romance/thriller. In addition, the IMDb's classification is based mainly on the plot and the characters of the film, whereas for the genre division of this study it was felt that the type of language used in the films should also be considered. Below is a list of the ten films, presented in alphabetical order with year of production, name of director, main production company and genre:

1. *Addicted to Love* (1997, Griffin Dunne, Warner Bros) Romantic comedy.
2. *American Pie* (1999, Paul Weitz, Zide-Perry Productions) College comedy.
3. *Fargo* (1996, Joel Coen, Working Title Films) Criminal drama.
4. *Legally Blonde* (2001, Robert Luketic, Metro-Goldwyn-Mayer Inc.) College comedy.
5. *Nurse Betty* (2000, Neil LaBute, Gramercy Pictures) Criminal drama.
6. *Primary Colors* (1998, Mike Nichols, Mutual Film Company LLC) Political drama.
7. *Pulp Fiction* (1994, Quentin Tarantino, Band Apart Productions) Crime/gangster.
8. *Se7en* (1995, David Fincher, New Line Cinema Corp.) Crime/gangster.

9. *Wag the Dog* (1997, Barry Levinson, Tribeca Productions) Political drama.
10. *While You Were Sleeping* (1995, Jon Turteltaub, Hollywood Pictures) Romantic comedy.

The complete transcriptions of the ten films were examined and each instance of *you know* was identified together with its (non-)translations. The identification of *you know* was done manually so as to avoid mistaking a DP function of *you know* for its referential function (see examples 1 and 2 below for a description of the differences between these functions). ST extracts with *you know* and corresponding (non-)translations were transferred to the Filemaker Pro database software and information of interest was added to each DP entry. This information includes discourse context, position, intonation and collocations of *you know* as well as corresponding subtitle, pragmatic main function (textual or interpersonal) and sub-function (frame-marker, mitigation marker, etc.) of the DPs and their translations. The division of functions into textual and interpersonal is based on the Hallidayan (2004) modes of functions (textual, interpersonal, and ideational functions) and the studies it has influenced, in particular Brinton's (1996:36-39) classifications of DP functions and Erman and Kotsinas's (1993: 81-88) division of DPs into phrase and textual levels. For the analysis of the textual and interpersonal functions, as well as their subfunctions, a cross-theoretical approach has been taken, encompassing relevance theory (Sperber and Wilson, 1986), coherence-based theory (Schiffrin, 1987) and politeness theory (Brown and Levinson, 1987). To make a division of DP functions it was important to study certain parameters like intonation, pauses, collocations and the position of the DP. The surrounding context of *you know* was also taken into consideration, which included studying body language and the personal traits of the characters portrayed in the films.

3. Subtitling of DPs

According to Aijmer and Simon-Vandenbergen (2006:113), DPs are "one of the most elusive aspects of language". As they are pragmaticalised, they do not have a well-defined lexical meaning but they do, however, have pragmatic meaning. This pragmatic meaning does not bestow any propositional content on the DP but may influence the proposition of the surrounding discourse by indicating how this discourse should be interpreted. In Example 1 below, *you know* is a subject + verb combination with referential use, i.e. this combination has propositional meaning. *You know* cannot be removed without rendering the utterance ungrammatical and is thus not to be considered a DP. On the other hand, *you know* in Example 2 is a

DP, as it does not have propositional meaning and can be removed without making the utterance ungrammatical, although removing it may, however, change the meaning of the proposition following it:

(1) You know what Richard's favourite song is?
(2) You know, Richard's favourite song is *My Way* with Frank Sinatra.

The notorious elusiveness of most DPs as well as the difficulty of pin-pointing their proper function in the discourse are the most likely reasons for their omission in subtitles. Another possible reason for their deletion is their lack of semantic meaning, a quality which causes DPs to be perceived as redundant features of language. They are usually considered a frequent component of spoken language that does not have much significance in written format in general. Certain socio-cultural norms at play in Swedish society consider DPs to be part of a spoken language which does not generally enjoy a high status and their (over)use is considered as 'bad language' (Kotsinas, 2002; Andersson, 2004). To a large extent, these norms govern the literary translation of DPs, which, in turn, dictates the subtitling of these features (Mattsson, 2007:7). A further reason for the omission of DPs in subtitling may be the fact that subtitles cooperate with the original film dialogue and "the meaningful and stroking presence of the parallel image" (Chaume, 2004:843). When dealing with audiovisual programmes, it is often argued that the various functions fulfilled by DPs can be replaced by means of intonation and gestures, as enough information is put across through the audio and visual dimensions of a film. However, if a DP is omitted in a subtitle, the information a viewer receives from the subtitle may in fact be at variance with the information received from the images and the soundtrack. This conflict between audiovisual information and subtitle can create "a discordance [...] which may need more processing time to resolve than the cinema [or TV] audience has available to it" (Hatim and Mason, 1997:89).

Ivarsson and Carroll (1998:87) in their influential work on subtitling state, under the heading 'Ellipsis', that:

> Words whose main purpose is to keep the conversation ticking over ("well", "you know") [...] can safely be omitted. But this does not mean to say that subtitlers should ignore those little words that often make all the difference or give the lie to a person's character. There can be a world of difference between "It's ridiculous", "It's just ridiculous" and "It's ridiculous, isn't it?"

The somewhat contradictory claim that, on the one hand, DPs can safely be omitted, but on the other hand, they should not be ignored, is a much quoted excerpt in Swedish subtitling guidelines. The Swedish public channel SVT (2002) states that the reduction of a ST is a must and, although it does not offer any rules, it gives advice on how to treat English DPs in Swedish subtitling: "There is usually no problem for not translating words that only fill pauses (well, you know, etc) [...]. However, one should not take away all those little words that add nuances to the language and characterise people. There is a difference between 'Han är hemma', Han är ju hemma', 'Han är väl hemma'"(my translation).

Another set of subtitling guidelines was produced by Subtitling International in 1990 and was still being used by SDI media, among others, in 2006 (Kenneth Johansson, 2006, personal communication). On the subject of reduction from English into Swedish, these guidelines state that it is up to each translator to choose what is most important to communicate to the viewer, and provide some suggestions: "As a rule, words that fill pauses, unnecessary repetitions [etc.] can be removed. However, one should not remove little words adding nuances to the language" (my translation).

As is clear from the above two quotes from the Swedish subtitling guidelines, they both quote Ivarsson and Carroll's excerpt more or less verbatim, illustrating how influential these authors' views are on the subtitling of DPs and other features devoid of semantic meaning. There seems to be a general tendency to consider DPs as only having the function of 'fillers' which can most often be removed in the subtitles. However, DPs are more than that. The two quotes from the guidelines explicitly mention the fact that *you know* and other DPs can be more than just fillers and, hence, should not be ignored completely. The issue is to discover which words simply 'keep the conversation ticking over' as fillers and which words 'make all the difference'. A possible way of doing this is provided below.

4. Functions of DPs

Ivarsson and Carroll's (1998) dichotomy presented above concerns the words that they believe can be omitted in subtitling and the ones that should not be ignored. This division can be seen as reflecting the two main functions of DPs, i.e. the textual function and the interpersonal function (Schiffrin, 1987; Stenström, 1994; Brinton, 1996; Bazzanella and Morra, 2000; etc.). The textual function of DPs 'keeps the conversation ticking over' while the interpersonal function may 'make all the difference' as far as the plot and characterisation in a film are concerned. The separation of these two functions is not definitive and they should be viewed as two opposite poles of a continuum. The dichotomy is influenced by the three modes concerning the function of language put forward by Halliday and Matthiessen (2004): interpersonal, textual and ideational. The textual function is concerned with

DPs as textual markers, i.e. as items used by speakers to structure their texts and utterances, to make their discourse cohesive. In Example 3 below, from *Wag the Dog* (00:54:42), the speaker uses *you know* to structure his utterance, initiating a parenthetical comment in the middle of a section of reported speech. The parenthetical function is also indicated here by the character's monotonous voice:

> (3) Years ago when I first went off to Hollywood, they said to me 'it's too theatrical', you know, I was from the theatre so everything was over their heads, 'it's too theatrical'.

In contrast, the interpersonal function is concerned with the relationship between interlocutors and is used when speakers express attitudes, judgements etc., as in Example 4 from *While You Were Sleeping* (00:17:59), where the speaker uses *you know* twice to appeal to the hearer's understanding of her situation as a single and quite lonely, but tolerant, woman:

> (4) Not, you know, not that I'm complaining or anything cos I, you know, I have, I have, I have a cat, have an apartment, uhm, sole possession of the remote control.

The two main functions of DPs can be further divided into a variety of sub-functions relating to either the textual meaning or the interpersonal meaning. The textual sub-function represented by DPs in general, and *you know* in particular, may include frame-markers (Schiffrin, 1987), repair markers (Jucker, 1993) and clarification markers (Erman, 1987), while interpersonal sub-functions are often represented by politeness markers (Lakoff, 1973), appealers for solidarity (Watts, 2003) and hesitation markers (Erman, 1987). The divisions between the sub-functions are not static and they show fuzzy boundaries as do the main functions.

Examples 5 and 6 each illustrate one sub-function of the textual and the interpersonal functions, respectively. The examples also show the Swedish subtitles of these functions for cinema, DVD, SVT and TV3/TV4 in an attempt to illustrate the effect that the inclusion or exclusion of the translation of *you know* may have on viewers.

In example 5, *you know* has a clarifying textual function. Conrad Brean, a political spin-doctor, does not understand the expression 'back end' and asks Stanley Motts, a Hollywood producer. Motts gives his explanation introduced by the clarification marker *you know*: Motts' utterance could be rephrased as *Yeah, that is, percentage, points, money*. In formal written language *that is* could in turn be paraphrased into *i.e.*, which demonstrates the quite unmistakable textual function of this sub-function of *you know*.

Example (5) – *Wag the Dog* (00:20:33)

Motts: Is there gonna be a back end on this thing?
Brean: What? Back end?
Motts: Yeah, *you know*, percentage, points, money.
Brean: Yeah, count on it.

Cinema, DVD, SVT	Back Translation
Blir det några fringisar?	[Will there be any fringe benefits?
Fringisar?	Fringe benefits?]
Procent, *alltså*. Stålar.	[Percentage, *that is*. Cash.
Visst.	Sure.]

TV4	Back Translation
Blir det nåt i slutänden?	[Will there be anything in the end?
I slutänden?	In the end?]
Du vet... provision, pengar...	[*You know...* provision, money...
Ja visst.	Yes sure.]

The cinema, DVD and SVT subtitles are identical and resort to the Swedish *alltså* [that is], which acts as a clarification marker. The TV4 subtitles, on the other hand, make use of a more literal translation, *du vet* [you know], which also acts as a clarification marker. All four TTs in this example have resorted to straightforward translations of the textual function of *you know*, which represents quite a common treatment of the textual function of *you know* in the corpus, since omitting DPs with a textual function may create a non-coherent text for a viewer.

Example 6 is an illustration of the interpersonal function of *you know*, in which three instances act as an appeal from the speaker to the hearer's solidarity and understanding. *You know* with an appealing function can be paraphrased into *you know how it is* (Erman, 2001) or *please understand me/agree with me*:

Example (6) – *Se7en* (00:55:29)

Somerset: Why don't you talk to him about it? Tell him how you feel. Tracy: I can't *(1) you know*, I can't be a burden. Especially now. I'll get used to things. *(2) You know*. I think I just…I wanted to talk to someone who's lived here for a long time. I mean, upstate, *(3) you know*, it's a completely different environment.	
Cinema, DVD, TV4	**Back Translation**
Prata med honom. Berätta hur du känner dig.	[Talk to him. Tell him how you feel.]
Jag kan inte ligga honom till last. Särskilt inte nu.	[I can't be a burden. Especially not now]
Jag vänjer mig *nog...*	[I'll get used to it *probably...*]
Jag ville prata med någon som har bott här länge.	[I wanted to talk to someone who's lived here for a long time.]
Jag menar, det är så annorlunda inåt landet.	[*I mean*, it's so different upstate.]
SVT	**Back Translation**
Varför talar du inte om för honom hur du känner dig?	[Why don't you tell him how you feel?]
Jag vill inte ligga honom till last. Särskilt inte nu.	[I don't want to be a burden. Especially not now.]
Jag vänjer mig.	[I'll get used to it.]
Jag vill bara prata med nån som har bott här länge.	[I just want to talk to someone who's lived here for a long time.]
Uppåt landet är det en helt annan miljö.	[Upstate it's a completely different environment.]

Tracy is talking to Detective Somerset, a friend of her husband's. She has just moved to where she now lives with her husband but does not like the city. Through her utterance she tries to keep up appearances by saying *I'll get used to things* and *I think I just wanted to talk to someone*. By using the DP *you know* it is clear, however, that Tracy is appealing to Somerset's understanding of her situation. She wants him to see her pain without telling him directly how she feels. However, none of the three instances of *you know* is overtly translated into any of the TTs. The cinema, DVD and TV4 versions show some kind of translation for the second occurrence of *you know*, by means of the Swedish modal particle *nog*, but it is not a straightforward

translation of the ST function of *you know*. *Nog* can here best be back
translated as a hesitating 'probably' or 'surely', reinforced by the addition of
the three suspension dots, illustrating uncertainty on the part of the speaker.
The Swedish modal particle is thus not a translation of the appeal for
solidarity so much as an indication of the insecurity of the speaker.

In the third instance, the DP *Jag menar* [I mean] is used in the cinema,
DVD and TV4 subtitles. This is a clear direct translation of *I mean*, perhaps
making up for the loss of translations of *you know* throughout the example.
The SVT subtitles, on the other hand, do not translate any of the instances of
you know. Hence, the cinema, DVD and TV4 subtitles seem to exhibit more
of the interpersonal function of *you know* than the SVT subtitles do.

Nonetheless, all the subtitles in Example 6 lose most of the
interpersonal function of *you know* in the ST. Omitting DPs with an
interpersonal function may cause confusion in the viewer when the audio and
visual information received from the film contradicts the information given in
the subtitles. More processing time on the part of the viewer may then be
needed to understand fully the seemingly contradictory message(s) provided.

5. Quantity and quality of *you know* and its translations

You know is one of the most frequently used DPs in spoken interaction. It is
also quite a frequent DP in film dialogue and, as such, the second most
common DP (after *well*) in the corpus. Table 1 below shows the number of
you know's in each film, and the number of translations in all four TTs,
together with the number of translation types in each TT (e.g. for the
American Pie cinema TT there are 5 translations, of 42 potential cases, and 3
different translation types). Examples of the most common translation type in
each subtitled film are also given. The figures of TV3 (17 translations in
total) and TV4 (15 translations in total) are combined to show the joint
number of the two commercial channels.

Table 1 – The distribution of ST *you know* and its translations

Film	ST You know	Cinema Tokens/ types	DVD Tokens/ types	SVT Tokens/ types	TV3+TV4 Tokens/ types	Most common translation type	Total number of translations
American Pie	42	5/3	5/4	8/5	8/5	alltså	26
While You Were Sleeping	36	4/4	4/4	2/2	4/4	ju	14
Wag the Dog	35	6/4	5/3	5/3	5/2	du vet	21

Primary Colors	32	2/2	3/3	3/3	3/3	ju/ni vet	11
Fargo	28	4/4	4/4	3/2	4/4	!	15
Addicted to Love	25	?	5/3	1/1	1/1	vet du	7 (+)
Nurse Betty	22	4/4	4/4	4/3	1/1	ju	13
Se7en	16	4/4	4/4	3/3	3/3	nog	14
Legally Blonde	15	2/2	3/3	1/1	3/3	men/du vet	9
Pulp Fiction	14	0	0	0	0		0
Total	265	31+	37	30	32		130 (+)

N.B.: The question mark in the cinema column for *Addicted to Love* indicates that this version has not been located and is thus not included in the total number of cinema translations.

All ten films show instances of *you know*, with a total of 265 tokens in the corpus, and all but one of the films, *Pulp Fiction*, have translations of this DP. The film with the highest frequency is *American Pie* with 42 tokens (15.8%) of the total 265 tokens, while the film with the lowest frequency is *Pulp Fiction* with 14 tokens (5.3%) of the total. *American Pie* also has the highest number of translations, whilst *Legally Blonde* has the lowest.

There is a discrepancy between the total numbers of translations in the different TT versions, although the difference is not great. The DVD translation shows the largest number of translations (37 instances), while the TV3+TV4, cinema, and SVT translations show 32, 31 and 30 instances, respectively. As previously mentioned, the variation in time and space constraints experienced by the different media may thus exert an influence on the subtitling of *you know*. The difference between the figures in Table 1 is not great, however, which may point to the fact that time and space constraints are not the only reasons for the omission of DP translations in subtitles.

6. The translation of the two main functions of *you know*

As indicated in Table 2 below, there are more tokens of *you know* in the STs exhibiting an interpersonal function (144 instances) than a textual function (121 instances). The interpersonal function of *you know*, exemplified by the appeal for solidarity in Example 6 above, is thus more common in the films than the textual function, exemplified by the clarification marker in Example 5. If, however, we consider the translations of these two functions, a different pattern emerges. On the whole, a larger number of translated instances of *you know* have a textual function (75 tokens) than an interpersonal function (55 tokens). In order to give a more accurate picture of the translations, the average number has been calculated. Table 2 thus illustrates whether the 265 occurrences of *you know* in the ST have a textual or an interpersonal function, and how many instances of *you know* with either function have been translated. The functions of the Swedish translations of *you know* are not included in the table. However, there seems to be a tendency for both textual and interpersonal occurrences of *you know* to be translated into a Swedish textual feature more often than a Swedish interpersonal feature.

Table 2 – Function of *you know* in the STs and number of translations

	STs	Number of translations in all four TTs	Average number of translations in each TT	Average % translated into each TT
Interpersonal function	144	55	13.8	9.6%
Textual function	121	75	18.8	15.5%
Total	265	130		

As can be seen in Table 2, an average of 9.6% of the instances of *you know* with an interpersonal function, and an average of 15.5% of the instances with a textual function are translated into each TT, pointing to the fact that most translated tokens of *you know* have a textual function, although the majority of the ST tokens fulfil an interpersonal function in the original film.

7. Conclusion

The main objective of this paper was to observe the subtitling in Swedish of the DP *you know* in order to discern what type of meaning is most often omitted and what effect this omission may have on the TT. Two main pragmatic functions of *you know* have been analysed, i.e. the textual and the interpersonal functions.

The study shows that the majority of the translated tokens of *you know* have a textual function, even though the majority of the ST tokens of *you know* carry an interpersonal function. A discrepancy is thus found between the subtitling of the two main functions of *you know* and the advice given by professional subtitling guidelines. What these guidelines define as 'fillers', and consider safe to omit from the subtitles, are in fact DPs with a textual function. Similarly, lexical items defined by the guidelines as adding nuances to discourse and facilitating the description of characters, and for these reasons considered important to retain in the subtitles, are in fact DPs with an interpersonal function.

Translating all the instances of *you know* or other DPs is not possible in view of the time and space constraints of subtitling, nor is it always desirable given the differences between spoken and written language. It is, however, important to bear in mind that DPs often mean more than they seem to at first glance. When subtitling, it is therefore important to be aware of whether or not the most relevant functions of DPs are in fact translated and to consider the effects that omissions of DPs may have in the final text.

References

Aijmer, Karin (2002) *English Discourse Particles. Evidence from a Corpus.* Amsterdam and Philadelphia: John Benjamins

Aijmer, Karin and Anne-Marie Simon-Vandenbergen (eds) (2006) *Pragmatic Markers in Contrast.* Amsterdam: Elsevier.

Andersen, Gisle (1999) *Pragmatic Markers and Sociolinguistic Variation: A Corpus-based Study.* Bergen: University of Bergen.

Andersson, Lars-Gunnar (2004) *Fult språk. Svordomar, dialekter och annat ont.* Stockholm: Carlssons bokförlag.

Bazzanella, Carla and Lucia Morra (2000) "Discourse markers and the indeterminacy of translation", in Ioern Korzen and Carla Marello (eds) *Argomenti per una linguistica della traduzione, On Linguistic Aspects of Translation, Notes pour une linguistique de la traduction.* Alessandria: Edizioni dell'Orso, 149-57.

Blakemore, Diane (1987) *Semantic Constraints on Relevance.* Oxford:Basil Blackwell.

Brinton, Laurel J. (1996) *Pragmatic Markers in English: Grammaticalization and Discourse Functions.* Berlin: Mouton de Gruyter.

Brown, Penelope and Stephen C. Levinson (1987) *Politeness. Some Universals in Language Use.* Cambridge: Cambridge University Press.

Chaume, Frederic (2004) "Discourse markers in audiovisual translation". *Meta* 49(4), 843-55.

Commission of the European Communities (2007) *High Level Group on Multilingualism. Final report.* Luxembourg: Office for Official Publications of the European Communities.
http://ec.europa.eu/education/policies/lang/doc/multireport_en.pdf

Erman, Britt (1987) *Pragmatic Expressions in English: A Study of You Know, You See and I Mean in Face-to-Face Conversation.* Stockholm Studies in English 69. Stockholm: Almquist and Wiksell.

Erman, Britt (2001) "Pragmatic markers revisited with a focus on *you know* in adult and adolescent talk". *Journal of Pragmatics* 33(9), 1337-59.

Erman, Britt and Ulla-Britt Kotsinas (1993) "Pragmaticalization: the case of ba' and you know", in Johan Falk *et al.* (eds) *Stockholm Studies in Modern Philology.* Stockholm: Almquist & Wiksell, 76-93.

Halliday, M.A.K. and M.I.M. Matthiessen (2004) *An Introduction to Functional Grammar.* London: Oxford University Press.

Hatim, Basil and Ian Mason (1997). *The Translator as Communicator.* London: Routledge.

Ivarsson, Jan and Mary Carroll (1998) *Subtitling.* Simrishamn: TransEdit.

Jucker, Andreas (1993) "The discourse marker *well*: a relevance-theoretical account". *Journal of Pragmatics* 19(5), 435-52.

Kotsinas, Ulla-Britt (2002) *Ungdomsspråk.* Uppsala: Hallgren och Fallgren Studieförlag AB.

Kovačič, Irena (1993) "Relevance as a factor in subtitling reductions", in Cay Dollerup and Annette Lindegaard (eds) *Teaching Translation and Interpreting* 5. Amsterdam and Philadelphia: John Benjamins, 245-51.

Kulturdepartementet [Ministry of Culture]. Slutbetänkande av Kommittén för svenska språket SOU 2002:27. 2002. *Mål i mun. Förslag till handlingsprogram för svenska språket.*
www.sprakradet.se/servlet/GetDoc?meta_id=2094

Lakoff, Robin (1973) "The logic of politeness; or minding your p's and q's". *Chicago Linguistic Society* 8, 292-305.

de Linde Zoe and Neil Kay (1999) *The Semiotics of Subtitling.* Manchester: St Jerome.

Lenk, Ute (1998) *Marking Discourse Coherence: Functions of Discourse Markers in Spoken English.* Tübingen: Gunter Narr Verlag.

Mattsson, Jenny (2007) "Linguistic variation in subtitling. The subtitling of swearwords and discourse markers on public television, commercial television and DVD", in Mary Carroll, Heidrun Gerzymisch-Arbogast and Sandra Nauert (eds) *Proceedings of the Marie Curie Euroconferences MuTra: Audiovisual Translation Scenarios.* Copenhagen 1-5 May 2006.
www.euroconferences.info/proceedings/2006_Proceedings/2006_Mattsso n_Jenny.pdf

Östman, Jan-Ola (1981) *You Know: A Discourse Functional Approach.* Amsterdam and Philadelphia: John Benjamins.

Owen, Marion (1983) *Apologies and Remedial Interchanges: A Study of Language Use in Social Interaction.* Berlin: Mouton de Gruyter.

Schiffrin, Deborah (1987) *Discourse Markers.* Cambridge: Cambridge University Press.

Sperber, Dan and Deirdre Wilson (1986). *Relevance: Communication and Cognition.* Oxford: Blackwell.

Stenström, Anna-Brita (1994) *An Introduction to Spoken Interaction.* New York: Longman.

Subtitling International (1990) *Översättarmaterial* [Translation material]. Sweden: Svensk Text AB.

SVT (2002) *Internt arbetsmaterial för SVT översättning och programtextning* [In-house material for SVT translation and programme subtitling]. Manuscript.

Watts, Richard (2003) *Politeness*. Cambridge: Cambridge University Press.

When do you go for benevolent intervention? How subtitlers determine the need for cultural mediation

Jan Pedersen

University of Stockholm, Sweden

Abstract
This paper deals with the problems involved in transferring a cultural reference in subtitling. The importance of appraising the transculturality level (i.e. how well known a reference is in the target culture) of these references is stressed, and also how such an appraisal is carried out. This is done in order to answer the crucial question of when a subtitler should go for benevolent intervention and help the viewers understand a cultural reference, and thus make sense of the text. There are indications that this is not always done anymore, and viewers are thus sometimes left in the dark.

1. Introduction

It is a well-known fact that translators not only transfer the meaning of words and sentences from one natural language to another when they translate. Equally importantly they also function as cultural mediators, helping the target language readers gain necessary insight into the source culture (SC). This raises the issue of how translators know when it is communicatively necessary to mediate cultural aspects of a text and when the target language audience can be expected to gain access to the target text without such mediation. Arguably, subtitlers in particular are faced with this question more often than other kinds of translator. This is because many audiovisual genres, particularly when it comes to subtitling for television, are very topical, and thus introduce many current cultural items, which the subtitler has to decide whether to mediate or not. A further complicating issue is the polysemiotic nature of the audiovisual texts of film and TV programmes (Gottlieb, 1997:143). Is the item in question seen in the picture and/or heard on the soundtrack? Finally, the time and space constraints of the medium limit the options that subtitlers have for mediating these items.

The cultural dimension of translation is of considerable interest to scholars like Leppihalme (1994, 1997), Katan (2004), and others. Studies have been carried out on specialised forms of translation such as subtitling (Nedergaard Larsen, 1993; Pedersen, 2007), and the whole field of localisation of new media (Pym, 2004) is arguably even more about cultural mediation than it is about translation. The common ground shared by these studies shows that cultural mediation is of great importance in translation, and many of the studies have focussed on which forms this mediation is currently taking or should take. In this paper, I would like to go one step further and explore one aspect of the process of cultural mediation that is sometimes neglected. The aspect in question is that of knowing when to go for benevolent intervention in the form of active cultural mediation and when not to do so.

2. Subtitling

When it comes to subtitling, these issues take on a multitude of new dimensions, or at least new modes. As subtitling is a form of audiovisual translation (AVT), it works within a multimodal, or polysemiotic, medium. This can be contrasted with literary translation, for instance, which is isosemiotic (Gottlieb, 2001:8), where a written source text (ST) is translated into a written target text (TT). In other words, there is only one channel of discourse, and this is recreated in a different text with more or less the same content. In audiovisual programmes, on the other hand, there is not only one, but four different channels of discourse: the verbal audio channel, i.e. the dialogue, the nonverbal audio channel, i.e. sound effects and background music etc., the nonverbal video channel, i.e. the images and the on-screen action and finally the verbal video channel, i.e. signs and captions (Gottlieb, 1997:143). All these channels interact to create the whole polysemiotic text, which means that in AVT, the term 'text' has a much wider sense than in other media. The subtitles become part of the polysemiotic text as an added channel, interacting or coexisting with the other channels in a meaningful way so that it translates the two verbal channels, ideally in synchrony with the two nonverbal channels. In this article, 'source text' refers to any text without translation, such as an untranslated film, whereas 'target text' refers to a translated text, e.g. a subtitled film.

As Gottlieb (2001:15, emphasis removed) puts it: subtitling is "prepared communication using written language acting as an additive and synchronous semiotic channel and as part of a transient and polysemiotic text". The fact that polysemiotic texts, and hence the subtitles that are part of them, are of a transient nature is particularly important when it comes to cultural mediation. The age-old debate in translation studies of whether translations should be source or target-oriented, a subject which was rekindled by Berman (1985/2000) and more prominently by Venuti (1995), is most pertinent when it comes to the translation of cultural items. No other translation feature puts the question of domestication or foreignisation – in Venuti's terminology – so much in relief. It is in this area where it must be decided if the reader should be moved towards the writer or vice versa, to use Schleiermacher's (1913/1998) metaphor.

However, due to the transient nature of subtitles, the choice is in many cases made for the subtitler by the medium. The predominant ideal of fluency in translation – so much despised by Venuti – is paramount in subtitling. It is simply just not possible to produce a 'resistant' TT (Venuti, 1995: 24), because the viewer has in most cases no opportunity of going back and rereading the text. The exception is of course in recorded subtitles, on DVDs for example, but this is not something that viewers tend to take advantage of and subtitlers should certainly not expect this of viewers. Hence, "subtitling's concern with clarity, readability and transparent references" as Díaz Cintas and Remael (2007:185) put it in their textbook on subtitling, which also echoes the age-old adage of subtitling fluency: "the best subtitle is the one the viewer reads unknowingly" (*ibid.*). This golden rule is also found in Gottlieb (2001:51) and Lindberg (1989), who consider that good subtitles are those that viewers never notice, meaning that subtitles should be 'invisible'. However, fluency does not necessarily mean domestication, as fluency and domestication are two different things. In a large study of Scandinavian subtitles, these were found to be ST-oriented, which suggests that they are not domesticated (Pedersen, 2007:251-2). The 'invisibility ideal' of subtitles does, however, mean that the TT needs to be fluent, and that entails mediating any cultural references in the ST that are incomprehensible to the TT viewer.

Another characteristic of subtitling further complicates the mediation process, namely the well-known technical constraints, i.e. limited time and space. If the common rule about an expected reading speed of 12 characters per second is followed, the subtitler only has a few more than 70 characters (including blank spaces and full stops) to recreate an utterance of five to six seconds. Normal dialogue is generally about a third (or more) faster than that. As an extreme example, the character Vicky Pollard in the sitcom *Little Britain* (2003) produced an utterance consisting (when transcribed) of 216 characters in 5 seconds, which was then subtitled using only 58 characters, a condensation of 73%. This is quite clearly exceptionally high, but a condensation rate of about a third is well attested. However, the 12 character per second rule is becoming somewhat dated, particularly on DVDs and in fansubs (where it was never established in the first place), and is being superseded by faster reading speeds. Faster reading speeds obviously give the subtitler more space to work with, but they also increase the need for fluency, as the reader is given less time to process the written message.

3. Rendering culture in subtitles

The time and space constraints of subtitling have a direct bearing on the cultural mediation process. If a cultural item is unknown to the TT audience, subtitlers have a few interventional strategies (Leppihalme, 1994:200) at their disposal for rendering it in a way that makes the message intelligible. For instance, the item can be specified, by adding more information; footnotes are of course out of the question in this medium, but the addition of bracketed information or some clarifying words is a possibility, as when 'Dorchester' became *staden Dorchester* [the city of Dorchester] in the Swedish subtitles of *Fawlty Towers* (1979). Replacing the cultural item with some other item that is better known to the TT audience is also a possibility, even if considered ethically dubious in some domains (Pedersen, 2007:261; and Example 1 below). The cultural item can also be paraphrased or in other ways generalised to make its meaning accessible to the TT audience. Most of these strategies involve making the subtitled message longer than the original, and that is why the time and space constraints of subtitling make this medium particularly challenging when it comes to cultural mediation.

Thus the subtitler has to balance the audience's need to understand the ST message, including 'accessing' cultural items, within the restrictions imposed by the constraints of the medium. This is often a frustrating task, not least for new subtitlers. Knowing when there is a need for intervention and when the cultural items can simply be transferred to the subtitles through minimum change strategies, such as retention or the use of an official equivalent, is therefore of great importance.

Deciding when to intervene in a TT in order to mediate some element of the source culture is basically a question of deciding how well-known the item is to the TT audience. This is rather a complicated issue, yet it is one that translators have to face every day, and practice shows that they have ways of answering this question, when they are faced with it. When a cultural item from the SC, for instance the brand name of a beverage or the name of a politician, appears in the ST, translators have to make an appraisal of how well-known this item is to the TT audience. If the answer is that it is well known, there is no need for any interventional strategy. Instead, it could simply be retained in the TT. However, if it is not very well-known, then interventional strategies may be required. In fact, this article focusses on this guessing of a cultural item's 'well-knownness'.

The 'well-knownness' of a cultural item is of course not a constant factor; in fact, it is not a property of the item itself, but of the relationship between the item and those that interact with it cognitively. In this particular case, when looking at cultural items in audiovisual programmes, it concerns the relationhip between the item presented (in the dialogue/image) on screen and the viewers. The question should thus be reversed so that it does not become a question of how well known an item is, but one of how many viewers know about it. It can be assumed that subtitlers work with a general notion of an average viewer and an assessment of that viewer's cultural literacy. Hirsch (1987:xiii) defines cultural literacy like this:

> To be culturally literate is to possess the basic information needed to thrive in the modern world. The breadth of that information is great, extending over the major domains of human activity from sports to science. It is by no means confined to "culture" narrowly understood as an acquaintance with the arts. Nor is it confined to one social class.

In other words, cultural literacy is the encyclopaedic knowledge that a person has acquired as being part of a culture.

One further problematic issue is the definition 'being part of a culture', as is the definition of 'culture' in fact, but that is beyond the scope of this paper, although suffice it to say that the broad definition used by Hirsch in the above quote will be used here. Culture works on many levels and people are part of different cultures depending on their interests, social class, occupation, etc. Furthermore, seen from a geographical perspective, people are part of their local, regional and national culture and, as citizens of the world, they are part of the global culture. It is this last distinction that directly concerns us here.

In today's world, with its varieties of globalisation, localisation and glocalisation, local and global cultures become ever more intertwined. Terms and issues such as 'intercultural communication' and 'intercultural competence' bear witness to this fact. The term 'intercultural' suggests a two-way communication that is not altogether relevant when it comes to audiovisual communication, as it is mainly a question of one-way communication (even if AVT in the new media is slowly changing that). Instead, the terms 'transcultural' and 'transculturality' are of more relevance here. Transculturality, in this context, refers to how cultures in the modern world "are extremely interconnected and entangled with each other" (Welsch, 1994:198). It can be used to describe how some cultural items transcend local cultures and are instead part of the global culture, which makes them not very culture-bound.

4. Describing transculturality

Leppihalme (1994:80) points out that:

> [a] message has its language component but it has many non-linguistic components as well, e.g. being linked to a time and place and requiring a

certain degree of extra-linguistic knowledge, usually intuitively accessed by ST receivers. Comprehension thus requires a close intra- and interlinguistic analysis as a prerequisite for interlingual operations.

This entails that before dealing with a cultural item, translators have to try to decide whether or not the TT audience has knowledge about it, or whether they need to intervene to help the TT audience to access the item. Leppihalme (1997) has attempted to capture this in her monograph about *Culture Bumps*. In it, she discusses, among other things, allusive names, which are most certainly cultural items of the kind that we are discussing here. She illustrates the transculturality of these names in the following figure:

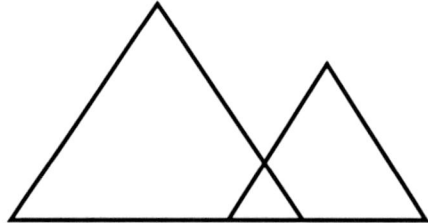

Figure 1: Overlap of allusive names in English and Finnish
(from Leppihalme, 1997:80)

The big triangle illustrates English allusive names, the smaller triangle illustrates Finnish allusive names, and the small triangle in the overlap between the two bigger ones illustrates transcultural names, i.e. names that are known in both cultures. She explains that the transcultural names would be those that are common to the Western culture, e.g. biblical names, and names known through other media like literature or film.

This model is very good for illustrating the general nature of transculturality but has some drawbacks for the translation situation, even though it was originally used to illustrate the translation of allusive names from English to Finnish. First of all, it lacks explicit directionality. The Finnish-only allusive names are of little consequence in this situation, as they would not normally be part of the Anglophone ST input. Also, the overlapping area would contain precious few elements from the Finnish side, as there is a considerable lack of reciprocity between the Finnish and English cultures. In other words, most Americans know infinitely less about Finnish culture than Finns know about American culture. Secondly, it arguably lacks one level of transculturality since it only illustrates transcultural items, and items that are known only in either of the cultures. However, it does not take into consideration that there are cultural items that are not known by all the members in the SC for whom the ST was produced. This may seem trivial, but it is of particular importance when it comes to AVT, and I will return to it momentarily, but let us first consider another illustration of transculturality in the translation situation:

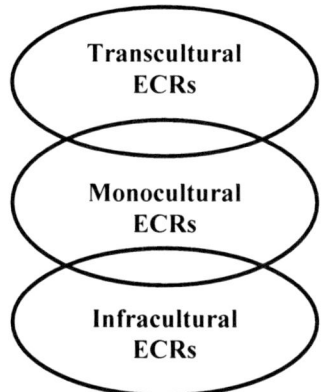

Figure 2: Levels of transculturality (from Pedersen, 2007:157)

Figure 2 is based on figure 1, but it is arguably better suited for illustrating transculturality in an AVT situation. It was developed specifically for illustrating how subtitlers deal with Extralinguistic Cultural References (ECRs) in films and TV programmes. ECRs would include Leppihalme's allusive names, but it is a term wider in scope, including everything that is cultural in the broad sense. The topmost ellipse illustrates transcultural ECRs, i.e. ECRs that are known in the SC and target culture (TC). In AVT, we can use the term 'transcultural' in a restricted sense, as the only cultures that are of importance are the SC and TC; in this situation, it is irrelevant whether the ECR would be known in other cultures as well. The second ellipse illustrates the problematic monocultural ECRs, which would be the ones only known in the SC; again, it is of no importance whether these are also known in other cultures. The bottom ellipse illustrates the more peripheral infracultural ECRs, which are not known in the TC, but which are not known by the majority of the original audience either. Examples of infracultural ECRs would include specialist gadgetry or very local geographical names. The ellipses overlap to illustrate that transculturality is a fuzzy feature; it is context-dependent and varies with time, genre and other variables.

The importance of the infracultural / monocultural distinction is that infracultural ECRs – like transcultural ECRs, but unlike monocultural ECRs for different reasons – do not normally cause translation problems, particularly not in AVT. It is rather obvious why transcultural ECRs do not cause translation problems as they are well known in both cultures and can be rendered straightforwardly in the TT. Infracultural ECRs do not cause translation problems either, because the ST producers cannot rely on their primary audience's encyclopaedic knowledge when introducing them. In other words, the referents of infracultural ECRs are not accessible to the ST audience through previous knowledge. Instead, the ST producers would normally take pains to make sure that the said referents are made accessible to their primary viewers, either through the context or the co-text. The co-text in AVT would be the rest of the dialogue and then there is the whole mesh of polysemiotic channels as context for making the infracultural ECRs accessible to the audience. Typically, the infracultural ECR would be visible on screen, or explained through the dialogue. The dialogue can then be subtitled, and the infracultural ECR would be made accessible to the TT audience; or it would already be accessible through the nonverbal visual channel (i.e. the image). Sometimes, however rarely, an infracultural ECR is left unexplained in the ST, but it could then be assumed that the ECR is peripheral to the text as a whole and the subtitler has a great deal of freedom in the treatment of it in the subtitles. Decontextualised infracultural ECRs are in fact fairly frequently omitted in subtitles for time and space reasons (Pedersen, 2007:190-4).

5. How to appraise transculturality

The preceding discussion raises the very relevant question of how a viewer of audiovisual material can access referents of cultural items. In a previous study (Pedersen, 2007:153), I argued that there are three ways for such a viewer to access such items productively:

> (i) Encyclopaedically or intertextually, i.e. through the viewer's cultural literacy of the world and other texts.
> (ii) Deictically, i.e. through deixis in the context or co-text, as explained above.
> (iii) Through benevolent intervention from the subtitler, working as a cultural mediator.

In other words, if the viewer does not know the cultural item through his/her cultural literacy (i.e. it is not transcultural), and it is not available from the dialogue or on-screen visuals (which would suggest that it is not infracultural), the subtitler would ideally intervene to help the viewer understand what the cultural item is. The implication of this is that knowing when a cultural item is monocultural is half the battle for producing culturally fluent subtitles.

The importance of successfully determining the transculturality status lies in the consequences this appraisal has for the viewers. If a transcultural item is treated as monocultural and thus explained in the subtitles, the subtitler may be accused of 'chewing the food' for the viewers or even of being condescending. This is because of the juxtaposition of ST and TT which makes subtitling such a vulnerable form of translation (Díaz Cintas and Remael, 2007:57). On the other hand, if a monocultural item is treated as being transcultural, the viewers simply do not get access to the whole message and this can cause quite some confusion (Pedersen, 2008:114; Example 2 below) as far as the viewer is concerned.

This brings us back to our original question of how subtitlers decide the transculturality status of an item and how they know when a cultural item is monocultural, and thus in need of intervention, or if it is infra- or transcultural and could thus be rendered using minimum change strategies. There are, broadly speaking, three sources for determining transculturality status.

Firstly, there is the ST, which gives information about the item's presumed transculturality status in the ST. If the cultural reference is introduced without any verbal or visual clues to its referent, the chances are that the reference is trans- or monocultural. This is based on the argument above, that infracultural references need to be explained deictically, either through the dialogue or the image, as they will be virtually unknown to the source audience. However, the ST gives no clue as to whether the reference is mono- or transcultural, as these categories are inseparable in the SC perspective. As it is possible, if not very common, for infracultural references to be introduced without their referent being present in the co-text or the context, the ST alone is not always sufficient for determining the transculturality status of a cultural reference.

Secondly, and perhaps most importantly, there is the TT audience. Subtitlers are also members of that audience (in most cases, anyway), but they cannot take their own cultural literacy as a yardstick when determining transculturality. The reason for this is simply that professional subtitlers are also cultural experts, with much more knowledge about the SC than the average viewer. This means that they cannot presume that, just because they understand a particular reference, everybody else in the TC does too. However, the fact that subtitlers are members of the TT audience means that they are likely to have a fairly good idea of what their acquaintances know about the SC. This helps the subtitler determine whether a reference is mono-

or transcultural, which is a most important distinction to make. Incidentally, this is an argument for producing subtitles locally.

Thirdly, there are TC sources that can be used for determining whether a reference is mono- or transcultural. Subtitlers can ask their acquaintances about their cultural knowledge. A more statistically accurate, but perhaps more rarely used, source of knowledge about the TC transculturality status of a SC item, are newspapers and other corpora. By searching original TL texts and finding how often the SC reference is mentioned, subtitlers can get an idea about its transculturality status. More importantly, by investigating how the SC reference is treated in the TL texts, whether it is known or unknown (i.e. whether the reference is explained in the texts or not), a very accurate picture of whether a reference is mono- or transcultural can be gleaned. Corpora are probably more used by researchers than by practitioners, as they are generally both restricted and time-consuming to use, although internet searches can easily be used in a similar way, even if the results are not quite as reliable.

6. The Scandinavian situation

When investigating a large subtitled corpus such as the Scandinavian subtitles corpus (Pedersen, 2007), it becomes apparent that subtitlers do indeed go through the process of determining the transculturality status of cultural items. This is seen mainly through the strategies they use for rendering the references in the subtitles. If the treatment of the reference in TL media is taken as a yardstick for the transculturality status, it becomes apparent that Scandinavian subtitlers in the vast majority of cases make what could be called 'accurate' transculturality decisions. This is hardly surprising, as the subtitlers who have produced the texts are professionals with a predominantly long experience as cultural mediators through their subtitling activities. Interventional strategies are indeed used on most monocultural references, and minimum change strategies are used on the infra- and transcultural ones, unless some other variables interfere, such as the constraints of the medium or the interplay between the channels of information in the text. The picture is not as simple as has been suggested here, but that need not concern us for the moment.

One example of how the interventional strategy of substitution has been used on a reference that was rightly appraised as monocultural is shown in Example 1. It is taken from a Danish TV2 2000 broadcast of the sitcom *Frasier* (1999). The main character, Dr Frasier Crane, is on the phone to his young son, Frederick, who lives with his mother in a different city. Frederick has apparently had a nightmare because Frasier is trying to calm him by saying: "Calm down, son. Listen to daddy. It's just a bad dream, I promise you..."

(Example 1)   ST: Senator Thurmond is not in your closet.
                Subtitle: Mogens Glistrup står ikke i dit skab.
                Back translation: Mogens Glistrup is not standing
                        in your closet.

In the subtitle, the very conservative Senator Strom Thurmond (1902-2003), who was, at the time, the oldest member of the US senate, and who looked scary, was replaced by the very conservative Danish politician Mogens Glistrup (1926-2008), who was also old and whose ugliness was almost legendary. This kind of translation license, to replace a SC person by a TC person used to be fairly common in Denmark up until the late 1980s (Gottlieb, 1994:50), but has since dwindled dramatically in usage, and is arguably ethically questionable. That is not the point here, however. The point is that the reference to Thurmond was rightly determined to be monocultural, with no support from the co-text or the context, and it was thus dealt with accordingly.

The trend, in Scandinavia at least, seems to be moving towards an increased use of retention and other minimum change strategies. There are many explanations for this. One very simple explanation is that most subtitled material in Scandinavia comes from the USA and the UK, and the Anglophone influence on Scandinavia has increased considerably in the last decades, and will probably continue to do so. This means that there are increasing numbers of transcultural references, as Scandinavians learn more and more about the British and American cultures.

Another explanation is that, in Sweden at least, there used to be a tendency for subtitlers to 'chew the food' for the viewers, mainly in the days when the public service companies were the only broadcasters in Scandinavia. These have a responsibility as educators, which might have led to a tendency for subtitlers to intervene more often than was strictly necessary. With a growing number of private broadcasters and TV channels, this imperative became less palpable.

A more unsettling reason for this development may be that the situation for subtitlers in Scandinavia has become more austere. Deadlines have become shorter and salaries have decreased drastically (Carp, 2006). This is of great importance here, because it takes time to determine the transculturality of a reference, and then, if it is judged to be monocultural, it takes even more time to research it and come up with a successful solution of use to the viewers. If subtitlers have a very narrow deadline, then they may have to forego this transculturality appraisal. Similarly, if subtitlers are poorly paid, they will have to produce more subtitles to make a living. This in turn means that they have less time to spend on each subtitle, which may also cause them to forego the transculturality appraisal and the attendant hunt for an ideal solution. The result would be more retention, as this can be seen as a constant option, the argument being that there is no harm in retaining a cultural reference. Instead, the viewer is receiving a verbatim account of the original utterance which s/he may not understand. The result may look like Example 2 below, which comes from the cop movie *Striking Distance* (1993). A dead body has been dragged out of the river, and the investigating officer gives an estimate of the time it had been in the water. He is then contradicted by another officer, the drunken, down-and-out character Tom Hardy, characteristically played by Bruce Willis, who gives what sounds like an expert opinion. The rather miffed investigating officer then replies sarcastically:

(Example 2) ST: Thank you, Jack fucking Webb.
       Swedish subtitle: Tack, jävla Jack Webb.
       Danish subtitle: Tack, fucking Jack Webb.

It should be clear without a back translation that the reference to Jack Webb has been retained with no attempt at cultural mediation from either the Swedish or Danish subtitlers, the latter having used a Swedish master template file for the translation. This is in spite of the fact that the reference is very clearly monocultural since Jack Webb was the actor who played Sgt Joe Friday in the US cop show *Dragnet* (1951-1959), a series which has never been aired in Scandinavia. The TT audience would thus be potentially confused by the subtitle. The subtitles were, perhaps typically, produced by what could be called a low-budget subtitling company.

7. Conclusion

This article has set out to explore how subtitlers know when to opt for benevolent intervention and act as cultural mediators and when not to do so, by appraising a cultural item's transculturality status. It has been shown how this is done through the use of intuition as being part of the TT audience, through the aid of the ST and also through the use of secondary sources. The trend, at least in Scandinavia, seems to be for this transcultural appraisal to become less demanding, partly because of globalisation, which has the effect of lowering the number of monocultural items. More unsettling, though, is the evidence of the tendency among some subtitlers occasionally to forego the transculturality appraisal due to the external pressures of deadlines and salaries. This arguably results in lower quality subtitles, as some viewers are left in the dark, without any means of accessing certain cultural referents, calling for more research into the correlation between subtitling quality and the (worsening) working conditions of subtitlers.

References

Berman, Antoine (1985/2000) "Translation and the trials of the foreign", in Lawrence Venuti (ed.) (2000) *The Translation Studies Reader*. London and New York: Routledge, 284-97.

Carp, Ossi (2006) "Programtextning kan bli sämre [TV subtitles may deteriorate]". *Dagens Nyheter,* 25 June.

Díaz Cintas, Jorge and Aline Remael (2007) *Audiovisual Translation: Subtitling.* Manchester: St. Jerome.

Gottlieb, Henrik (1994) *Tekstning – synkron billedmedieoversættelse* [Subtitling – synchronous media translation]. Copenhagen: University of Copenhagen.

Gottlieb, Henrik (1997) *Subtitles, Translation & Idioms.* Copenhagen: University of Copenhagen.

Gottlieb, Henrik (2001) *Screen Translation: Six Studies in Subtitling, Dubbing and Voice-Over.* Copenhagen: University of Copenhagen.

Katan, David (2004) *Translating Cultures: An Introduction for Translators, Interpreters and Mediators* (2nd edition). Manchester: St Jerome.

Leppihalme, Ritva (1994) *Culture Bumps: On the Translation of Allusions.* English Department Studies 2. Helsinki: University of Helsinki.

Leppihalme, Ritva (1997) *Culture Bumps.* Clevedon: Multilingual Matters.

Lindberg, Ib (1989) *Nogle regler om TV-teksting* [A few rules about TV subtitling]. Manuscript.

Nedergaard-Larsen, Birgit (1993) "Culture-bound problems in subtitling". *Perspectives: Studies in Translatology* 2: 207-42.

Pedersen, Jan (2007) *Scandinavian Subtitles: A Comparative Study of Subtitling Norms in Sweden and Denmark with a Focus on Extralinguistic Cultural References.* Stockholm: Stockholm University. PhD Thesis.

Pedersen, Jan (2008) "High Felicity: a speech act approach to quality assessment in subtitling", in Delia Chiaro, Christine Heiss and Chiara Bucaria (eds) *Between Text and Image. Updating Research in Screen Translation.* Amsterdam and Philadelphia: John Benjamins, 101-15.

Pym, Anthony (2004) *The Moving Text. Localization, Translation and Distribution.* Amsterdam and Philadelphia: John Benjamins.

Schleiermacher, Friedrich (1813/1998) "Om de olika metoderna att översätta" [On the different methods of translation]. Translated by Lars Bjurman, in Lars Kleberg (ed.) (1998) *Med andra ord. Texter om litterär översättning.* Stockholm: Natur och Kultur, 115-30.

Venuti, Lawrence (1995) *The Translator's Invisibility: A History of Translation*. London and New York: Routledge.

Audiovisual material

Dragnet (1951–1959) Jack Webb, USA, NBC.
Fawlty Towers (1975-1979) John Cleese and Connie Booth, UK, BBC.
Frasier (1993-2004) David Angell, Peter Casey and David Lee, USA, NBC.
Little Britain (2003-2006) David Walliams and Matt Lucas, UK, BBC.
Striking Distance (1993) Rowdy Herrington, USA, Columbia.

Towards a creative approach in subtitling: a case study

Anna Foerster

Imperial College, London, UK

Abstract
This article revolves around new trends in subtitling practice and explores the aesthetic dimensions provided by subtitles. The English subtitles of the Russian film *Night Watch* (2004) are analysed and compared with the way conventional subtitling practice is carried out. The aim of this paper is to discuss whether aesthetic subtitling has the potential to become a professionally recognised approach and to illustrate the requirements that are needed for such recognition.

1. Introduction

Conventional subtitling, loosely based on the Code of Good Subtitling Practice (Ivarsson and Carroll, 1998:157-59), is the approach that has dominated the subtitling profession up until now, becoming the industry's standard. However, new ideas and influences are emanating from outside the mainstream, such as arthouse-productions and fansubs, giving birth to new trends which then enter the commercial realm. Whether these new trends have the potential to become more usual in subtitling remains to be seen. The aim in these pages is to analyse the subtitles of the Russian film *Night Watch* (Timur Berkmambetov, 2004) and to compare them with conventional subtitling practices in an attempt to map out the strategies implemented when adopting a highly creative stance.

The following observations and findings have been carried out with interlingual subtitles, Russian into English. Although the findings may be applicable to intralingual subtitling or subtitling for the deaf and hard-of-hearing (SDH), the actual scope of transferability deserves a closer look and exceeds the scope of this paper.

2. The conventional subtitling practice

In the words of Benjamin (in Stolze, 1997:35): "The true translation is transparent, it does not cover the original". Though referring to literary translation, this statement sums up the ultimate goal of translation as it is understood today, not only by publishers, reviewers and readers, but also by film production companies, distributors and movie-goers. The result has been a particular code of subtitling practice that aims at the 'invisibility' of subtitles by insisting on the fact that "subtitles should ideally blend in with the film in such a way that the viewer doesn't notice them and they must never distract the viewer from the story" (Subtitling International UK, 1994:3).

Today, most of the subtitles found on TV, DVD, and in the cinema, tend to adhere to the above mentioned Code of Good Subtitling Practice, which offers guidelines to the industry in an attempt to preserve the quality of subtitles. The Code is widely regarded as standard in the profession (Díaz Cintas and Remael, 2007:80), but the proposed guidelines are not binding and subtitling companies have their own style guides that tend to deviate slightly from the Code of Good Subtitling Practice on some points.

This conventional subtitling practice recommends that subtitles occupy a maximum of two lines at the bottom of the screen and are either centre or left aligned. Their colour is usually white with a black drop shadow, and the typeface is Arial or Arial Narrow, size 29 to 32. Most subtitles consist of a maximum of some 37 to 40 characters per line, staying on screen for a minimum of one second and a maximum of six seconds and adhering to an overall reading speed of between 150 and 180 words per minute. Subtitles appear generally when someone starts to speak and disappear when the speaker stops completely. The linguistic register is mostly neutral, accents and dialects are almost never rendered, and harsh and rude language is toned down. The result is a register and a design for subtitles that never call attention to themselves. This is the desired effect as subtitles are generally regarded solely as a means of understanding what is being said on screen.

3. The invisibility paradox

For a long time subtitles have been aiming, as translations in the printed media, at invisibility because many people, mostly in dubbing and English speaking countries, think that subtitles are a necessary evil (Marleau, 1982) and only detract from the enjoyment of the film. I agree with Venuti (1995:1-2), who successfully argues, when discussing translations in the printed media, that invisibility is an illusion:

> A translated text, whether prose or poetry, fiction or non-fiction is judged acceptable by most publishers, reviewers, and readers when it reads fluently, when the absence of any linguistic and stylistic peculiarities makes it seem transparent, giving the appearance that it reflects the foreign writer's personality or intention or the essential meaning of the foreign text – the appearance, in other words, that the translation is not in fact a translation but the "original". [...] What is so remarkable here is that this illusory effect

conceals the numerous conditions under which the translation is made, starting with the translator's crucial intervention in the foreign text.

Subtitles have never been and will never be invisible. Aiming for invisibility becomes a paradox verging on the absurd for several reasons. Firstly, because, as Gottlieb (1994:104) puts it, subtitling is an instance of diagonal translation where two dimensions cross, from speech in the source language (SL) to written text in the target language (TL). The shift from spoken language to written language is one between two different channels of communication and, as such, one could never give the illusion of the other. Subtitles bridge the gap between those two channels. On the one hand they are written text; on the other hand they derive from oral discourse and therefore take on some characteristics of spoken language, such as a more colloquial tone, unfinished sentences, etc.

Secondly, this is because subtitles must be always visible as they are inscriptions of words and sentences that cover part of the screen. As Thompson (2000:1) puts it: "subtitles are an intrusion into the visual space of a film". Critics of subtitles are often concerned that "they have the potential to 'drown' the images [and] instead of watching images, the audience starts literally to see only the texts" (Sinha, 2004:174).

Finally, because the source text (ST) and the target text (TT) are available at the same time – one heard, one read – the audience is always aware of the fact that they are reading a translation. Thus, the illusion of the translated text being the original is never the case in subtitling – as opposed to dubbing and even that is arguable. So, where does the idea of trying to make something invisible that, by its very nature, draws so much attention to itself originate?

I would like to argue that the answer lies in the translational approach that dominates the Western and the Anglo-American culture in particular. Translational approaches can be divided into two main groups: those that are faithful to the ST and serve the intention of the original author, and those that focus on the communicative intention with regard to the TT audience. The most appropriate approach is, among other factors, determined by the skopos of the ST. And, although in many modern schools of thought, like the Pragmatic Turn and the Cultural Turn, the importance of the translator and the visibility of the translation are promoted, for example by Vermeer, Hönig, Nord or Venuti (Stolze, 1997:155), in practice, the transparency of the TT and the invisibility of the translator still dominate the commercial world, where the aim is to produce a fluent text in the TL giving the reader the illusion of the original. This is especially so in the case of the film industry as it is highly commercialised and clearly dominated by the Anglo-American culture and ideology. This industry does not pay much attention to the actual process of translation, and tends to adhere overwhelmingly to domesticating translation theories and to producing the illusion of transparency.

4. New trends in subtitling

There have always been films which have defied the dogma of invisibility in subtitling and have used the added dimension that subtitling provides in an unconventional, creative manner, becoming a diegetic element of the plot. Monty Python's 2004 DVD version of *Monty Python and the Holy Grail* (1974) features "subtitles for people who don't like subtitles", according to the information provided on the cover of the DVD. These subtitles are not a translation of the film dialogue, they do not have a direct connection to the film as the text is literally taken from Shakespeare's *Henry IV*, Part II. In *Vivre sa vie* (1962), director Jean-Luc Godard robs his main character, Nana, of her voice in a very moving scene and lets her speak through subtitles only. Another example of this kind is in *Annie Hall* (1977) where Woody Allen subtitles the unspoken thoughts of his main characters while they are having a superficial conversation, thus giving us an insight into the psyche of these people.

A prime example of subtitles being completely integrated into the aesthetics and language of the film is *Desperanto* (1991). Patricia Rozema (2004:65-67), the director, explains her use of subtitles in the following way:

> In *Desperanto* I tried to make visible the experience of trying to access another culture when I can't speak the language. [...] In her dreams she finds subtitles, those imperfect little life lines that straddle, bore through and circumvent the walls. She notices the subtitles explaining everything she didn't know before. Finding it difficult to read the subtitles at the bottom of the frame that are oriented towards the viewer, she squeezes in between us and the subtitles to better connect to the world on the other side.

Beyond cinema, contemporary fansubs for anime also appear to be breaking the rules of conventional subtitling in an effective way: "Fansubs share some of the characteristics of professional subtitling but they are clearly more daring in their formal presentation, taking advantage of the potential offered by digital technology" (Díaz Cintas and Muñoz Sánchez, 2006:51).

Pérez González (2006:270-1) elaborates on three topics in which fansubs divert from conventional subtitles, basing his study on a more detailed account of fansubbing conventions presented by Ferrer-Simó (2005). In fansubs, different type, style and size fonts coexist within the same programme. To ensure that the visual styling of the subtitles is compatible with the aesthetics of the programme is a top priority. In an approach that is inconceivable in conventional subtitling, fansubbers introduce foreign words in the TL with definitions that sometimes cover most of the screen, by resorting to glosses at the bottom and notes at the top of the screen, which we could call 'headnotes' (Díaz Cintas and Remael, 2007:141). According to Nornes (1999:32) this strategy helps fansubbers to deal with untranslatable cultural references. As for their positioning, subtitles appear not only at the bottom of the screen, but virtually anywhere.

The popularity of unconventional forms of subtitling seems to be on the increase, as not only arthouse films or anime but also mainstream TV productions and advertisements are beginning to use them. In the TV series *Heroes*, different colours for the subtitles from Japanese into English are used and are no longer restricted to the bottom of the screen. They appear in different positions and sometimes even consist of three lines. A similar trend can be witnessed in advertising. The advertisement industry seems to have discovered the potential of subtitles and uses them in inventive and rule-breaking ways, for instance Carlton Draught's *Big Ad*. This TV-spot features a chorus that sings the advertisement text *Big Ad* to the melody of *O Fortuna* taken from Carl Orff's *Carmina Burana*. The subtitles appear in the form of karaoke subtitles with characters and words coming into view on screen rhythmically as they are being sung, using stylistic devices such as suspension dots and capitals to mark musical characteristics or emphasise words, for instance 'HUGE' (Figure 1). Words with longer rhythms are marked with multiple characters, like 'blooooooooody' (Figure 2):

It's just so freak...ing HUGE!

blooooooooody...

| Figure 1 | Figure 2 |

I call this unconventional form of subtitling aesthetic subtitling, as it draws attention to the subtitles via aesthetic means exploring semiotic possibilities, which include the semantic dimension without being restricted by it. Whereas the abusive subtitling promoted by Nornes (1999:online) is centred around the approach of making translations linguistically visible – "abusive subtitles encroach on the word-for-word end of the spectrum, because they take into consideration the array of qualities that make up the material basis of language" –, in aesthetic subtitling the subtitles are predominantly designed graphically to support or match the aesthetics of the audiovisual text and consequently develop an aesthetic of their own.

5. *Night Watch*: a case study

In order to get a better insight into the ways aesthetic subtitling can be implemented into audiovisual texts, examining the advantages and weaknesses of such implementations, I take a closer look at the subtitles of the Russian film *Night Watch*, directed by Timur Bekmambetov in 2004, with the aim of focussing on technical aspects and special effects and leaving linguistic considerations aside.

    Night Watch, a fantasy action thriller, is the first film of a trilogy based on Russian author Sergei Lukyanenko's *Nochnoj Dozor* series. For the English-language release, the voice-over in the opening-sequence is narrated in Russian-accented English whereas the dialogue in the film itself is subtitled. The subtitles deliberately break the conventional rules of subtitling practice and are integrated into the visual design of the film in a similar way to graphic novels. This approach has enjoyed a very positive response with audiences, even in the United States:

> The subtitles, for instance, are the best I have encountered. Far from palely loitering at the foot of the screen, they lurk in odd corners of the frame and, at one point, glow scarlet and then spool away, like blood in water. I trust that this will start a technical trend and that, from here on, no respectable French actress will dream of removing her clothes unless at least three lines of dialogue can be made to unwind across her midriff. (Lane, 2006:online)

Fox Searchlight, a specialty film division of 20th Century Fox and distributor of the film, collaborated on this experiment with director Timur Bekmambetov. Given that this new approach seems to be very popular with audiences and critics alike, I will examine the subtitles from a professional point of view, taking the Code of Good Subtitling Practice as put forward by Ivarsson and Carroll (1998:157-9) into consideration.

5.1. Temporal considerations

In order to measure the reading speed and get a clearer picture about the cueing of the subtitles I have reproduced them with a subtitling programme (WinCAPS) by using the same in and out times as the original subtitles as well as their line breaking and positioning on screen.

The film features 1,139 subtitles, an average number for a feature film, although an action or horror movie usually has fewer subtitles. This higher number of subtitles results from individual, one-line subtitles being used for each utterance in scenes with two or more protagonists, whereas, usually, two speakers share a subtitle, denoted by dashes, in order to avoid excessive reading speeds. Whenever a character in *Night Watch* starts to speak, a new subtitle comes in, resulting not only in rather a high number of subtitles, but also in extremely high reading speeds throughout the film. The average reading speed for cinema and DVD ranges from 160 to 180 words per minute (wpm). In this film, 156 subtitles out of 1,139 (13.7%) have a reading speed of 190 wpm and higher, often way above 230 wpm. Even when taking into consideration the fact that the subtitles in question are made for cinema where the reading speed is usually higher than for DVD releases due to the superior definition of film screens (Ivarsson and Carroll, 1998:65-6), and that the target audience for this film is aged between 15 and 30 and quite used to words on screen and rapid image changes, a reading speed above 190 wpm can still be considered very high. Sometimes this problem could have easily been solved by leaving the subtitles stand for longer or merging two subtitles into one, which would have also had the effect of giving the whole flow of the subtitles a better rhythm, especially as some of them are shorter than one second.

Concerning the cueing of the subtitles there are quite a few deviations from standard subtitling practice. The normal practice is to leave two to four – sometimes even up to six – frames between subtitles to make it easier to distinguish between individual subtitles (*ibid.*:76). Many subtitles in this film follow the previous subtitle without a space being left in between. On other occasions too many frames, often up to seven, are left between subtitles.

The high fluctuation in the reading speed and the frames between subtitles makes for a very irregular rhythm which is hard to follow as the eyes cannot settle for a certain reading speed and projection of the subtitles. The audience has to be alert and watch the subtitles intently in order not to miss one. The in and out times before and after shot changes also seem to be irregular and do not follow standard subtitling practice. A common rule is that subtitles either cue out or in with the shot change or two to four frames before or after. If the subtitle needs to remain in vision over a shot change it should stand for at least 10 to 20 frames before and after, again, to maintain a certain rhythm. In *Night Watch* the subtitles often come in only two frames before a shot change or disappear two or three frames after.

All these cueing issues result in a subtitle file that goes against the rhythm of the film and against the reading habits of the audience. Giving subtitles a rhythm that is relaxing to the eye and matches the rhythm of the film is a highly demanding requirement of subtitling and is usually only mastered by professionals. From the cueing of these subtitles one gets the impression that they have been done by someone inexperienced, who might not understand the underlying reasons for the conventions applied in standard subtitling practice.

5.2. Special effects

As mentioned above, the film stands out because of the special effects of the subtitles. Temporal considerations aside, about 30 percent of them deviate from conventional subtitling practice in some way, notably in terms of layout.

The subtitles that deviate from the Code of Good Subtitling Practice fall into two categories: (i) those that have a diegetic function and underline the content of the story and (ii) those that have a purely stylistic purpose.

Diegetic Subtitle Design

The subtitles designed to accentuate certain diegetic elements in the film are easily recognisable, as they are clearly related to the plot. One prime example is a subtitle design that is related to one particular recurring aspect of the story and appears in the very same way every time. A vampire lures people to her, particularly a young boy, through a whispering voice that only the victim and the audience can hear. This voice is always subtitled in red and the subtitles take on the form of clouds of blood before they disappear. These subtitles are not placed at the bottom of the screen, in their usual position, but can appear virtually anywhere. In the example shown below, they appear in the water and when they turn into clouds of blood they are automatically connected to the boy's nose bleeding. They take on the same form as the blood in the water (Figures 3–6):

Figure 3

Figure 4

Figure 5   Figure 6

This is the only subtitle design that recurs throughout the film in the very same way and is always linked to this one aspect. These subtitles seem to be perfectly integrated into the visual environment in which they are embedded.

The other subtitles in this category are more individually designed and their function is to underline particular aspects of the story. Some fade out slowly, instead of cueing out, in an attempt to emphasise what has been said, foreshadowing future events. For example the subtitle 'And destroying an innocent child' fades out and with the fading emphasises the next subtitle 'is a great sin' which foreshadows the events. The fading of the subtitle, basically the slowing down of the disappearance from the screen, has the effect of resonating in the audience's mind.

Some take on a prominent position on the screen like the subtitle 'Go ahead' which is positioned in the middle of the screen right next to the potion the protagonist is supposed to drink. Others have a comic style design to underline urgency or the screaming of a character, as in Figures 7-9:

Figure 7

Figure 8

Figure 9

Other subtitles change their colour from white to red to highlight a word (Figures 10-12). In this example the word 'warning' in 'TORNADO WARNING FOR MOSCOW' gradually turns red. This design is reminiscent of karaoke subtitles, the difference being that the whole word gradually turns from white into a light red and then into a dark red instead of a word changing its colour instantly as is the case in karaoke.

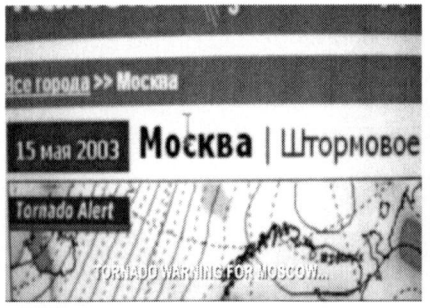
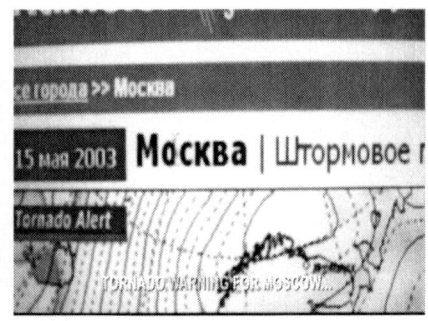

Figure 10

Figure 11

Figure 12

The protagonist in this film is portrayed as living between consciousness and unconsciousness, sometimes hearing people speaking from a distance and echoing in his mind. In what can be interpreted as an attempt to mirror his state of mind, some subtitles exploit the dynamic nature of film, as opposed to the static nature of printed material, and fade in and out, float across the screen, flicker and blink. This subtitle design underlines the main character's fragile state of mind, unstable and unbalanced like the written text on the screen.

Another subtitle even provides a 'picture in a picture'-effect. It appears on a TV screen in vision and looks as if the TV programme itself has been subtitled. The subtitle reads 'We'll show you the proper techniques for using live bait.' and features the translation of the narrator in the TV programme on fishing. However, the sentence also refers back to the film's plot as the drama begins to unfold over the accusation by the dark side that the light side breaks the rules of the agreed truce by using live bait to catch vampires (Figure 13):

Figure 13

In the subtitle 'It's safer to go through The Gloom' the words break apart and fly away resembling the swarm of mosquitoes in the picture. The Gloom is a twilight place that exists alongside the real world and is depicted in the film through visual transitions, from small swarms of mosquitoes to networks of blood vessels. Here the subtitle design explains the words of the subtitle, what it means 'to go through The Gloom'.

In the subtitle 'So you really did want to kill me.' the words 'kill me' stay on screen longer than the rest of the subtitle, which disappears before the shot change. After the shot change the protagonist appears and, by remaining in vision, the words 'kill me' are emphasised and seem to echo in the protagonist's head. The shot change here is not only a visual story telling device for the photographer, it is utilised by the subtitle to emphasise the words.

As different as the subtitle designs described above are, they all have a quasi-diegetic function, underlining the plot of the story and drawing attention to themselves. They stand out in a way that makes the audience fully aware that they are reading subtitles and in their function they are similar to book illustrations which are often used to provide another layer of the story and to leave an impression on the readers' mind. Some of the subtitles are designed to reinforce the characters feelings and to 'illustrate' them graphically. This way, subtitles provide another layer of meaning that would otherwise be missing. They become an artistic device in their own right.

Stylistic Subtitle Design

The film also features many subtitles with a design that has no diegetic function but mirrors the style of the film, the way it is shot. Henceforth I will call this category 'stylistic subtitles'. Some subtitles are positioned in a way that suits the aesthetics of the picture composition such as the subtitle '... Anton'. It is positioned underneath the character Anton who can be seen on his wedding photo standing next to his wife (Figure 14):

Figure 14

Another subtitle comes in word by word and resembles the chopping of an onion, as seen in Figures 15–18. This design is related to cumulative subtitles, also known as add-on subtitles used in SDH. Add-on subtitles allow the display of a new subtitle on the screen – that is cued in in synch with the speakers' utterance – before the previous one has vanished. This allows two, sometimes three, speakers' utterances to appear in the same subtitle, although not at the same time (Díaz Cintas and Remael, 2007:140). The subtitle design here works in a similar way but instead of different speakers coming in at one time, the subtitle is displayed on screen word by word:

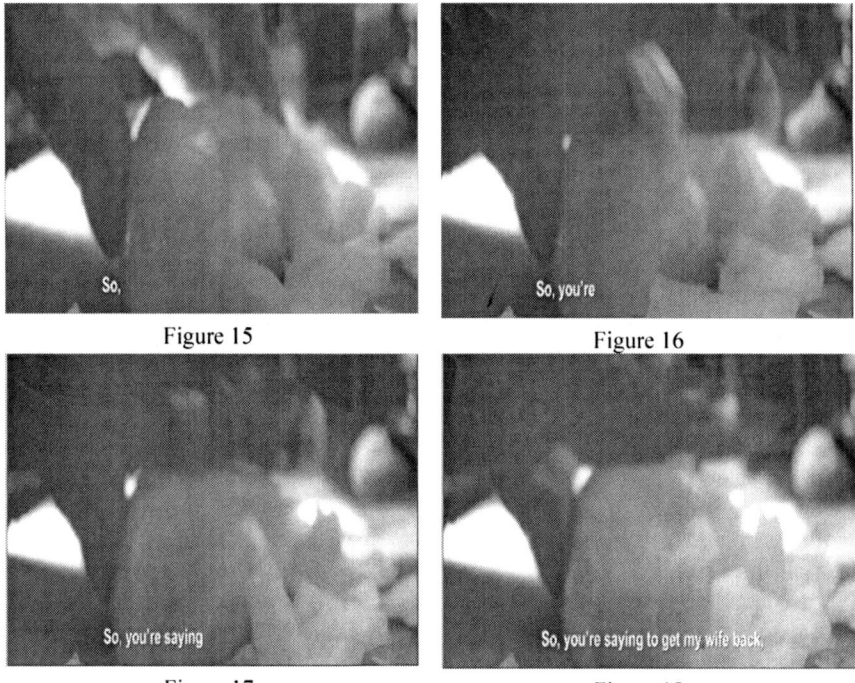

Figure 15   Figure 16

Figure 17   Figure 18

Other subtitles follow certain movements in vision, thus moving in the same way as a particular object which can be a hand, a bottle or, in another instance, an owl. The subtitles do not have a fixed position but move across the screen in the same way as the object moves. This does not necessarily mean horizontally from right to left, as some subtitles or news on news channels do, but also from the bottom to the top of the screen, the other way around or diagonally across the screen.

Furthermore, there are subtitles where the in and out times are determined by the composition of the picture. For example, they are revealed in synchrony with the opening of a fridge door and cue out as the fridge door closes. The light inside the fridge determines the in and out time of the subtitle.

One subtitle even follows the focus of the camera. The focus of the camera is on the foreground to begin with, and with it the subtitle comes into focus. As the camera focusses on the background, both the foreground and the subtitles go out of focus, as if the subtitle had ceased to be part of the representation of the story on film and had become part of the three dimensional story itself.

This stylistic subtitle design resorts to some of the same strategies as the diegetic subtitle design, but rather than being attached to the content, it underlines the film's aesthetics. Many of these seem justifiable, as they are pleasing to the eye and in harmony with the pictures. Others contribute something to the film design. How much of these stylistic subtitle designs can be implemented in a film and what designs are being used, also depends on the film's genre, so as to avoid damage to credibility or atmosphere. A period film, for example, would resort to different effects and designs from an action film.

As the director Timur Bekmambetov said in the audio commentary of the film, this film was made solely with a Russian audience in mind. Only after Fox Searchlight became interested in the film for the American market did they start thinking about the subtitles and decided to "create special subtitles which help to tell the story" (Bekmambetov DVD). So only the theatrical version of the film for the English speaking markets features the added dimension of aesthetic subtitles. The film as it is shown in Russia misses out on any form of aesthetic inserts on screen. On the DVD we can find three versions of the film. The Russian version without subtitles, the theatrical version with the aesthetic subtitling approach and an English dubbed version. Interestingly, as with other DVDs it is possible to watch the Russian version with standard interlingual DVD subtitles, although the theatrical version is available as well.

Evaluation

Seeing the film's subtitles as an independent entity, it can be concluded that they are in parts very innovative, creative and well executed. However, a close inspection also reveals some major weaknesses. As with many innovative trends, the balance between the advantages and disadvantages of the conventional way and the innovations does not seem to have been found yet. The recurring high reading speeds and the lack of rhythm due to rather chaotic subtitle cueing is a clear disadvantage. Whether this happened unintentionally, for lack of proficiency, or whether it deliberately broke the rules cannot be fully ascertained, although the first hypothesis seems more likely.

Since the rules for reading speeds and the timing of the subtitles as applied in conventional subtitling make particular sense, breaking them would almost always lead to loss of quality. A lot of testing has been done to establish appropriate reading speeds for different media and, although reading speeds nowadays tend to be a bit higher than twenty or thirty years ago, the numbers customary in the industry are still well-grounded. The special effects applied throughout the subtitles were often appropriate but resorted to too many different designs. When watching the film one gets the feeling that many subtitles feature an effect just for the sake of it.

The idea of aesthetic subtitling is an interesting start, but in order for this trend to have a future, it is my contention that it has to develop from a simply aesthetic approach to a creative subtitling approach. According to Preiser (1976:5): "A creative achievement emerges from the awareness of a problem and presents something new that in a certain time within one culture is accepted as sensible by experts". Or as Stein (1953) phrased it: "A creative product is a new product that is regarded usable or satisfactory at a certain time by a certain group". The evaluation of a creative solution is thus based on two pillars: the awareness of a problem, as innovations generate out of discontent; and sensibility, as innovations have to meet certain parameters and norms to eliminate the discontent and to be regarded as satisfactory by experts (Kußmaul, 2000:17).

The subtitling approach in *Night Watch* meets the first requirement of a creative product. It presents something new which emanates from an awareness of the problem – the unpopularity of subtitles in the target market, USA. However, it does not meet the second requirement. It does not meet all the criteria necessary to be regarded as satisfactory by experts. The reasons are the weaknesses of the subtitles described above. The cueing of the subtitles, as well as the high reading speed, do not seem to have a diegetic or stylistic function that supports the film. The same can be said about the overuse of different designs that appear to be rather sporadic and seem to be implemented just because it was technically possible. Therefore the subtitling of *Night Watch* is an aesthetic approach but, according to the parameters of a creative product as defined above, cannot yet be called creative on every level. A creative subtitling approach would be a combination of new aesthetic elements and features from the standard subtitling practice that are proven to be sensible. Together, they might form the essence of an approach that is professional and yet of artistic value.

6. Outlook and conclusion

I would like to argue that this creative approach should not be restricted to films or programmes that because of their nature lend themselves to it. The extent to which there will be deviations from standard subtitling practice will naturally vary from one programme to another, but every audiovisual programme and every target audience deserves a subtitle layout that is intentionally tailored, similar to what happens in print. In print every task needs a different solution. The way the text is being read determines the design. Willberg and Forssman (1997:14-5) already distinguished between eight different readings that determine only the design of commodity books – let alone artistic books, visual poetry and others. Whether a reading is linear, informative, consulting etc. determines the design of the text. Margins, typeface, text structure, length of a line, headings and other factors are adjusted to ensure the text is being transported to the reader in the best way possible.

If we want to explore new trends further, not only those which exist on the margins of the industry and among fansubbers, the traditional approach that regulates professional practice needs to be reconsidered. A more inventive approach is needed to keep up with recent developments and trends, one that allows more creative room for both diegetic and stylistic design, that becomes 'visible', but at the same time takes into account traditional practice where it is sensible.

Such a translation would make the audience even more aware of the subtitles and equally of the differences between text and speech. The fact that images and language always interact could be taken as a chance to explore the possibilities of subtitling more creatively, as in the case study discussed here. However, more creative space means more responsibility and the obligation to fully understand traditional practice in order to be able to divert from it successfully.

The arrival of digital media, digital TV, HDTV and the like offers plenty of scope to be creative (Díaz Cintas, 2010). Subtitlers do not have to deal with old technical restrictions any more, when only a couple of different fonts were available, animation was not possible or too expensive, and there was not enough disk space to contain the data. Nowadays, we have the luxury to play around with different fonts, sizes, colours, shapes, effects, etc. without reducing the legibility or making the process too expensive. In my opinion such an approach would be contemporary and in line with the technical and aesthetic developments of our time.

References

Díaz Cintas, Jorge (2010) "The highs and lows of digital subtitles", in Lew N. Zybatow (ed.) *Translationswissenschaft – Stand und Perspektiven. Innsbrucker Ringvorlesungen zur Translationswissenschaft VI.* Frankfurt am Main: Peter Lang, 105-30.

Díaz Cintas, Jorge and Aline Remael (2007) *Audiovisual Translation: Subtitling.* Manchester: St Jerome.

Díaz Cintas, Jorge and Pablo Muñoz Sánchez (2006) "Fansubs: audiovisual translation in an amateur environment". *The Journal of Specialised Translation* 6, 37-52.
   www.jostrans.org/issue06/art_diaz_munoz.pdf

Ferrer-Simó, María Rosario (2005) "Fansubs y scanlations: la influencia del aficionado en los criterios profesionales". *Puentes* 6, 27-44.

Gottlieb, Henrik (1994) "Subtitling: diagonal translation". *Perspectives: Studies in Translatology* 1, 101-21.

Ivarsson, Jan and Mary Carroll (1998) *Subtitling.* Simrishamn: TransEdit.

Kußmaul, Paul (2000) *Kreatives Übersetzen.* Tübingen: Stauffenburg.

Lane, Anthony (2006) "Evil touch". *The New Yorker*, 27 February.
   www.newyorker.com/archive/2006/02/27/060227crci_cinema?currentPage=2

Marleau, Lucien (1982) "Les sous-titres... un mal nécessaire". *Meta* 27(3), 271-85.
   www.erudit.org/revue/meta/1982/v27/n3/003577ar.pdf

Nornes, Abe Mark (1999) "For an abusive subtitling". *Film Quarterly* 52(3), 17-34.

Pérez González, Luis (2006) "Fansubbing anime: insights into the 'Butterfly Effect' of globalisation on Audiovisual Translation". *Perspectives: Studies on Translatology* 14(4), 260-77.

Preiser, Siegfried (1976) *Kreativitätsforschung.* Darmstadt: Wissenschaftliche Buchgesellschaft.

Rozema, Patricia (2004) "Little life lines in 'Desperanto'", in Atom Egoyan and Ian Balfour (eds) *Subtitles: On the Foreignness of Film.* Cambridge, Massachusetts: MIT Press, 65-7.

Sinha, Amresh (2004) "The use and abuse of subtitles", in Atom Egoyan and Ian Balfour (eds) *Subtitles: On the Foreignness of Film.* Cambridge, Massachusetts: MIT Press, 171-90.

Stolze, Radegundis (1997) *Übersetzungstheorien. Eine Einführung.* Tübingen: Narr.

Subtitling International UK (1994) *Subtitling for TV and Video: A Short Manual.* Manuscript.

Thompson, Peter (2000) *Notes on Subtitles and Superimpositions.*

www.chicagomediaworks.com/2instructworks/3instruct_writings/wrsubtit
.doc

Venuti, Lawrence (1995) *The Translator's Invisibility.* London: Routledge.

Stein, Morris I. (1953) "Creativity and Culture". *Journal of Psychology: Interdisciplinary and Applied* 36, 311-22.

Willberg, Peter and Friedrich Forssman (1997) *Texttypographie.* Mainz: Hermann Schmidt.

Audiovisual films and programmes cited

Annie Hall (1977) Woody Allen. USA.

Big Ad (2005) George Patterson and Partners. Australia.

Desperanto (1991) Patricia Rozema. Canada.

Heroes (Since 2006) Tim Kring. USA.

Monty Python and the Holy Grail (1974) Terry Gilliams and Terry Jones. UK.

Night Watch – Nochnoy dozor (2004) Timur Berkmambetov. Russia.

Vivre sa vie (1962) Jean-Luc Godard. France.

The subtitling profession in Croatia

Kristijan Nikolić

University of Zagreb, Croatia

Abstract
This paper is based on personal experience, a survey carried out among subtitlers and an interview with the Head of the Translation and Subtitling Department of Croatian state television *Hrvatska Televizija*. The main goal is to find out the kind of professional training that practising subtitlers have received and, if none, whether they would be interested in any potential form of professional training. It also aims to gauge their opinion as to whether research is important and relevant for their daily work.

1. The history of public subtitling in Croatia

The information in this section is based on an interview with Ms Bojana Zeljko-Lipovscak, Head of the Translation and Subtitling Department at the state Croatian Radio and Television (HRT).

Hrvatska televizija (HTV), part of HRT, the Croatian Radio and Television state broadcasting corporation formerly known as RTVZ (Radio Television Zagreb), began broadcasting in 1956. In the first couple of years the company rebroadcast Austrian and Italian programmes without translation, and in the 1960s it began producing and broadcasting its own programmes, which included foreign films and TV series with Croatian subtitles, signalling the birth of television subtitling in the country. Until the 1970s, programmes were broadcast live and subtitlers had to be present in the studio during transmission so that they could perform the time cueing of subtitles. As is the current practice at most film festivals today, they were responsible for technically launching the subtitles live: this inevitably compromised the accurate synchronisation of dialogue and subtitles.

The profession gathered momentum with the establishment of the Translation and Subtitling Department (TSD) at HTV in 1989, the use of VHS tapes and the introduction of new subtitling technology that enabled better quality subtitles. The separation of Croatian Radio and Television from the network of TV and radio broadcasters of the former Yugoslavia was also a positive step for the growth of the subtitling profession, since it meant that all foreign programmes were to be broadcast from Zagreb and not by the various TV and radio broadcasters in the Yugoslav republics, as had previously been the case. Zagreb was thus confirmed as the principal media centre, with Croatian as the main language. In addition, there was a considerable increase in the number of foreign programmes that were broadcast with Croatian subtitles.

The TSD currently handles about 100 hours of programmes a week and provides subtitles for films, TV series, documentaries (partly dubbed), cartoons (occasionally dubbed), news reports and domestic productions for the overseas market (i.e. subtitled into the foreign language). To cope with the demand, over the past two decades several hundred subtitlers have been trained at HTV. Since subtitling is a freelance profession and beginners are generally young, the turnover of subtitlers is rather high and constant recruitment is necessary.

According to the Head of the TSD, the following characteristics are desirable in a subtitler: high linguistic competence in both the target and source languages, the ability to condense text, and an adherence to the company's language standards, PC literacy, manual and technical dexterity, willingness to work to short deadlines and at unusual times. In her opinion, professional and practical training in subtitling is necessary and the steps taken by HTV in this respect have shown good results. However, this is not a simple task since good supervisors are needed and prospective subtitlers must ideally be monitored for a certain period of time at the beginning of their careers, which, in most cases, is impossible.

TDS cooperates with some 70 subtitlers who translate into a wide range of languages, English being the main source language of most programmes. Of these, around 40 work exclusively for HTV as freelancers. However, new developments in the Croatian TV market have opened up new opportunities for Croatian subtitlers. In 2000, national commercial television stations were introduced in Croatia (Nova TV and RTL Televizija), as well as foreign owned cable and satellite channels – such as HBO, Hallmark, Viasat History, Viasat Explorer, National Geographic and TV 1000 – and local TV broadcasters. Given that Croatia has traditionally been a subtitling country, all of these new stations decided to subtitle their foreign language programmes in Croatian. In addition, the growth of the DVD market and easier internet access have allowed Croatian subtitlers to work for companies based overseas. This means that the number of professional subtitlers has increased greatly and, given the potential of new technological advances, like internet television, it can only be expected that, as the number of subtitled channels increases, so will the demand for new subtitlers. However, one of the main drawbacks in Croatia is that there is no formal, institutional subtitling training in the country, though some agencies do organise their own in-house training. This situation is not unique to Croatia and is shared by many other countries, as is highlighted by Díaz Cintas and Remael (2007:41-

2). The question is whether any form of training is perceived as necessary from the perspective of the subtitlers themselves.

2. Survey

A survey was carried out in 2007 in the form of a questionnaire distributed amongst professional subtitlers working for Croatian Television's Subtitling Department (TSD) and colleagues who work for a large multilingual subtitling company based in the USA (henceforth The Company).

2.1 Methodology

The questionnaire was sent by email to all 70 subtitlers who work for HRT and to 15 who work for the subtitling company. As far as HTV was concerned, the subtitlers were sent the questionnaire by the head of the TSD, in order to make sure that they all received it. As for The Company, I personally sent the questionnaire to all the colleagues.

I decided to use open questions because they enabled respondents to be more descriptive in their answers. All participants were asked the following questions:

1. How long have you been working as a subtitler?
2. Do you consider yourself a full-time subtitler?
3. Have you finished or taken a course at a specialist translation school?
4. If available, would you study subtitling or take a course in subtitling?
5. Do you think that research in translating for TV is necessary and would you be interested in the results?
6. What are the advantages and disadvantages of being a subtitler? What would you change if you could?

2.2 Findings: subtitlers working for HTV

A total of 27 completed questionnaires were received, 21 from HTV's subtitlers and six from The Company's. HTV's subtitlers gave the following answers:

1. How long have you been working as a subtitler?

Answers varied from one year (two subtitlers) to 19 years (two subtitlers). The average period was seven years of experience. However, it was very obvious that, at least among those subtitlers who returned the questionnaires, there were very few subtitlers who had worked for more than 10 years.

2. Do you consider yourself a full-time subtitler?

Nine subtitlers answered 'yes' and twelve answered 'no'. Out of those who said 'yes', one mentioned that that s/he also worked as a translator but considered her/himself to be a full-time subtitler; another one said that s/he was a subtitler but also translated for the theatre; and the last one stated that whilst s/he had another full-time job, s/he was involved in both jobs full-time and considered her/himself to be a full-time subtitler. One of the main reasons for this ambivalence was the fact that subtitlers tend to earn less nowadays than they used to some ten years ago, which forces most of them to have a 'day job' and work in subtitling as an extra job.

3. Have you finished or taken a course at a specialist translation school?

Only two subtitlers answered 'yes' to this question, which represents 9.5% of the respondents, although on closer inspection, the schools they mentioned were specialist centres for the training of conference interpreters, not subtitlers or translators. Nonetheless, this state of affairs was actually expected because of the lack of specialist translation schools on Croatian territory. Not only are there no schools in the country, but in the rapidly growing literature on subtitling (Gottlieb, 1994:263) there are virtually no works dealing with Croatian subtitling.

4. Would you, if it were possible, study subtitling or take a course in subtitling?

Out of 21 subtitlers, ten said 'yes' (47%), nine said 'no' (43%), and two said 'maybe' (10%). Eleven subtitlers (52% of the total number of respondents) had four or less years of experience and nine of these less experienced professionals (i.e. 85%) showed a willingness to enrol for a subtitling course.

On the other hand, only one subtitler with 15 years experience or more, out of the six in this group, answered 'yes'. The rest from this group of experienced subtitlers answered 'no'.

The four subtitlers in the group of professionals with four to 15 years experience (21% of the total number of respondents) answered 'no'. This distribution was to some extent understandable as a subtitler with many years of experience, for example 19, would not be interested in becoming a subtitling student, while those with only a couple would be more willing to do so.

5. Do you think that research in translating for TV is necessary and would you be interested in the results?

Only two subtitlers were of the opinion that research was not important, whilst the other 19 answered 'yes'. In this particular case, respondents provided more detailed responses such as: "yes, I would be interested if competent people were involved". One subtitler said that she would not only be interested in the results, but would be willing to participate in such research and another said that s/he would be interested in research and the attitude of viewers towards subtitling and dubbing. The conclusion therefore is that research, at least in principle, would be interesting to practitioners of subtitling.

6. What are the advantages and disadvantages of being a subtitler? What would you change if you could?

Respondents felt this question was stimulating and engaging, which resulted in an array of more detailed answers. The advantages can be grouped into both personal and professional considerations.

With respect to their personal considerations, the subjects mentioned an individual approach to work and sometimes wonderful films which were a pleasure to subtitle as being among the advantages of the job. Some said that it enabled them to see programmes they would otherwise never have seen and many considered that the diverse formats of films, TV series and cartoons enabled them to express their creativity. For some, the job was not too difficult and some professionals thought that permanent contact with the source language and the various cultures and subcultures was a real plus point. Regular exposure to new words; constant improvement through one's own work and learning to express thoughts in a concise way were also seen as very positive. Interestingly, "taking a holiday when one wants" was a great bonus for one of HRT's subtitlers.

Regarding working conditions, some of the main advantages included the ability to accept as much work as one wanted as well as the possibility of working from home. For some, the television format was short, which was seen as an advantage, so that it would only take a couple of days to subtitle a film, as opposed to translating a book. Some subtitlers felt that the fact that they did not have to work for one employer was an asset, meaning that if one has a 'day job', one has one employer, and if one is a freelancer, one can have one, two or more employers.

The disadvantages were also grouped into personal and professional considerations. However, the principal and the most frequently expressed disadvantage was perhaps both personal and professional. According to all subtitlers, the job was underpaid, or 'painfully underpaid' as was pointed out by one subtitler.

Personal reasons included having to work sometimes with terribly bad films ("shallow content, a lot of aggression and vulgarity", said one subtitler). For another subtitler, it was "an autistic job unacceptable to many". Some respondents thought that the subtiler was a figure on show, allowing viewers to praise someone's work or, more regularly, to criticise subtitlers very rudely.

As far as professional considerations were concerned, there were various disadvantages according to the respondents, one being that a guess or a careless translation never goes unnoticed, a point that has also been discussed by Ivarsson and Carroll (1998:105). The "total ignorance of the viewing public about who and under what circumstances subtitles are created" was also a negative point according to one of the subtitlers.

The fact that subtitlers were often left to rely on their own resourcefulness was a disadvantage for some, as well as the fact that it was a freelance job, which, as mentioned before, was perceived as an advantage by other subtitlers. Short deadlines and poor and outdated equipment were disadvantages of the job, the latter being mentioned by almost all the subtitlers, i.e. the use of VHS cassettes in an age of DVDs. Some language restrictions were also perceived as being negative: "such as the restrictions when using slang which are unnecessary, sometimes even damaging because they impoverish the translation", as was stated by one of the respondents. This agrees with what Assis Rosa (2001:219) calls centralization, that is an attempt to use standard language as much as possible, as opposed to local variants, resulting in an impoverished translation.

There were subtitlers who thought that it was a stressful job, for example when they had to deal with texts out of context, referring to segments used in various TV programmes, like the statements of politicians. Working nights, weekends and on holiday was a disadvantage for many, as well as the fact that subtitlers had no professional body representing their interests, meaning that there was nobody to help negotiate better prices with employers, a fact which added to the lack of networking and communication amongst colleagues.

Most respondents thought that the contracts signed by subtitlers stripped them of any rights as authors although, under the Berne and World Conventions, translators are entitled to the same copyright as writers and therefore have the right to be given credit for their work (Ivarsson and Carroll, 1998:59). Working on the principle of 'take it or leave it' and the unpredictability of the job market were criticised by many. "The names of Croatian proofreaders of subtitles do not appear on the screen at the end of a programme together with the subtitler's name and the fact that nobody knows that they are the ones who work on the text before broadcasting" was a disadvantage according to one subtitler.

2.3 Findings: subtitlers working for the multilingual subtitling company (The Company)

The six subtitlers working for the subtitling company had all been working as TV subtitlers for less than a year except one, which was understandable as The Company only started operations in Croatia in June 2006, just one year before this survey was carried out. It opted for hiring primarily new, unqualified subtitlers, presumably to cut costs.

None of the six respondents considered themselves to be a full-time subtitler and none had finished or attended a specialist school in Translation. Four of the subtitlers mentioned that they would be interested in following a programme of study in subtitling, whereas the other two declined this opportunity, arguing that they thought they were too old for such a training course. All six were unanimous in showing an interest in the results of research. When it came to commenting on the advantages and disadvantages of this profession, the answers were very similar to those put forward by HRT's subtitlers. Significant, though, was the negative statement given by one of the subtitlers: "since it will never be a well paid job, this discipline will always be treated with disrespect, the same as any other form of translation of material that is truly interesting".

An advantage, according to one subtitler, was that "subtitling is incomparably better than other types of translation, like the translation of legal documents, regulations, manuals etc.".

3. Challenges in the profession

Just a mere glance at the above comments and results leads to the conclusion that there seem to be more disadvantages than advantages to the job according to HTV's subtitlers. Whether this is really the case in practice is difficult to ascertain since people tend to complain a lot about their jobs. Nonetheless, the general conclusion was that the job is not an easy one and that is not very well paid in relation to the difficulty and responsibility entailed. On the other hand, subtitlers new to the profession are mostly positive about it.

Subtitling for television is in many ways specific differing from other translation forms. At first glance, it is the size of the audience that makes it specific, since a programme shown on Croatian Television is available to millions of viewers, unlike printed translations. Furthermore, it is a translation format in which consumers (viewers) immediately see the results and they are able to compare it with the original. Most foreign programmes subtitled into Croatian are originally in English and there is a prevalent feeling that 'everyone speaks English', which seems to empower many people to comment on a subtitler's work. HTV is a state-owned company for which viewers pay an annual licence fee and they therefore feel free to comment on the service provided by the TV station, including the subtitles. The internet boom has made this process even easier and viewers can post their comments on the HTV's official on-line forum expressing whatever they wish, under a pseudonym if they so desire. Subtitlers are always credited at the end of a programme meaning that their identity is in the public domain, a situation that new subtitlers find especially sensitive. This can make the job rather stressful for the subtitler.

Although the immense wealth of resources available on the internet has made the job a lot easier for subtitlers, the speed at which some commissions must be carried out in order to meet impossible deadlines means that subtitlers simply do not have time to carry out proper research and revise their translations before submitting them. This is obviously a recipe for poor translations, particularly when working with audiovisual programmes in which slang or any specialised jargon abound.

Working for television means working to very tight deadlines, and a couple of subtitlers pointed out that this is not always a very positive thing since it generates a lot of stress. Although deadlines vary depending on the distribution channel (Díaz Cintas and Remael, 2007:38), the professional reality is that they tend always to be very stringent and some subtitlers find it very hard to cope. Clients can impose short deadlines for a variety of reasons that can be attributed to the nature of the medium itself and, as part of a team, subtitlers must be prepared to complete their translations in a given time. Many respondents commented on the fact that, because the work is freelance, clients do not consider the conditions in which subtitlers work, whether at night, at weekends, on holiday or for very long hours, and consequently these 'extras' will not be reflected in the rates they pay. This is one of the main reasons why subtitlers quit the profession. On the bright side, it is an ideal job for those who dislike 9 to 5 jobs or who like to work at 'unusual, unsocial hours'.

According to the answers provided in the questionnaires, all subtitlers feel that they are underpaid and that the rates do not reflect the difficulty of the job they have to perform. Subtitling rates probably reflect the attitude of employers towards subtitling as a profession and there is no sign that this will change in the near future. If subtitlers want to make a living solely from subtitling, they must work hard and long hours, which again brings us back to the question of quality. Some subtitlers tend to take on more work than they perhaps should.

When it comes to the use of language, many subtitlers feel that they are not independent enough in their work given the language constraints imposed by some of the broadcasters. Usually, it is not subtitlers who are the last see their subtitled work, but rather a proof reader at HTV or a simulator at The Company. Since these professionals also work to stringent deadlines, there is often not enough time to check the changes that they want to introduce with the subtitler before proceeding to implement them. Subtitlers are very unhappy about this situation, as it is their name that is shown at the end of a programme. Having said that, the fact that someone else checks the subtitled material tends to improve the quality of the final product eliminating ' typos' and other punctuation mistakes.

As an activity, subtitling is, as many subtitlers stressed in their questionnaire, repetitive. However, it is a form of translation that enables them to learn many new things not only in linguistic terms. Subtitlers may subtitle a mind-numbingly dull film one day and work on something completely different, like a documentary on the Roman Empire or a corporate video on the banking system the next. All the subtitlers employed by the subtitling company pointed out in their questionnaires that they liked their job precisely because of the quality of the programmes. Seen from this perspective, subtitling has the potential to expand a subtitler's knowledge and views. Other commercial TV stations do not usually broadcast such high quality programmes (Nikolić, 2005:33). So the opportunity to learn does, in many ways, depend on the client.

As mentioned before, new technologies like ADSL high-speed internet connections, integral subtitling programmes and the DVD have enabled subtitlers to produce better quality translations. However, this can also be a negative factor since most subtitlers, especially those who work for subtitling companies, do not have to leave their PC in order to subtitle. This can make it a very solitary job and not everyone is very comfortable doing it as a freelancer, which is why some subtitlers give it up after a couple of years.

4. The future of the profession

The consolidation of the DVD industry has undoubtedly changed the profile of the profession (Díaz Cintas and Remael, 2007:35). Since there is a growing number of TV companies in Croatia, it seems logical to expect that the demand for subtitlers will increase in the years to come. As technology gets better and more user friendly, clients will probably expect subtitlers to work to even shorter deadlines, for more 'challenging' fees and with no errors. However, subtitlers are only human, and will probably expect more money for their work, better working conditions and more realistic deadlines.

It remains to be seen how these two opposing views will be reconciled in the future.

Bibliography

Assis Rosa, Alexandra (2001) "Features of oral and written communication in subtitling", in Yves Gambier and Henrik Gottlieb (eds) *(Multi) Media Translation. Concepts, Practices and Research.* Amsterdam and Philadelphia: John Benjamins, 213-22.

Díaz Cintas, Jorge and Aline Remael (2007) *Audiovisual Translation: Subtitling.* St. Jerome: Manchester.

Ivarsson and Carroll (1998) *Subtitling.* TransEdit: Simrishamn.

Gottlieb, Henrik (1994) "Subtitling: people translating people", in Cay Dollerup and Annette Lindegaard (eds.) *Teaching Translation and Interpreting 2: Insights, Aims and Visions.* Amsterdam and Philadelphia: John Benjamins, 261-74.

Nikolić, Kristijan (2005) "Differences in subtitling for public and commercial TV". *Translating Today* 4, 33-6.

Localising Cockney: translating dialect into Italian

Irene Ranzato

Imperial College, London, UK and
Università di Roma Sapienza, Italy

Abstract
The wide field of sociolinguistics and dialectology applied to translation and to AVT in particular is one of the most fertile, lively and creative objects of research today. Audiovisual texts offer a varied and exhaustive number of examples of linguistic variation at phonological, syntactical, and lexical levels. In the case of Italian, the attitude of translators towards linguistic varieties is multi-faceted but is still markedly influenced by the strong emphasis placed, in the foreign language and translation classroom, on the study of Standard English and Received Pronunciation. Examples taken from films of various genres and dubbed in different periods help illustrate some of the strategies which have been used in the past to translate the Cockney variant of English into Italian. The paper also tries to offer the most appropriate solutions that help achieve a pleasant exotic effect without falling into any of the two potential extremes of incoherent localisation or banalising neutralisation.

1. Introduction

The problem of the translatability of the linguistic varieties of a geographical, ethnic and social type is particularly felt in the field of audiovisual translation (AVT) where, if linguistic problems are the main concern, issues related to the policies of penetration and dissemination of audiovisual products within a national market are also crucial factors which affect the process of translation.

A limited percentage of the English population – between 3 and 5% – has an accent without a dialect inflection (Trudgill, 2000:2-3). It is the 'nonregional' accent defined as 'Received Pronounciation' or RP. This accent, peculiar to such a restricted group of speakers, is the main object of study in schools, language institutes and universities, and English courses all over the world refer almost exclusively to it. When we use the more extensive term of 'dialect', the spectrum is wider as we refer not only to accent, and thus variations in pronounciation, but also to lexical, morphological, and syntactical variations which, for purposes of study and analysis, are commonly considered against the yardstick of so-called Standard English. Standard English, which could be defined as the most successful of English dialects, is the English normally used in the written form and spoken by the majority of the cultured population in England – again, the English normally studied in schools and language institutes –, but it is actually spoken by no more than 12 to 15% of the English population (*ibid.*).[1]

It is obvious that, besides the geographical variants, every region also offers a social spectrum of variations, with Standard English being the 'prestigious' dialect, spoken by people at the top of the social spectrum, and a number of nonstandard variations in the other social strata. Although the word 'dialect' refers to a way of speaking a language which is different from the standard, and not to an incorrect way of speaking a language, as it is often erroneously perceived, nonstandard dialects are often associated with the language spoken by the 'have nots' of society: those without power, less economically well off and less socially prominent, with little or no education. While legitimate linguistically, these dialects tend to be stigmatised by the 'haves' of society.

The wide field of sociolinguistics and dialectology, applied to translation and to AVT in particular, is one of the most fertile, lively and creative objects of research today. The particular interest in applying it to AVT lies in the fact that, thanks to the audio and visual dimensions, no other texts offer such a complete, varied and exhaustive number of examples of all sorts of linguistic variations and, thus, a practically infinite number of phonological, syntactical, and lexical objects of analysis. The films by British directors Ken Loach and Mike Leigh, for instance, are prime examples of the wealth of material available to researchers, since both directors take a stark look at society and at people as they really are and as they really speak.

Nonetheless, despite the wealth of information available in the fields of sociolinguistics and dialectology, the approach to the translation of dialect is generally superficial, dilettantesque or simply heedless of the problem. It is no wonder that if, as has been argued, the focus in the study of the English language is exclusively on Standard English and RP, the translator will not be sufficiently trained to pay much attention to any variations from the norm. It is thus of crucial importance to expose students, from a very early stage, to literary and audiovisual programmes which reflect the varied linguistic and social specificities of other cultures.

2. New trends in dubbing

The situation in Italy concerning the attitude of translators towards linguistic varieties is a complex one. Holmes (1988:49) makes the following distinction between the diachronic and the synchronic axes in the course of the 20th century:

a marked tendency towards modernization and naturalization of the linguistic context, paired with a similar but less clear tendency in the same direction in regard to the literary intertext, but an opposing tendency towards historicizing and exoticizing in the socio-cultural situation.

Trying to apply Holmes's reflection to feature films, the tendency that seems to be the most explicit and generalised in Italy nowadays goes in the direction of a modernisation of the linguistic context, accompanied by an exoticizing of the socio-cultural content, which is achieved by keeping unaltered some lexical items and by using stylistic devices which succeed in maintaining the linguistic flavour of the original. This tendency is more evident if we compare films from the 1980s onwards to the films produced in the decades before the 1970s, though the change has been gradual and never abrupt, and it allows for a number of exceptions.

Two recent examples, based on Spanish films, are in this sense particularly interesting. In the film *Mar Adentro*, a multi-awarded 2004 feature film by Alejandro Amenábar, dealing with a euthanasia case, the effort in translating and adapting the film into Italian was to keep in the dubbed version the original flavour of the original work. This is achieved by maintaining the cadence of the Spanish language at various moments in the dialogue, a characteristic which is evident especially in the dubbing of the main character who, as a result, has in Italian a voice and a way of speaking that are very similar to the original. *Però, perché?*, the protagonist's nephew protests in one scene in the film; *però, no*, we hear in other instances. This is not, strictly speaking, Italian: an Italian would say *Ma perché?*, as *però* is too emphatically adversative to be used in such an instance. The message that the adaptation of this film intends to convey is that it is a Spanish film and proud to be so.[2]

Another example comes from the film by Pedro Almodóvar, *La mala educación* (2004). The adapters into Italian have chosen to let one of the main characters keep his Spanish identity and speak Italian with a strong Spanish accent. The idea of having the Spanish actor Javier Cámara dub his own role in Italian was Pedro Almodóvar's himself, as dubbing director Francesco Vairano stated in an interview (in Bonardelli, 2004/05). This unusual policy serves to emphasise the exoticism of the product, reminding the viewers of the Spanish nature of the original. This relatively new trend in the Italian adaptation of audiovisual programmes is certainly very different from past approaches in which adapters would replace the then almost unknown 'peanut butter' of the original with the word *formaggio* [cheese] in *Some Like It Hot* (Billy Wilder, 1959), or mention the generic *università* [universities] instead of specifically Harvard, to meet the tastes of a public presumably ignorant and scarcely receptive towards the new (Bovinelli and Gallini, 1994:93).

The tendency to allow the exoticism of another language and culture to surface in the translated text is not accompanied by a similar effort when dealing with dialects. Considering that dialects are a clearly exotic element that translators could be tempted to preserve, their absence from the dubbed versions could be regarded as a countertendency. Indeed, dubbed cinema seems to have opted for the standardisation of dialectal variants and has generally abandoned the 'parodistic' tendency to translate foreign dialects with Italian dialects, a choice which, according to Di Giovanni *et al.* (1994), has now become unpopular and is often stigmatised for being politically incorrect and absolutely arbitrary.

As Galassi (1994) remarks, the use of dialect in Italy has a comic connotation. Generally it is not intended to convey a socio-cultural message, maybe because of its humoristic origins in the *Commedia dell'Arte*. Its use is thus generally perceived as unsuitable for dramatic films, with the exception of the (often artificial) Sicilian mafia which is deemed suitable to all genres, from *The Godfather* (Francis Ford Coppola, 1972) to *The Sopranos* (David Chase *et al.*, 1999-2007). Apart from this exception, dialects are often neutralised in translation or resolved synctactically by utilising 'wrong' expressions and lexically by resorting to a highly informal way of speaking, geographically unlocalised and socially unmarked.

It is worth remembering that the effacement of dialects has deep historical roots in Italy, ever since 1933 when a piece of legislation was passed forcing the dubbing of films to take place on Italian territory. From then on, the government would exert greater linguistic control over the 'purity of the Italian language' and insist on the disappearance of dialects, regionalisms and accents. American films, the majority of the films imported, were to be dubbed in an 'abstract' Italian, thus contributing to the effort of cultural homogenisation and regional uprooting which was one of the aims of fascism. From this point of view, as mentioned by Gili (1981:37), the foreign film to be dubbed was a more flexible product than an original Italian film.

3. Cockney and Estuary English

In what follows, I would like to concentrate on some of the solutions adopted by Italian translators in the dubbing of the London accent, both in its traditional Cockney form and in its modern development of rapidly expanding Estuary English. The traditional Cockney dialect includes a number of typical phonetic and grammatical features, among which are:

- 'th' fronting, which involves the replacement of the dental fricatives, /θ/ and /ð/ by labiodentals [f] and [v] respectively, as in words like 'mother' (muvver) and 'think' (fink);
- dropped 'h', as in 'house' ('ouse);
- 't'-glottalisation: use of the glottal stop as an allophone of /t/ in various positions, especially the use of a glottal stop for intervocalic /t/, as in 'bottle' or 'butter'. Also /p,t,k/ are almost invariably glottalised in the final position;
- many vowel and diphthong alterations, including /eɪ/ → [æɪ~aɪ] as in *take* = tyke; /aʊ/ may be [æə] or a monophthongal [æː~aː] as in *round* = raand, *house* = 'aase;
- vocalisation of dark 'l', thus [mɪɔk] for 'milk';
- use of 'ain't' instead of 'isn't', 'am not', 'are not', 'has not', and 'have not';
- use of 'me' instead of 'my'.

Cockney English is also characterised by its distinctive rhyming slang. In this traditional feature, you take a pair of associated words, 'porky and pies', where the second word rhymes with the word you intend to say, 'lies', then use both or sometimes only the first word of the associated pair to indicate the word you originally intended to say. Some rhymes have been in use for years, for example: "apples and pears" = stairs, "plates of meat" = feet. There are others, however, that became established with the changing culture, for example "John Cleese" = cheese.

Since the mid 1990s, a number of studies have reported dialect levelling, by which differences between local accents/dialects are reduced, features which make them distinctive disappear, and new features are developed and adopted by speakers over a wide area. Levelling is thought to centre on large urban areas, such as Tyneside or London in the UK, from which new features disseminate, and within whose reach high degrees of contact and mobility may lead to linguistic homogenisation. Estuary English is the only regional levelling process to receive a name and to become the subject of public debate. It is a popular variety of spoken Standard English with phonetic features placing it between RP and broad London Cockney. First described by Rosewarne (1984), it was characterised as follows:

> Estuary English is a variety of modified regional speech. It is a mixture of nonregional and local south-eastern English pronunciation and intonation. If one imagines a continuum with RP and popular London speech at either end, Estuary English speakers are to be found grouped in the middle ground. They are 'between Cockney and the Queen', in the words of *The Sunday Times* (Rosewarne, 1994: 3).

Estuary English actually spans a very wide range of accents, from near-Cockney to near-RP, so it is difficult to call it a 'variety'. A realistic approach to Estuary English is to see it as referring to a set of levelled (relatively homogenised) regional – as opposed to local – accents or dialects spoken in the south-east of England. These varieties, and their counterparts throughout the British Isles, are a result of greatly heightened mobility since the period just after the Second World War, and a change in ideology that allowed non-RP users to take up a range of occupations, especially in broadcasting, from which they had been formerly barred (Kerswill, 2006:14).

4. *My Fair Lady*

The dubbing of the 1964 film *My Fair Lady* is both a typical and extreme way of treating dialect in dubbing translation; an example which, whatever the opinion on the final result, might encourage translators to find more creative strategies beyond that of the levelling of register to deal with dialectal specificities.

The film by George Cukor, based on George Bernard Shaw's *Pygmalion*, deliberately keeps the theatrical atmosphere of the play on which it is based: the use of stage settings as opposed to filming in realistic locations contributes to the 'artificiality' of the film. This is an important detail as 'unrealistic' plots and settings tend to encourage a certain latitude in the way dialects are translated. In other words, if dialects are not used to describe the 'real' world, translators feel less constrained by problems of coherence.[3]

To make the film more interesting for the purpose of analysis, it is important to remember that its main theme is the use of the English language. This is programmatically set out in the very first song of the musical:

> An Englishman's way of speaking absolutely classifies him. The moment he talks he makes some other Englishman despise him. One common language I'm afraid we'll never get. Oh, why can't the English learn to set a good example to people whose English is painful to your ears?

In the Italian version of the film, the main character, Eliza Doolittle, who in the original speaks an already quite forced, 'laboratory' Cockney, adopts a mixture of Neapolitan and Barese (from the city of Bari, in the South of Italy). The end result is a non-existent Italian language that attempts to translate a London dialect which, in essence, is very far from natural; as far, one could say, as Audrey Hepburn is from a Covent Garden flower girl. In the following example, the typical Barese vowel shift from /a/ to /e/, as in *pega'* instead of the standard Italian *paga[re]*, is happily mingled with other features unknown to this dialect, like the expression *E' figlie vostre* [he's son of yours] below, which is (more or less) Neapolitan but certainly not Barese:

Eliza: 'e's your son is 'e? Well, if you'd done your duty by 'im as a muvver should you wouldn't le' 'im spoil a poor girl's flow'rs and run away without pyin'.	
Ah! E' figlie vostre. Se gli spezzavate le chiappe quand'era piccolo adesso non arruvinava li fiori a 'na povera figlia scappanno via senza pega'.	[mixed accents] Ah, he's son of yours. If you had broken his ass when he was a child now he wouldn't ruin a poor girl's flowers and run away without paying.

In 2005, the stage version of *My Fair Lady* directed by Massimo Romeo Piparo toured the Italian theatres. On this occasion, the translation chose to give Eliza a Sicilian accent, but the protagonist, the inexperienced Roman actress Gaia De Laurentiis, was unable to reproduce the Sicilian accent perfectly and, hence, spoke a strange language from nowhere land. Against all odds, her performance achieved, unknowingly, that excess of foreignisation that can be so appealing and stimulating. The key to the success probably derives from the fact that the accent is not from London, it is not really Italian, but something 'other'. It is that being 'other' in an unlocalised sense that the public perceives: while the London context is visually portrayed, the linguistic information is estranging. Would it have been better to hear Eliza speak with a perfect Sicilian accent under the Covent Garden portico to have had her speak an aseptic, grammatically 'wrong' Italian as generally adopted in dubbing? Or is it not better to hear the character speak another language variation, a language which does not really exist and that tells us that a dialect has been translated with a new variation invented *ad hoc*?

However difficult it may be to achieve this result consciously, I would like to argue that this 'experiment' goes in the right direction of achieving an exotic effect which gives the measure of a cultural distance while avoiding the arbitrary and risky solution of choosing a real dialect from the range offered by the target language.

Coming back to the film version of *My Fair Lady*, if the choice of the Italian dubbers is in many ways surprising and probably unconscious (did they really 'design' that dialect?), it is also true that the result is interesting in itself. The strange language spoken by the Covent Garden flower girl is far both from Naples and from Bari, and it is certainly very far from the geographical context of the original. It is an extreme choice which, while emphasising the unrealistic atmosphere of the whole work, also adds something to it: an extra-geographical dimension. This new dimension does not belong to the target culture or the original, which bases the whole plot on precise geographic and linguistic coordinates: areas and streets of London are precisely mentioned in the film (and in the play), some of the main characters speak Cockney, the male protagonist, Doctor Higgins, recognises anyone's exact place of birth only by hearing their accents etc.

Dubbing certainly manages to unsettle the balance between images and dialogue but it does so in a stimulating way, although one may argue that the choice of Southern dialects to describe the 'have nots' of society is politically incorrect as 'the poor' are often portrayed as coming from the South of Italy rather than from the North. If one really wished to localise it, the natural choice would probably be to translate Cockney by the Roman accent. *Romanesco* is commonly defined as being 'gross' and 'loud' as is Cockney: it is the dialect spoken by the inhabitants of the capital city and its popularity in Italy is only rivalled by Neapolitan, a popularity measured in terms of its use in comedy films and TV sketches (the same as Cockney's popularity is only rivalled by some Northern accents like Liverpudlian). This is not scientifically consistent but, as we have seen, localising can be effective even if it can hardly be defined as a coherent strategy.

5. *Secrets and Lies*

The problem is very different when we have to translate dialects in films with a dramatic, political or social content. In films by realistic directors such as Mike Leigh, dialect is used not only to provide a geographical context, but also to define the various characters from a socio-cultural point of view. The original version of Mike Leigh's masterpiece, *Secrets and Lies* (*Segreti e bugie*,1996), lets the nuances of the language take the burden of conveying the subtle differences of social status among the characters: the protagonist, Cynthia, speaks in a working class London accent, of which the most prominent characteristic is the glottal stop; slightly different is the accent spoken by her brother, who has climbed the social ladder by a few rungs and is married to a Scottish woman who evidently has higher social aspirations. We can also hear, among others, the more formal middle-class English – but with distinctive London and Black British traits – spoken by Cynthia's natural daughter, a black girl who was adopted as a baby by a well-to-do family. All of this and much more is lost in the Italian adaptation which opted for a standard Italian characterised by a few colloquial expressions in the dialogue exchanges between the protagonist, Cynthia, and her daughter Roxanne: for example, the effective choice of the working class *gioia* [joy] to translate some of Cynthia's repeated 'sweetheart' and 'darling'. But in spite of the effort made in trying to keep at least some of the flavour of their exchanges, the loss of information in the dialogues of these two most 'colourful' characters is quite evident, as we can see from the following transcript, which of course cannot convey the marked London accent:

Cynthia: Ain't you seein' him tonight then?

Roxanne: I'm havin' an early night.

Cynthia: Keep me company.

Roxanne: I've got a hangover.

Cynthia: You should stop in more often. You are lookin' after yourself with him, ain't you sweetheart?

Roxanne: What d'you mean?

Cynthia: You know, taking care. I don't wanna ask you nothing personal, darling, but are you taking the pill?

Roxanne: That IS personal.

Cynthia: Why don't you bring him round?

Roxanne: Leave it out.

Cynthia: I'd like to meet him. I wouldn't know him if he stood up in me soup.

Roxanne: Don't hold your breath.

Cynthia: You don't wanna leave it up to him, darling, men are all the same.

Cynthia: Che fai, non lo vedi stasera?	Cynthia: What, you're not seeing him tonight?
Roxanne: Voglio andare a letto presto.	Roxanne: I want to go to bed early.
Cynthia: Tienimi compagnia.	Cynthia: Keep me company.
Roxanne: Mi sono presa una sbronza.	Roxanne: I've got a hangover.
Cynthia: Dovresti startene di più a casa. State facendo attenzione, vero tesoro?	Cynthia: You should stay home more often. You are taking care, aren't you sweetheart?
Roxanne: Che vuoi dire?	Roxanne: What do you mean?
Cynthia: Sai, le precauzioni. Non mi voglio impicciare degli affari tuoi ma, prendi la pillola?	Cynthia: You know, precautions. I don't want to poke my nose into your own business, but are you taking the pill?
Roxanne: Ecco, questi sono affari miei.	Roxanne: Now, this is my business.
Cynthia: Perché non lo fai venire a casa?	Cynthia: Why don't you bring him round?
Roxanne: Sono cavoli miei.	Roxanne: Mind your own business.
Cynthia: Mi piacerebbe conoscerlo. Non lo riconoscerei neanche se me lo ritrovassi nella zuppa.	Cynthia: I'd like to meet him. I wouldn't know him if I found him in my soup.
Roxanne: Risparmia il fiato.	Roxanne: Don't hold your breath.
Cynthia: Non aspettare che sia lui a preoccuparsi, gli uomini sono tutti uguali.	Cynthia: Don't expect him to worry about that, men are all the same.

These lines, delivered in standard Italian, show the tendency to neutralise the local and social flavour of the film by choosing to eliminate two idiosyncratic 'darling' from Cynthia's sentences; by changing the register of the original when translating the expression 'taking care' with the more formal *precauzioni* [precautions]; by translating literally, and thus conveying what is an unusual image in Italian, the idiomatic phrase 'I wouldn't know him if he stood in me soup'; and by ignoring all the grammatical deviations from standard English (two negatives, use of 'ain't', and the like).

As Taylor (2006:38) correctly points out when discussing the translation of the films by a similarly realistic British director, Ken Loach, the defining features of an original film dialogue marked by dialects and sociolects as well as by other local features are always diluted to the point of neutralisation when translated into Italian.

6. *Lock & Stock and Two Smoking Barrels*

The 1998 film *Lock & Stock and Two Smoking Barrels* by Guy Ritchie about petty criminals and humorous swindles, captures the audience from its very first scene drawing them into a context which, while showing no places and only people, is unmistakably London. The funny opening monologue delivered by the protagonist, the small time criminal Bacon, who is selling stolen goods at a market, perfectly illustrates the work that has gone into the Italian adaptation:

Bacon: Let's sort the buyers from the spiers, the needy from the greedy, and those who trust me from the ones who don't. 'Cos if you can't see value here today, you're not up here shopping, you're up here shoplifting. You see these goods? Never seen daylight, moonlight, Israelites, Fanny by the gaslight. Take a bag, come on take a bag. I took a bag home last night - cost me a lot more than ten pounds, I can tell you. Anyone like jewellery? Look at that one there. Hand-made in Italy, hand-stolen in Stepney. It's as long as my arm, I wish it was as long as something else. Don't think 'cause these boxes are sealed, they're empty. The only man that sells empty boxes is the undertaker. By the look of some of you here today, I'd make more money with my measuring tape. Here, one price, ten pound (…)	
Squeeze in if you can. Left leg, right leg, your body will follow. They call it walking. You want one as well, darling? You do? That's it, they're waking up. Treat the wife - treat somebody else's wife. It's a lot more fun if you don't get caught. Hold on. You want one as well? OK darling. Show me a bit of life, then. It's no good standing out there like one o'clock half struck. Buy 'em, you'd better buy 'em. These are not stolen - they just haven't been paid for. Can't get 'em again, they've changed the locks. Can't come back – I'll have sold out. (…)	
"Too late, too late" will be the cry when the man with the bargains just passed you by. If you've got no money on you now you'll be crying tears big as october cabbages.	
La prima cosa che bisogna fare è dividere chi compra da chi vuole guardare, quelli che di me si voglion fidare da chi non ci vuole neanche provare.	The first thing one has to do is to sort the buyers from the onlookers, the ones who want to trust me from those who don't even try to.
E se queste cose non sapete apprezzare, non siete venuti a comprare.	And if you can't appreciate these things, you're not here to buy.
Sono cose nuove, sono cose belle, non	They're new things, they're beautiful

hanno mai visto il sole né le <u>stelle</u>, né le <u>modelle</u> sulle <u>passerelle</u>.	things, they've never seen the sun nor the stars, nor the models on catwalks.
Prendete una busta, su, prendete una busta. Una donna ieri a casa ho <u>portato</u> e mi è costata dieci sterle, datelo per <u>scontato</u>.	Take a bag, come on take a bag. I took a woman home last night and she cost me ten pounds, I can tell you.
A chi piacciono i gioielli? Guardate questa qui. E' stata fatta a mano in Italia e poi rubata a mano armata. E' lunga quanto il <u>braccio</u>, più lunga di qualcos'altro, <u>accidentaccio</u>.	Anyone like jewellery? Look at that one there. Hand-made in Italy, then hand-robbed. It's as long as my arm, longer than something else, damn it.
Le scatole non sono <u>sigillate</u> perché sono state <u>svuotate</u>. Solo le pompe funebri vendono le scatole vuote. Ma guardandovi in faccia mi fate <u>pensare</u> che a prendervi le misure più ricco potrei <u>diventare</u>. Prezzo unico, dieci sterle belli. (…)	The boxes aren't sealed because they're empty. The only man that sells empty boxes is the undertaker. But by the look of you, you make me think I'd make more money with my measuring tape. Here, one price, ten pound. (…)
Non <u>esitare</u>.	Don't hesitate.
Prima la destra, poi la sinistra, e il resto non dovrai <u>aspettare</u>. Sai, si chiama <u>camminare</u>.	Right leg, left leg, for the rest you won't have to wait. You know, they call it walking.
Ne vuoi una anche tu tesoro? Bene, vi state svegliando a quanto pare.	You want one as well, darling? That's it, you're waking up it seems.
Se un regalo a vostra moglie o alla moglie di un altro volete <u>fare</u>, è più divertente se non vi fate <u>beccare</u>. Aspetta ne vuoi una anche tu? D'accordo <u>amore</u>, allora mettici un po' di <u>vigore</u>. Se stai lì ferma come un palo prenderai un <u>raffreddore</u>. <u>Comprate, comprate</u> che non <u>sbagliate</u>. Non sono cose <u>rubate</u> - solo che non sono state <u>pagate</u>.	Treat the wife - treat somebody else's wife. It's a lot more fun if you don't get caught. Hold on. You want one as well? OK darling. Show me a bit of life, then. If you stand there like a pole you'll catch a cold. Buy them, you'd better buy them. These are not stolen - they just haven't been paid for.
Ma averne ancora sarà <u>dura</u> perché hanno cambiato la <u>serratura</u>. (…)	It will be hard to get them again, they've changed the locks. (…)
Più tardi avrò venduto <u>tutto</u>, mi dispiace per chi sarà rimasto a becco <u>asciutto</u>.	Later on it will all be sold out, sorry for those who'll be left with nothing.
Troppo tardi, troppo tardi. Io sarò <u>lontano</u> e il buon affare ti sarà scappato di <u>mano</u>.	Too late, too late. I'll be far away and the bargains just passed you by.
E se adesso i soldi con te non <u>hai</u>, più tardi lacrime amare purtroppo sono certo <u>piangerai</u>.	If you've got no money on you now unfortunately I'm sure you'll be crying bitter tears later.

The most obvious feature of this translation is the use of the rhyme. The dubbing adapters, while basically faithful to the semantic content of the text, have chosen to emphasise this particular stylistic dimension, interpreting it as the dominant feature of the source text. As mentioned above, it is the opening monologue of this fast-paced film and, as such, it sets the tone of the dialogue which follows. It was particularly important to find a solution which is both striking and humourous. The result is undoubtedly exotic. The wealth of rhymed words (underlined in the text – 38 in Italian compared to a total of only ten rhyming words in the source text) is certainly unusual but it perfectly conveys the flavour of the Cockney's rhyming slang that is sometimes used in the original. Caught by the charm of the Italian version, viewers do not really mind if a few funny wordplays are lost: 'bag' translated with *busta* [*bag*, but with no double meaning] loses its second meaning of 'prostitute'; the Italian audience will never recognise one of the quotes from Anthony Asquith's British film *Fanny by Gaslight* (1944), or know the idiomatic meaning of 'standing like one o'clock half struck', a Geordie expression meaning 'looking like an idiot'. Nor will they mourn the loss of the geographic, thus exotic, trait offered by the mention of the East London area of 'Stepney'. The main achievement of this translation is that the exotic feature of the source text Cockney rhyming slang is most preciseley transferred into Italian by exaggerating the number of rhymes. The result is that the audience hears a linguistic variety which is not a new dialect, is not an Italian dialect, but is so far from the standard use of the language that it sounds unlocalised and, to some extent, 'foreign'.

Incidentally, it is worth noting that the use of rhyming lines to translate non-standard English into Italian seems to be growing: the TV series *Skins* (Jamie Brittain *et al.*, 2007)[4] depicts the lives of a group of young people from Bristol, characterised by a speech full of dialect, slang and idiomatic expressions. The Italian version makes ample use of rhymes which are not present in the original text. The result is, also in this case, what could be labelled as 'exotic'.

7. Conclusion

The exclusive emphasis in the foreign language and translation classroom on the study of Standard English and Received Pronounciation does not create the basis for developing a sensitivity towards other linguistic variations. It is no wonder that some translators seem to be unprepared and untrained at solving the task of dialect translation in a way which, if not completely satisfactory, can be at least intellectually stimulating.

There are examples of solutions and strategies in dialect translation which achieve unusual but imaginative and intelligent results that might lead the way to further developments. One of them is the use of rhyming which, used in the instances discussed above, to translate Cockney's rhyming slang or even other non-rhyming dialects, achieves a pleasant effect of exoticism. It can be concluded that one of the solutions to translating dialects in a carefully selected number of cases might be that of playing with the potential of the target language – its syntax, its standard lexicon – in such a way as to come up with an unusual prosody that achieves the effect of an 'unlocalised' variant of the standard language.

Notes

1. It is not possible to delve here into the complexities of this interesting field of research. It will suffice to point out that RP, unlike Standard English, appears to be changing quite rapidly. This leads to problems in finding criteria for determining what are changes and variations within RP, and what features make a person's speech non-RP. Trudgill's (2002:175) own criterion is simply to say that, for inclusion as part of RP, a feature must not be a regional feature.

2. The dubbing director of *Mare dentro (Mar adentro, The Sea Inside)* was Maura Vespini. However, it is important to note that dubbing, like everything in cinema, is the product of a collective effort. In this sense, Andrea Occhipinti, the distributor of the film, took personal care of the dubbing and made sure that the film's Hispanicity was linguistically evident in the Italian version. An earlier comment on this film was contained in Ranzato (2006).

3. Among the many examples in this sense, in Italian dubbing translation, we might mention the inconsistent but effectively funny translations of dialects in cartoons like *The Simpsons* and *South Park* or in comedies which make wide use of language variations like the Monty Python films. The use of Cockney in a Palestinian setting, as in *Monty Python's Life of Brian* for instance, certainly called for an equivalently incongruous localisation in the Italian version.

4. *Skins* is a teen drama premiered in 2007 on the digital TV channel E4. Its fourth series is now in production.

References

Bonardelli, Marco (2004/05) *Speciale.*
    www.antoniogenna.net/doppiaggio/film/lamalaeducacion.htm
Bovinelli, Bettina and Serena Gallini (1994) "La traduzione dei riferimenti culturali nel doppiaggio cinematografico", in Raffaella Baccolini, Rosa Maria Bollettieri Bosinelli and Laura Gavioli (eds) *Il doppiaggio – trasposizioni linguistiche e culturali*. Bologna: Clueb, 89-98.
Di Giovanni, Elena, Francesca Diodati and Giorgia Franchini (1994) "Il problema delle varietà linguistiche nella traduzione filmica", in Raffaella Baccolini, Rosa Maria Bollettieri Bosinelli and Laura Gavioli (eds) *Il*

doppiaggio – trasposizioni linguistiche e culturali. Bologna: Clueb, 99-104.

Galassi, Gianni (1994) "La norma traviata", in Raffaella Baccolini, Rosa Maria Bollettieri Bosinelli and Laura Gavioli (eds) *Il doppiaggio – trasposizioni linguistiche e culturali*. Bologna: Clueb, 61-70.

Gili, Jean A. (1981) *Stato fascista e cinematografia*. Roma: Bulzoni.

Holmes, James S. (1988) *Translated! Papers on Literary Translation and Translation Studies*. Amsterdam: Rodopi.

Kerswill, Paul (2006) "Standard English, RP and the standard - non-standard relationship", in David Britain (ed.) *Language in the British Isles*. Cambridge: Cambridge University Press, 34-51. Also available on: www.ling.lancs.ac.uk/staff/kerswill/pkpubs/Kerswill2006RPStandardEng lish.pdf

Ranzato, Irene (2006) "Tradurre dialetti e socioletti nel cinema e nella televisione", in Nigel Armstrong and Federico M. Federici (eds). *Translating Voices, Translating Regions*. Roma: Aracne, 141-60.

Rosewarne, David (1984) "Estuary English". *Times Educational Supplement*. 19th October.

Rosewarne, David (1994) "Estuary English: tomorrow's RP". *English Today* 37, 10(1): 3-8.

Taylor, Christopher J. (2006) "The translation of regional variety in the films of Ken Loach", in Nigel Armstrong and Federico M. Federici (eds). *Translating Voices, Translating Regions*. Roma: Aracne, 37-52.

Trudgill, Peter (2000) *The Dialects of England*. Oxford and Malden: Blackwell.

Trudgill, Peter (2002) *Sociolinguistic Variation and Change*. Edinburgh: Edinburgh University Press.

Translating postmodern networks of cultural associations in the Polish dubbed version of *Shrek*

Agnieszka Chmiel

Adam Mickiewicz University, Poznan, Poland

Abstract

Screen translation in Poland has long focussed on voiceover, its market position being strengthened by rather unsuccessful dubbing attempts. A major breakthrough in the general perception of dubbing came with the Polish dubbed version of *Shrek* (2001). The dialogue exchanges were much domesticated and they appealed to Polish viewers since they abounded in jocular allusions to Polish reality and culture. This paper focusses on examining, comparing and juxtaposing selected networks of cultural associations created by original (American culture-oriented) and translated (Polish culture-oriented) utterances of the film characters in *Shrek*. The dubbed text is set in the context of screen translation in Poland and the Polish polysystem of films, the nature of audiovisual translation operations and the intertextuality of the original work.

1. Introduction

Poland is typically a voiceover country with few films translated with other audiovisual translation (AVT) techniques, such as dubbing or subtitling. However, the viewers' generally negative attitude to dubbed films changed slightly due to the immense popularity of the Polish dubbed version of *Shrek* (Andrew Adamson and Vicky Jenson, 2001). This paper focusses on examining, comparing and juxtaposing selected networks of cultural associations created by original (US culture-oriented) and translated (Polish culture-oriented) utterances of the film characters in *Shrek*. The analysis of original and translated dialogues seeks to answer a host of questions: What do Polish viewers lose in the domesticated dubbed version of *Shrek*? Do they lose anything at all or would they be able to decipher most of the source culture allusions in the original text? What do Polish viewers gain? How are the discrepancies between messages sent through the domesticated audio channel and the non-domesticated unadjusted visual channel perceived? For the purpose of the analysis, the dubbed text is set in the context of screen translation in Poland and the Polish polysystem of films, the nature of audiovisual translation operations and the intertextuality of the original work.

2. Screen translation in Poland

Screen translation in Poland, as in many formerly communist states in Central and Eastern Europe, is mainly based on voiceover, a cost-effective audiovisual translation technique that deafens actors' voices with an emotionless reading by a narrator. Voiceover is used for virtually all translations on state-owned television regardless of the genre – be it a feature film, a documentary or a quiz show – and is predominant on private TV channels. In cinemas, subtitling is used for the majority of productions. Dubbing is applied solely to TV shows and films for children (both on TV and in cinema). Additionally, when films are released on DVD, their voiceover versions are now usually available. In fact, Polish DVD releases of foreign films used to be advertised by focussing on the availability of the voiceover version as added value. This, as unbelievable to the viewers from non-voiceover countries as it may be, probably shows that Poles are so accustomed to voiceover that they simply disregard its disadvantages when compared to subtitling.

There is very little data as regards types of AVT applied by various Polish mass media. According to a 1991 study by the European Institute for the Media, 100% of TV programmes in Poland were translated via voiceover while 100% of films screened in cinemas were subtitled (Dries, 1995). Since then, the situation has not changed much and television shows – at least the ones offered by TVP, the Polish national broadcaster – are still predominantly voicedover while cinemas use subtitling overwhelmingly and dubbing only for films for children.

According to a survey conducted in 2002, voiceover is preferred by 50.2% of Poles, dubbing is favoured by 43.3% and subtitling is chosen by 8.1% of Poles (Bogucki, 2004). Polish viewers seem to be well accustomed to voiceover and rather unwilling to change their preferences. This might be partially due to the fact that early dubbing attempts in the 1980s were rather unsuccessful and strengthened the market position of voiceover. Private broadcasters did not have enough expertise and were not willing to allocate sufficient funds to produce professional dubbing. Moreover, when attempting to introduce dubbing and subtitles on television, the Polish national broadcaster met with a lot of criticism on the part of the viewers (Garcarz, 2006:115).

Dubbing has been considered by many viewers as something 'damaging', an obstacle that detaches the viewer from the original voice and acting. The general criticism raised against dubbing in Poland was in its nature similar to that mentioned by Whitman (1992:118, in Chaume, 2003:104) in the early 1990s: "Artificiality is one of the main faults pillored in denouncements of dubbed versions: the audience can hear that this is not an original. Dubbed language simply does not correspond to the way normal people talk". Additionally, when poorly translated, entertainment programmes lost their main popularity-generating factor.

Dubbing is also widely criticised by viewers on the internet. According to many negative opinions expressed in 2008 on various fora frequented by fans about the poor quality dubbing of *The Simpsons* – screened by TV Puls, one of Polish public broadcasters –, the low popularity of this otherwise immensely successful cartoon was precisely due to the irritating and unamusing translation. In fact, low popularity ratings and criticism of the dubbed version forced the broadcaster to discontinue the series.

These open criticisms are somehow at variance with the most recent survey conducted among Polish viewers. According to the 2005 opinion poll, their preferences changed slightly as compared to the 2002 results with dubbing ranking first (46%), followed by voiceover (45%) and subtitling (5%) (Garcarz, 2006). This trend might show that Polish viewers have started noticing the advantages of dubbing as an AVT technique over voiceover in general but are also dissatisfied with the quality of many domestic dubbed productions. It remains to be seen if this change in preferences is the beginning of a long-term trend, also in the context of the very successful dubbing of *Shrek* to be analysed below.

An overview of listings of Polish cinemas in one large city (Poznań), carried out by the author in April 2006 and repeated in November 2008, shows that only approximately 20% of films are dubbed; mainly films directed at young audiences or families with children. However, as mentioned above, the perception of dubbing has changed slightly thanks to excellent dubbed versions of animated movies directed mainly at children, but also – due to their postmodern intertextual nature – at adults. A major breakthrough came with the Polish dubbed version of *Shrek* (original version written by Joe Stillman, Roger S.H. Schulman, Ted Elliott and Terry Rossio; Polish version by Bartosz Wierzbięta), released in 2001. The dubbed version of this film will be analysed in more detail in the second part of this chapter. In the first part, the analysis will be preceded by more general remarks about the scope of AVT, the position of dubbed movies in the Polish film polysystem and the postmodern nature of popular culture.

3. AVT – operations on semiotic complexes

Audiovisual translation, especially when analysed in the context of cultural and postmodern intertextuality, should not be treated as an operation on language and culture only. According to Tomaszkiewicz (2006:98), AVT involves much more than operations between the source language and the target language (on the linguistic level only), between the source message and the target message (i.e. involving communication, context, utterance, intentionality, etc.), or even between the source text and the target text. She claims that due to its intersemiotic nature, AVT includes operations between the source semiotic complex and the target semiotic complex. It is a specific type of translation that combines elements of traditional interlingual and intersemiotic translations (*ibid.*:100). Although the translator changes only the verbal layer of the film, the translation has to fit the whole semiotic context of the film and the semiotic complex of the target culture.

Zabalbeascoa (1993:222-3, in Chaume, 2003:70) applies a similar approach to dubbing, by claiming that "the translation (a process performed only on the verbal signs) is only one part of the dubbing process (which should take into account verbal and nonverbal signs); the words are just part of the final product".

In his pragmatic plot-oriented approach to translation in dubbing, Luyken *et al.* (1991:162) suggest that one should not translate sentence by sentence, but rather scene by scene. The scene should be treated as a translation unit. Such an approach gives the translator more freedom since the objective is to provide the faithful translation of a scene, which means that omissions, additions and shifts between sentences within a scene are perfectly acceptable. As is demonstrated below, the translator of *Shrek* did apply the above mentioned theoretical assumptions in his global strategy.

4. The Polish polysystem of films

When analysing translations of any artistic works, it is very useful to put both the former and the latter in the context of the target culture artistic landscape. Only then can it be seen if the translated work under scrutiny complies with the established norms, breaks certain rules or sets new standards if there have been none previously. In the case of AVT, it is helpful to resort to Even-Zohar's (1978) literary polysystem theory as applied by Díaz Cintas (2004) to films. A film polysystem, as one of the "semiotic systems that co-exist dynamically within a particular cultural sphere" (Díaz Cintas, 2004:22) includes national and translated products and the relationships among them. Translations "shake off the mantle of a secondary, deficient product" and are "in principle at the same social and cultural level as the national ones" (*ibid.*:24). This statement is quite crucial for current deliberations since, as we hope to show, the analysed film has shifted in the Polish polysystem from the location traditionally reserved for dubbed films.

The Polish polysystem includes, apart from national films, foreign films that are translated mainly using subtitles (in the cinema) or voiceover (on television) with US films enjoying a central position, especially in the popular culture. Dubbed films used to be rather peripheral due to poor quality dubbing. Therefore, no standards or norms have been developed as regards this type of AVT in Poland, as opposed to other countries with long established dubbing traditions, where isochrony can be a flexible restriction like in Italy or one of the major dubbing constraints as in Spain (Chaume, 2004:47). Additionally, there is a high level of acceptance of Anglicisms and foreignisation in Poland and some movie titles are not even translated (e.g. *Good Night and Good Luck* or *The Flintstones*, the latter being a curious case since the TV cartoon was also very popular in Poland and it had a translation well established in popular culture: *Jaskiniowcy* [*The Cave People*]). This overall acceptance of foreignisation might stem from generally pro-American sentiments that are strong across Poland or from the viewers' previous experiences of very bad or strange translations of some film titles (e.g. *Reality Bites* translated as *Orbitowanie bez cukru* (sic!) [*Orbiting Without Sugar*] or *Dirty Dancing* translated as *Wirujący seks* (sic!) [*Spinning Sex*]). It is very interesting to analyse the dubbed version of *Shrek* against this background for the following three reasons: it is the first immensely successful example of a dubbed movie that is no longer peripheral to other translated movies with subtitles or voiceover; it has set some standards as regards dubbing strategies; these strategies are based mainly on domestication, which is surprising in the context of the wide acceptance of foreignisation in Poland.

5. The postmodern nature of popular culture

Before moving on to the analysis of the translation of *Shrek* to see how postmodern networks of cultural associations and various intertextual allusions were rendered by the Polish translator, let us briefly consider the nature of modern popular culture of which this film is such an excellent example. According to Johnson (2005:xi), popular culture has grown more complex and intellectually challenging over the past years. Modern works of popular culture, be it computer games, television series or films, are more sophisticated and present us with increasingly demanding cognitive challenges.

Films abound in intricate narrative paths, multiple layers of information built into the plots, intertextual references and allusions to other works and to reality. Johnson (2005) compares the structure of TV crime series from the 1970s (such as *Starsky and Hutch*) with their younger counterparts (such as *The Sopranos*) or popular children's films (*Bambi* from 1942 and *Mary Poppins* from 1964) with more recent box office hits (*Monsters Inc.* from 2001 or *Finding Nemo* from 2002). The analysis shows that current series and films include more complex narratives with multiple plots and threads, a greater number of characters with more developed social networks and more pronounced intertextuality.

The upward trend visible in more complex narratives, called the Sleeper Curve by Johnson (*ibid.*), is particularly apparent in children's films, such as *Toy Story, Shrek, Monsters, Inc.* or *Finding Nemo.* According to Johnson (*ibid.*:127): "creators of these recent films build distinct layers of information into their plots, dialogue, and visual effects, creating a kind of hybrid form that dazzles children without boring the grownups". While visual allusions may be perfectly detectable to native and foreign audiences (such as the jocular allusion to *Matrix* in *Shrek* or to *Beverly Hills Cop* in *Shrek 2*), postmodern intertextual networks of cultural associations created on the linguistic level set a great challenge to audiovisual translators who cannot resort to lengthy explanations or footnotes. This challenge is also observed by Agost (2004:66), who states that: "if the analysis of culture reveals a complex network of ideas and highlights a relationship between the various systems, the intercultural situation that translation represents is an additional difficulty". Set in this context, *Shrek* is a perfect object of study to see how the author of the dubbed script managed to overcome technical and linguistic constraints and to weave the intertextual network of domesticated or foreignised allusions into the fabric of the dialogue exchanges.

6. The translator's strategy

The text for the dubbed version of *Shrek* was created by Bartosz Wierzbięta who is now a well-known audiovisual translator and dialogue writer. He tackled the challenge presented by the postmodern, intertextual film by applying a target culture adaptation strategy. Tomaszkiewicz (2006:202) claims that animated films translated by Wierzbięta are a very good example of domesticated dubbing:

> We are facing a new dimension of film dialogues that are friendly to Polish viewers, i.e. dialogues that are fully understood thanks to their references to our linguistic and cultural background. A skilful translator, such as Wierzbięta, smuggles some information that refers to the Polish reality into translated dialogues. Thus, foreign characters are assimilated for the viewers. As a result, the translator introduces a national dimension to the dialogues and creates *additional* comic effects (my translation and emphasis).

Therefore, the criterion of fidelity seems to have lost its priority when confronted with other functions played by the dubbed film.

Zabalbeascoa (1997:336) lists criteria and restrictions that refer to the translation of television situation comedies. Some of them, such as the following, pertain also to the translation of children's films and comedies:

1. popularity ratings – the commercial dimension of the film and its translation is important;
2. the translation should be funny, entertaining and should elicit laughter;
3. it should 'integrate the words of the translation with other constituent parts of the audiovisual text';
4. implicit and explicit allusions to other TV programs or films work only if they are part of the required 'shared knowledge'.

As will be demonstrated, the translation strategy and solutions applied by the translator of the analysed film comply with the above priorities and restrictions. Wierzbięta (in Wojtowicz 2002:online) presents his overall translational strategy as follows:

> Dialogues have to be comprehensible to the Polish audience; thus, it is *not always appropriate* to produce a complete equivalent of the original dialogues. If nuances of the original language and puns are not funny, they *should be adapted* to the Polish reality. The development of my translation skills meant that I became aware of the fact that I can enjoy more freedom and that I can afford more freedom. [...] It is not about the Polish text being the perfect reflection of the original text. What counts is that the text is synchronized, attractive and comprehensible. I know from my own experience that the more detached the Polish dialogue is from the original, the better it is. It is not a rule but the movies with the greatest number of such differences were the most popular (my translation and emphasis).

The translational equivalence is thus subjected to domestication. The text has to be first of all attractive, entertaining, easily understood by the target audience, and only then faithful to the original. Wierzbięta's most favourite strategies include: adaptation, addition and compensation. They will be discussed in more detail in the subsequent sections.

The translator's freedom in translating an animated film is further justified because of a special status of the film as a work of art. When watching a dubbed film, viewers agree to two illusions, the first being 'the willing suspension of disbelief' (a term coined and originally applied to poetry by Coleridge 1817/1985:312) and the second being 'the suspension of linguistic disbelief' (Romero-Fresco, 2006). The former pertains to any work of art. In the case of films it means that viewers accept the depicted world as real and look past certain limitations of the film as a medium. The latter pertains to the language spoken in dubbed films. Even if a film is set in the USA, the viewers consent to the illusion that the characters speak Polish, German or French and that the given language is natural to them. The suspension of the linguistic disbelief is even easier to obtain in an animated film, such as *Shrek*. Characters are not real and the plot is not set in any real country. Thus, it is easy for the viewers to believe that the characters speak fluent Polish and that some of them sound just like very famous Polish actors. The illusion created by the animated film gives more freedom to the translator. Since the viewers accept the fact that the characters speak Polish, they will also suspend their disbelief in the fact that the characters naturally allude to Polish reality in their conversations.

6.1. Adaptation

The original dialogue includes numerous allusions to films, fairy tale characters and other source culture-specific items. Their inexhaustive list includes: *The Matrix*, Cinderella, Big Bad Wolf, Three Little Pigs, *Beverly Hills Cop*, Robin Hood, Pinocchio, Sleeping Beauty, The Dating Game, and The Muffin Man. Some of these films or characters are part of the 'shared knowledge' referred to by Zabalbeascoa (1997:336). In such cases, the translator simply resorts to using well-established translations such as *Pinokio* [Pinocchio] and *Śpiąca Królewna* [Sleeping Beauty]. The problems arise when the culture-specific knowledge is not shared and the translator must adapt the source culture to the target culture and trigger a comic effect by creating completely new allusions and intertextual networks of postmodern associations.

One of the examples is a song sung by the flying Donkey that alludes to Dumbo, a flying elephant well-known to US children. Instead, the Polish version introduces a completely different allusion, not to a character of children's movies and the related song, but to a song performed by Jerzy Stuhr, the actor playing Donkey in the Polish version of *Shrek*. Jerzy Stuhr is much appreciated by Poles mainly for his comic characters. In 1977, he performed a song entitled *Śpiewać każdy może* [Anyone can sing] at the Polish Song Festival in Opole. The lyrics convinced the listeners that anyone can sing, no matter if the singing is good or bad, and Stuhr's singing was deliberately bad to create a comic effect. He plays a person who cannot really sing but is sure of his talent and has to give vent to it for fear of suffocation. The song is very popular in Poland and the title (anyone can sing) has been used in many contexts and talent shows. By activating a whole network of cultural associations, this substitution is very entertaining to Polish adult audiences.

The dubbed dialogue exchanges abound in Polish culture-specific references. The original allusion to a children's song about a 'Muffin Man' who lives on 'Drury Lane' is completely opaque to the Polish audience and is thus replaced by an allusion to cartoon characters Żwirek and Muchomorek.

'Parfaits' mentioned by Donkey are substituted with *kremówki*, a typically Polish cake that again triggers a network of entertaining associations, including even the childhood memories of Pope John Paul II, who largely contributed to the immense success of *kremówki* on the Polish market by reminiscing about them at one of his televised meetings with thousands of young people during his pilgrimage to Poland. The majority of the Polish audience would not know that 'Heimlich manoeuvre' mentioned by one of the characters is an abdominal thrust used to prevent choking. Thus, it is replaced with a phrase: *Czy jest na sali lekarz?* [Is there a doctor here?] that is fixed in Polish and sometimes used in jokes.

The above examples of translational adaptations show that some Polish solutions include even richer and funnier allusions than those in the original script and they definitely create different networks of postmodern associations. When evaluated according to Zabalbeascoa's (1997) criteria for the translation of entertainment shows, these solutions seem to be very efficient and successful in evoking intended comic effects.

6.2. Addition or compensation?

Apart from the domesticated translations analysed above, the translator frequently resorted to adding to the translated text elements absent in the orginal. An addition is considered by Tomaszkiewicz (2006:206) as a translation error that involves an unjustified introduction in the target text of unnecessary information or stylistic effects not present in the source text. The domesticated dubbed version of *Shrek* in Polish abounds in unfaithful translations or additions of short linguistic items and even whole lines. In accordance with Luyken's *et al.* (1991) pragmatic approach to dubbing mentioned earlier, the translator justifies his approach in the following way: "If I have no good idea for translating a funny line, it's not crucial for me to have the Polish viewer laugh exactly at the same time as the American viewer. Let the Polish viewer laugh two lines later when there is nothing funny for the American viewer but there is something that could be a source of laughter for the Polish viewer" (in Wojtowicz, 2002:online, my translation). It remains to be seen if additions in the dubbed version should be treated as errors or rather a manifestation of a key translation strategy, i.e. compensation. What follows is an analysis of selected examples to settle the above issue.

Example 1

Shrek: Grab your torch and pitchforks.	
Jontek, łap za widły.	[Jontek, grab your pitchfork.]

The translator adds a name here, Jontek. This is an allusion to a famous Polish opera, *Halka* by Moniuszko, in which Jontek was one of the main characters of a rather impetuous nature. Humour in this line comes from the unexpected use of an old Polish name of an opera character in the film's context.

Example 2

Pinocchio: Oh, gosh, no one invited us.	
Hej, ty, no nie bądź taki drewniak.	[Hey, you, don't be such a stiff.]

The sense of this line has been changed completely and a pun – a wooden character accusing someone of being stiff – is introduced to compensate for other comic effects present somewhere else in the original film and lost in translation.

Example 3

One of the three little pigs: He huffed and he puffed and he... signed an eviction notice...	
Dmuchał, chuchał i zarządził, świnia, eksmisję.	[He huffed and he puffed and he... signed an eviction notice, what a pig.]

As in example 2, the pun, in this case related to a pig, is not present in the original and is deliberately added by the translator for a comic effect.

Example 4

Shrek: All right. You're going the right way for a smacked bottom.	
Słuchaj, jeszcze chwila, a otworzę wytwórnię salami.	[Listen, you do that once again and I'll open a salami production plant.]

This threating statement is used in the film by Shrek in his conversation with Donkey. Salami is known in Poland as a sausage made originally of horse meat. However, it was quite common in communist Poland to manufacture products of substitutes due to the overall scarcity of goods. Thus, the inference here is that donkey meat can be a good substitute for horse meat, making the utterance funny to the Polish audience. As reported by the translator himself (in Wierzbięta, 2002), this phrase was a bone of contention with the representative of the US major supervising the Polish dubbing production. Example 5 below can be seen as an extreme instance of the translator's freedom:

Example 5

Donkey: ---	
Idę po precelki.	[I'll get some little pretzels.]

The original character says nothing, while the dubbed character has been given a new line. The synchronisation requirement is fulfilled because the character's lips are not visible during this utterance. The only justification for such an addition is that it actually compensates for lost comic effect somewhere else in the film, either before or after that added line. Polish morphology allows for the creation of a variety of diminutives by resorting to suffixes. When used often, as is the case in the Polish version of *Shrek*, diminutives can create a comic effect. This is what happens in this particular instance in which *pretzels* are used in the diminutive form. Additionally, the (ab)use of diminutives can be seen as an allusion to the distinctive speaking style of Maks, a character from the unforgettable 1984 Polish comedy entitled *Seksmisja* and directed by Juliusz Machulski. Maks was played by actor Jerzy Stuhr, whose many comic lines are still alive in Polish popular culture. As mentioned above, Jerzy Stuhr is the voice talent behind Donkey, and it is this duality that enables adult Polish viewers of *Shrek* easily to recognise the reminiscences of Maks in Donkey.

Example 6

Donkey: I'm right behind ya.	
A co tu będę siedział?	[Why would I sit around here like that?]

This line is an allusion to a very popular line from another well-known Polish comedy entitled *Psy*. In one scene, an unpopular rookie cop is addressed by his older colleagues, renowned for bending the rules, in the following way: 'What are you looking at? We're not here', to which he replies: "Then I'll go. Why would I sit around here like that alone?"

Example 7

Donkey: Listen, keep breathing!	
Pamiętaj, wdech i wydech!	[Remember, breathe in and breathe out!]

This phrase alludes to a nasty blonde joke in which a blonde refuses to take off her headphones while at a hairdresser's. The irritated hairdresser finally takes the headphones off the blonde's head and she drops dead. Shocked, the hairdresser picks up the headphones to check what the blonde was listening to and is even more surprised to hear: 'Remember, breathe in and breathe out!'. Such jokes were very popular in Poland at the time the dubbing was produced.

The following line alludes to TV commercials for beer in Poland:

Example 8

Shrek: Can't we settle this over a pint?	
Może omówimy to przy bezalkoholowym?	[Can't we settle this over alc-free beer?]

When a ban was introduced on the advertising of alcohol on television many beer producers counteracted by launching alcohol-free lines of their most well-known brands and advertising them legally. However, in a typical tongue in cheek twist, the producers made it obvious in their commercials that alc-free beer was not really what the advertising campaign was all about and people endorsing alc-free beer in the commercials could be seen winking an eye at viewers when saying 'alcohol-free'.

These examples show that the additions are justified and should be considered as instances of a compensation strategy, in which the translator has opted for a pragmatic approach. He clearly uses scenes, rather than sentences, as translation units and takes into consideration the whole intersemiotic complexity of audiovisual translation when deciding on his solutions.

Obscure source culture allusions are lost in translation and replaced with target culture allusions that trigger new intertextual values. However, certain elements of the original dialogue, like accents, do get lost irretrievably. Such is the case of Shrek's Scottish accent that was not replaced by any Polish regional accent, perhaps because of the smaller regional variations in Polish and the different associations assigned to regional accents.

7. Conclusions

The above analysis shows that the function of the translated film, i.e. to activate entertaining and comic effects, has been preserved by replacing some source culture elements with domesticated elements. The loss of source culture allusions is not damaging since they would be largely undecipherable to Polish viewers. By compensating and introducing target culture oriented solutions, the intricate intertextual network of allusions in the original has also been recreated in the target culture, thus maintaining the intended effect.

The translator's overall approach turned out to be immensely popular and the successful domesticated dubbing of *Shrek* seems to have introduced certain shifts in the Polish polysystem of films when it comes to dubbed animations. As mentioned by Urbańska (2004, in Tomaszkiewicz, 2006:203, my translation): "the technique of polonization has in recent years become much desired and anticipated not only by the audience, but also by producers. [...] All translators of film dialogues are now required to polonize original film versions". Hence, dubbed animations have acquired a more central position in the polysystem and certain norms, standards and audience expectations have been identified and followed in subsequent productions. Thanks to the successful translation of *Shrek*, the previously negative opinion of dubbing held by most Polish viewers was transformed into an enthusiastic one, as reflected in the results of the 2005 survey on AVT preferences among Polish viewers mentioned in the initial part of the paper (Garcarz, 2006).

Despite obvious advantages of dubbing over voiceover in the translation of films, the popularity of dubbed versions of animated films and feature films for young audiences generated by *Shrek* did not permeate into other film genres and did not bring about any major changes in AVT techniques applied in Poland. Nine years after the premiere of *Shrek*, most television productions are still broadcast with voiceover, DVD releases include both subtitling and voiceover versions, while most films screened in cinemas are only subtitled. Economic factors that determine the preponderance of voiceover may be less crucial nowadays than they were some decades ago, especially for private broadcasters. It seems, therefore, that old translation traditions and viewing habits die hard in Poland.

References

Agost, Rosa (2004) "Translation in bilingual contexts. Different norms in dubbing translation", in Pilar Orero (ed.) *Topics in Audiovisual Translation.* Amsterdam and Philadelphia: John Benjamins, 63-82.

Bogucki, Łukasz (2004) "The constraint of relevance in subtitling". *The Journal of Specialised Translation* 1: 71-88.
www.jostrans.org/issue01/art_bogucki_en.pdf

Chaume, Frederic (2003) *Doblatge i subtitulació per a la TV*. Vic: Eumo Editorial.

Chaume, Frederic (2004) "Synchronization in dubbing. A translational approach", in Pilar Orero (ed.) *Topics in Audiovisual Translation.* Amsterdam and Philadelphia: John Benjamins, 35-52.

Coleridge, Samuel T. (1817/1985) *Biographia Literaria: Biographical Sketches of My Literary Life and Opinions*, Princeton: Princeton University Press.

Díaz Cintas, Jorge (2004) "In search of a theoretical framework for the study of audiovisual translation", in Pilar Orero (ed.) *Topics in Audiovisual Translation.* Amsterdam and Philadelphia: John Benjamins, 21-34.

Dries, Josephine (1995) "Breaking Eastern European barriers". *Sequentia* 2 (4): 5-6.

Even-Zohar, Itamar (1978) "The position of translated literature within the literary polysystem", in James Holmes, José Lambert and Raymond van den Broeck (eds) *Literature and Translation.* Leuven: ACCO, 117-27.

Garcarz, Michał (2006) "Polskie tłumaczenia filmowe". *The Journal of Specialised Translation* 5: 110-9.
www.jostrans.org/issue05/art_garcarz.pdf

Johnson, Steven (2005) *Everything Bad is Good for You. How Popular Culture is Making Us Smarter,* London: Penguin.

Luyken, Georg-Michael, Thomas Herbst, Jo Langham-Brown, Helen Reid and Hermann Spinhof (1991) *Overcoming Language Barriers in Television: Dubbing and Subtitling for the European Audience,* Manchester: European Institute for the Media.

Romero-Fresco, Pablo (2006) "The Spanish dubbese: a case of (un)idiomatic *Friends*". *The Journal of Specialised Translation* 6: 134-51.
www.jostrans.org/issue06/art_romero_fresco.pdf

Tomaszkiewicz, Teresa (2006) *Przekład audiowizualny*, Warsaw: PWN.

Whitman, Candace (1992) *Through the Dubbing Glass.* Frankfurt: Peter Lang.

Wierzbięta, Bartosz (2002) *An interview.*
www.interia.pl

Wojtowicz, Grzegorz (2002) "Bardzo dobre dialogi są. Rozmowa z Bartoszem Wierzbiętą".
www.stopklatka.pl

Zabalbeascoa, Patrick (1993) *Developing Translation Studies to Better Account for Audiovisual Texts and Other New Forms of Text Production.* Lérida: University of Lérida. PhD Thesis.

Zabalbeascoa, Patrick (1997) "Dubbing and the nonverbal dimension of translation", in Fernando Poyatos (ed.) *Nonverbal Communication and Translation*, Amsterdam and Philadelphia: John Benjamins, 327-42.

Section 2

Media accessibility

Accessibility to the media by hearing impaired audiences in Poland: problems, paradoxes, perspectives

Agnieszka Szarkowska

University of Warsaw, Poland

Abstract

The present article examines the accessibility to audiovisual translation (AVT) of hearing impaired viewers in Poland. After offering an overview of AVT modes in Poland – including subtitles for the deaf and hard of hearing (SDH) and sign language interpreting (SLI) – and of the Polish target group, the article explores the availability of SDH and SLI on television, DVDs and in cinemas. Although SDH has been available on Polish public TV since 1994, its provision is still inadequate. Similarly to other countries, it is also subject to stormy debate on edited vs. verbatim subtitles, as demonstrated by preliminary results of an SDH reception study discussed in the article. Unlike other countries, SLI available on public TV does not use Polish Sign Language, a natural means of communication among Deaf Poles, but Signed Polish, a system of signing based on the Polish oral language. This has also fuelled controversy within the Deaf community since not only is Signed Polish incomprehensible to many viewers, but it is also ideologically unacceptable. The article ends with a discussion of legal regulations on media accessibility and some suggestions for improving accessibility to AVT products for hearing impaired viewers.

1. Introduction

Poland is an EU country of 38 million people. Given the estimate that about 10% of any population has some problems with hearing (Szczepankowski, 1998), the number of hearing impaired Poles with limited access to the media could total about four million. The figure comprises not only those who were born deaf or hard-of-hearing, but also a rapidly growing number of people with age-related hearing loss. Despite the large scale of the problem, the needs of people with hearing impairments are not catered for sufficiently.

This article sets out to present the current situation of the deaf and the hard-of-hearing in Poland in terms of accessibility to the media, particularly television. Eastern Europe still seems to be a no-go area for many researchers and so far publications on accessibility have tended to focus mostly on the 'old' EU (Remael, 2007; EFHOH, 2005). Poland itself is not without blame, as it is only just beginning to wake up to the notion of media accessibility and the pressing need to provide appropriate services on a wider scale so that they become the rule rather than the exception.

2. Audiovisual translation in Poland

Before discussing media accessibility, let us briefly describe the audiovisual landscape in Poland – a country which is widely believed to be a stronghold of voiceover (Gottlieb, 1998:244).

The overwhelming majority of Polish TV channels are indeed voicedover. To the bewilderment of the rest of Europe, this includes both fiction and non-fiction programmes. The use of voiceover for translating feature films has never had good press in Western Europe, as is shown by the following quote from Dries (1995:6):

> This means that few, sometimes only one, actor(s) speak for all characters in the film with (sic) the original sound is often still audible in the background. Although the costs for voice-over are estimated to be slightly higher than subtitling, these countries seem to prefer re-voicing their imported programmes. Research on audience preferences on this matter have never been carried out so far, however, some professionals regard it as the worst possible method. It is seen as too simple a way of getting the message across. The viewer simply gets the dialogue 'read' with the moving image, most of the time without any difference in intonation or acting attempts. Doing this, the characters in the film lose their identity and acting quality can only be transmitted visually and not orally. Therefore, language transfer using this method can in no sense maintain or do justice to the quality.

Since Dries's article was published, a number of surveys on audience preferences have been conducted (Bogucki, 2004:69; Garcarz, 2007:131; Subbotko, 2008), demonstrating that despite its numerous drawbacks, the substantial majority of Poles still claim voiceover to be their preferred mode of audiovisual translation on television. Nonetheless, a survey carried out for the *Dziennik* daily shows that one in five Poles supports subtitles and as a result of their lobbying for subtitles on television, in 2008 Polish public television (TVP) began its first broadcast of a programme in the original English version with open interlingual subtitles (Fig. 1). The programme was an American TV series for teenagers entitled *The Suite Life of Zack & Cody* (translated into Polish as *Nie ma jak hotel*) on channel TVP2:

Figure 1: Open interlingual subtitles on Polish television

Polish state television also operates a satellite channel TVP Polonia, which is the only channel to provide open English subtitles to Polish programmes. The subtitles are interlingual and, according to their official website (www.tvp.pl/polonia/o-antenie), the target audience "are Poles living and staying outside Poland, Polish communities in different parts of the world, citizens of other countries who speak Polish as well as foreigners interested in Polish culture. It is with these viewers in mind that English-language versions of the programmes are prepared" (my translation).

All in all, a brief look at mainstream TV channels in Poland presents a rather bleak picture for viewers with hearing impairments, for whom the vast majority of both foreign and domestic productions are equally inaccessible since the former are voicedover and the latter are aired without subtitles. Digital television seems to be the light at the end of the tunnel for deaf and hard-of-hearing viewers, as they are able to switch off the voiceover and switch on subtitles instead. This option is presently only available on some cable and satellite channels, which provide subtitles aimed at hearing audiences, but is not yet available on major terrestrial channels and will not be for some time, as the predicted date for the completion of the digital switchover in Poland has been postponed until June 2015 (www.poland.gov.pl). Curiously enough, viewers of cable digital TV in Poland can watch programmes subtitled into a number of different languages, such as Czech, Romanian, Hebrew or Swedish, but very rarely into Polish. An exception to this state of affairs are closed interlingual teletext subtitles (page 777) available for some films on a private TV film channel *Ale Kino!*, accessible via satellite and cable TV. Although they are very popular among the deaf and the hard-of-hearing, the subtitles are prepared with a view to making the original soundtrack available for hearing viewers. They differ from SDH aired by the state television as they have no colours, they are all centred, a much larger font is used and dialogue exchanges are marked with a dash.

In Polish cinemas most foreign films are screened with interlingual subtitles, except for children's films, which are dubbed. Domestic productions do not have any subtitles, which naturally excludes the deaf and hard-of-hearing, consequently leading to the situation that they are more familiar with foreign cinematography than with Polish works.

3. Hearing impaired audiences

Audiences with hearing impairments do not comprise a homogenous group. Some were born deaf, others acquired hearing loss at a later stage in life. Hearing loss can be classified according to various parameters, such as audiological measurements, the severity and the cause of the impairment, and it can also be approached "in terms of social integration and language use" (Neves, 2007a:262).

Based on audiological parameters proposed by the International Bureau for Audiophonology, the following four major types of hearing loss can be distinguished (Szczepankowski, 1998:28):

Type of hearing loss	Hearing loss in dB
Mild	between 20 and 40 dB
Moderate	between 41 and 70 dB
Severe	between 71 and 90 dB
Profound	over 90 dB

Another classification, related to people with severe and profound hearing loss, is based on the onset of hearing loss in relation to language development (*ibid.*:35):

- *Prelingual hearing loss* – before acquiring an oral language, usually up to 2-3 years of age.
- *Perilingual (interlingual) hearing loss* – in the period of acquiring language, between 3-5 years of age.
- *Postlingual hearing loss* – after the process of acquiring oral language has been completed, aged 5+.

These classifications come in useful when defining the addressees of media accessibility services. People with severe and profound hearing loss are usually referred to as *deaf*. This term covers those who "cannot hear well enough to process aural information conveniently" (Neves, 2005:84). It is not synonymous with the *Deaf* (with a capital D), which stands for those who were born deaf and/or lost hearing before acquiring an oral language, whose first language is usually sign language, who usually attended Deaf schools and who consider themselves part of Deaf culture and in a linguistic minority (Neves, 2007a:262; Stone, 2007:71). A similar distinction also exists in Polish and the equivalent term for *deaf/Deaf* is *głuchy/Głuchy*. There is also another term, *niesłyszący* [non-hearer(s)], which is a neutral description of all those people who cannot hear.

People with mild to moderate hearing loss are often termed *hard-of-hearing* (Padden and Humphries, 1988; Szczepankowski, 1998; Neves, 2007a), a group referred to in Polish by *niedosłyszący* and *słabosłyszący* [poor hearer(s)]. Their mother tongue is usually the oral national language (Polish in Poland, English in the UK). The hard-of-hearing were either born with hearing loss or acquired it at a later stage; they usually have residual hearing and/or hearing memory (Neves, 2008:131). The elderly comprise a large number within this group.

It is difficult to obtain reliable data on the number of d/Deaf and hard-of-hearing people. According to Szczepankowski (1998:41), while it is easier to estimate the number of those with severe and profound hearing loss, as they usually rely on state benefits, it is practically impossible to give an exact number of people with mild and moderate hearing loss. Generally speaking, the milder the impairment, the more difficult it is to account for it in figures. Gambier (2003:175) notes that in the EU alone, depending on the definitions used, "there are between 4 million and 80 million hearing impaired members of the population, out of a total of 390 million!"

According to Kazimierz Diehl (personal communication), former President of the Polish Association of the Deaf (*Polski Związek Głuchych*, PZG), in 2006 the association had about 30,000 fee-paying members and about 80,000 registered *protégés* (deaf and hard-of-hearing people who are not fee-paying members but may benefit from assistance programmes offered by the Association). Szczepankowski (1998:42-3) puts the figure of Deaf Poles at about 45,000 (based on the deafness indicator for Poland it is 0.12-0.13% of the population), the hard of hearing at around 800,000-900,000, and those with mild hearing loss at ca. 2.5-3 million. This roughly corresponds to the estimates that about 10% of any population has some sort of hearing impairment.

All the groups have varying linguistic needs and abilities and, consequently, different expectations when it comes to their preferred type of audiovisual translation mode. Research has shown that d/Deaf viewers with sign language as their mother tongue tend to be slower readers than those whose first language is oral (Conrad, 1977; Jensema, 1998; de Linde and Kay, 1999:11; Jelinek Lewis and Jackson, 2001). Hence, it can be hypothesised that this group will most probably call for sign language interpreting, whereas the hard-of-hearing, the deaf and those with milder hearing impairments are more likely to prefer subtitles.

Neves (2007a:252) lists three types of programme through which people with hearing impairments can obtain access to television: (1) subtitled programmes, (2) spoken language programmes with sign language interpreting, and (3) sign language programmes. Below is an overview of these forms in the Polish context.

4. Subtitling for the deaf and hard-of-hearing (SDH) on television

Polish SDH began on 1 January 1994 when the state television broadcast the western *Rio Grande* (John Ford, 1950) with closed teletext subtitles. Since then, hearing impaired people have been provided with SDH on two major public television channels – TVP1 and TVP2 – constituting about 8% of TVP1 and TVP2 air time in 2009. So far, no private broadcaster has decided to provide SDH on any channel.

There are no digital subtitles for the deaf and hard-of-hearing, and the only subtitles are available as analogue teletext on page 777 with priority being given to prime time programmes. The SDH offer covers a variety of genres such as feature films, TV series and soaps, current affairs programmes, television theatre, documentaries as well as two news programmes per day. Most programmes are subtitled intralingually but some foreign feature films are provided with interlingual SDH.

The overwhelming majority of subtitles are pre-recorded. In the case of feature films and some TV series, the main characters are allocated one of the three colours: yellow, green or blue. Subtitles are also justified to the left or to the right depending on the location of speakers on screen. Dialogue subtitles are not marked with a dash at the beginning of each line, but an empty line is used instead (Fig. 2). Important information about off-screen sounds relevant to the understanding of a film is displayed at the bottom of the screen in white capital letters against a blue background (see Fig. 3):

Figure 2: Use of colours (white and blue on black
background) and displacement

Figure 3: Description of sounds [SINGING]
(white letters on blue background)

News programmes like *Teleexpress* and *Wiadomości* are broadcast with semi-live subtitles, which are always left-aligned and take up to three lines of text (Fig. 4):

Figure 4: Semi-live SDH of *Teleexpress*

The subtitles do not contain timecodes and are based on the script to be read by the news presenter from the autocue and on the audiovisual clips to be broadcast. When the programme is on air, they are manually keyed in by a subtitle operator.

As no speech recognition system for the Polish language has yet been fully developed, it is not possible at this point to provide realtime subtitling with respeaking. For truly live broadcasts, one subtitler at the studio strives to summarise quickly the gist of what is being said on screen and to convey it in the form of subtitles. Time pressure and other constraints result in the fact that the hurriedly typed subtitles tend to contain major spelling errors, not to mention the lack of synchrony with the image and coherence between subtitles. This only adds fuel to the flames and leads to protests from viewers with hearing impairments, discontented at both the quantity and quality of the subtitles they are presented with. From the perspective of the broadcaster, news subtitling appears to be one of the most difficult types of SDH, whereas from the perspective of deaf and hard-of-hearing viewers it is one of the most needed, yet under-rated.

There is also another problem with SDH in the news. Although it is technically viable not to cover the labels with the names and positions of the people interviewed (Fig. 5), such labels are often covered, which prevents hearing-impaired viewers from learning the identity of the speakers (Fig. 6):

Figure 5: SDH and uncovered speaker's identity

Figure 6: SDH covering the speaker's identity

5. SDH in cinemas and on DVD

Polish cinemas are flooded with foreign productions screened with open subtitles, so many viewers with hearing impairments are frequent cinema-goers even though cinema subtitles are meant for hearing audiences and, as such, contain no additional information about sounds. However, given the fact that Polish films are screened without any subtitles, not many hearing impaired Poles can enjoy domestic productions.

The situation may hopefully change thanks to new initiatives such as *Kino poza Ciszą i Ciemnością* [Cinema beyond Silence and Darkness] organised by the charity *Fundacja Dzieciom 'Zdążyć z Pomocą'* [Foundation for Children 'Help on Time'], which invites the d/Deaf and hard-of-hearing as well as the blind and partially sighted to cinema screenings of recent Polish productions with electronically displayed SDH and live audio description (AD).

The first DVD film with Polish subtitles for the hearing impaired was *Katyń*, a WW II historical drama by the Oscar-winning director Andrzej

Wajda, which was only released in 2008. Soon afterwards other distributors followed suit and began to release films with SDH, but their number is still very limited.[1] Sadly, it is still more common for a Polish film released on DVD to have subtitles in English than in Polish.

6. Sign language interpreting (SLI) on Polish television

According to Neves (2007a:256), however difficult it is to pinpoint precisely the time when sign language interpreting first appeared on television, she suggests it may have begun in the early 1980s in the UK and the US. In Poland, the first in-vision SLI took place in 1979, while in 1980 it began to be used on a regular basis (Szczepankowski: personal communication). Since then, three bilingual sign interpreters (Zbigniew Grzegorzewski, Józef Hendzel and Mirosława Sosnowska), all of whom are children of deaf adults (CODAs), have been regularly interpreting news (Fig. 7), TV series and soap operas (Fig. 8) as well as religious and current affairs programmes for the Deaf:

Figure 7: Sign language interpreting on TVP INFO

Figure 8: Polish soap opera *M jak miłość*
[*The Name of Love*] with sign language interpreting

As in the case of SDH, public television is the only broadcaster to provide programs with sign language interpreting. SLI on television may be considered to be "a genre of its own" (Neves, 2007a:256). What is more, different 'sub-genres' may be distinguished since interpreting news is different from interpreting fiction. As discussed by Romero-Fresco (this volume), televised news broadcasts usually have a significantly higher speech rate than spontaneous speech, which together with the use of a great deal of proper names considerably raises the level of difficulty for signers. On the other hand, when translating news, the problem of speaker identification does not usually arise, unlike in the case of translating soaps, where a number of speakers are often present on screen and sometimes speaking simultaneously.

Sign language interpreting on Polish television has been a source of heated debate within the Deaf community. The problem stems from the fact that television interpreters do not use Polish Sign Language (PSL), which is a natural way of communication among Deaf people, but Signed Polish, an artificial system of signing based on the Polish oral language.[2] It needs to be stressed that Signed Polish is not a language – it is a system of manual communication which consists of signs representing the Polish spoken language. In contrast to PSL, Signed Polish never appears on its own, but is always presented simultaneously with speech following the Polish word order, thus forming a message in two parallel codes: speech and signs (Szczepankowski, 1998:137).

Signed Polish was developed in the 1960s by Stanisław Siła Nowicki and Bogdan Szczepankowski from the Polish Association of the Deaf in order to introduce signing in deaf schools. At that time, signing was not allowed to be used in schools owing to the dominant philosophy of oralism, an approach to deaf education which recommended teaching based on lip-reading and gave priority to teaching speaking skills to deaf children. The prohibition of signing resulted in high illiteracy rates among deaf school graduates. Signed Polish was meant to be a way of counteracting illiteracy and enabling deaf people to continue their education above primary and vocational levels. The authorities were initially unwilling to allow any manual communication to be introduced into schools, but in the 1980s finally capitulated. This is how Signed Polish made its way into schools. But it also made its way into television. Although it may work well in the context of direct communication, it has some serious drawbacks when used on television.

Many Deaf people complain that they do not understand programmes interpreted in Signed Polish, as it is not their natural every day means of communication (Woźniak, 2007:85; Czajkowska-Kisil, secretary of the Polish Sign Language Institute: personal communication). Others state that it would be impossible to convey the televised broadcast by means of

PSL, as it works well only for simple everyday communication, but is not suitable for the more complex information in the news (Roczan-Maciejska, president of the Warsaw division of the Polish Association of the Deaf: personal communication).

Critics of the present SLI also point out that the figure of the translator placed at the bottom right-hand corner of the screen is too small to be understood, as sign language makes use of three-dimensional space and facial expressions. The signing thus "becomes confined to the space provided and takes on a screen format, removing amplitude to arm and hand movement and placing all signing at an unnatural chest level" (Neves, 2007a:256). As a result, it may be more difficult for Deaf viewers to see the movements and facial expressions of cornered signers, and consequently, to comprehend the signed messages.

Disappointed with inadequate SLI on traditional television, the Deaf community has taken an active approach by launching the first online television in Poland to broadcast in Polish Sign Language on the Deaf portal www.onsi.tv. Clips with news snippets presented in PSL and giving more prominence to the signer are posted daily with subtitles in Polish (Fig. 9):

Figure 9: Internet TV with news in sign language

The subtitles do not conform to the traditionally recognised standards. The number of lines varies from one to four, demanding very fast reading speeds from viewers. Line breaks are not made at the highest syntactic nodes and the information distribution within lines is rather arbitrary. Some subtitles contain spelling and grammatical errors, which probably stems from the fact that they were prepared by Deaf subtitlers for whom Polish was not the mother tongue. It is nevertheless a fascinating case where the usual roles are reversed: in order to understand the message, it is the hearing viewers who find themselves in the position of those who need translation.

Sign language interpreting may be "a means of disseminating the language and gaining visibility" for the Deaf community (Neves, 2007a:263). Given the fact that SLI on public television cannot serve this purpose as it promotes Signed Polish, this role has been taken on by onsi.tv. It would be interesting to see if the development of nationwide television broadcasting in Polish Sign Language will also bring about the unification of PSL itself, as the language in its present form has many local variations.

7. Reception of accessibility services

Many viewers with hearing impairments have repeatedly voiced their negative opinions about the accessibility of services on television, both in relation to SDH and SLI. Subtitles are generally criticised for excessive editing, frequent omissions and inconsistencies with lip movements. Many viewers are calling for verbatim subtitles (visit www.deaf.pl or www.itvp.pl/blog). According to Neves (2008:135-6), "Deaf, and particularly hard of hearing viewers, demand verbatim, word for word subtitles, in the belief that only so will they be on an equal stand with hearers". This is also confirmed in a recent web survey I carried out among deaf and hard-of-hearing viewers,[3] where 70% of participants said they preferred verbatim subtitles to edited ones. Any form of editing is often seen as an attempt at censorship, as declared by a participant who wrote: "we have the right to full information, why should this access be restricted?"

Interestingly, while numerous hearing impaired viewers fiercely criticise teletext SDH for Polish programmes on TVP, they praise interlingual subtitles highly, be it on DVD, in the cinema or on premium digital TV channels like HBO or Canal+, for their faithfulness, readability, spotting, succinctness and richness of vocabulary. Can it be attributed solely to the quality of the DVD and cinema subtitles? Is it in any way related to the level of proficiency in the foreign source language? Does it have anything to do with the fact that both hearers and non-hearers are shown exactly the same subtitles, the implication being that nothing has been censored? Answering these and other questions by investigating differences in the reception of interlingual and intralingual SDH among deaf and hard-of-hearing viewers seems to be a new promising line of research.

When asked for the preferred mode of making audiovisual programmes accessible to hearing impaired audiences, 93% participants in the online survey opted for subtitling. Some suggested they would prefer sign language interpreting provided that it was done in Polish Sign Language and not in Signed Polish. Others stated they would like to have both options

(SDH + SLI) to choose from. Offering the choice between SLI and SDH seems to be a satisfactory solution, albeit not a very cost-effective one. Along those lines, viewers could also be offered a choice between edited and verbatim subtitles, as is already done in the US by PBS in the case of the children's cartoon *Arthur* (Debra Toffan, 1996-2009). Neves (2007b:92) conjures up an image of subtitling in the future, where viewers will be able to "interact with the original text adjusting it to their particular needs and wishes", for instance by selecting the subtitle characteristics (verbatim/edited), the appearance of the subtitles (the use of colours and displacement or the size of the subtitles), or by being able to switch on/off additional information on sounds and music. However, owing to the postponement of the analogue switch-off, combined with the lack of financial resources and legal regulations on media accessibility services, it is highly unlikely that any of these solutions will be implemented in Poland in the near future.

8. Legal situation on media accessibility in Poland

There is currently no legislation in Poland on how much SDH and SLI should appear on television. As a member of the EU, Poland is obliged to implement the Directive 2007/65/EC of the European Parliament and of the Council of 11 December 2007, amending Council Directive 89/552/EEC (known as *TV without Frontiers*). Under Article 3, all Member States are obliged to "bring into force laws, regulations and administrative provisions necessary to comply with this Directive" by 19 December 2009. Poland has not introduced any regulations so far, but the National Broadcasting Council (*Krajowa Rada Radiofonii i Telewizji*, KRRIT, www.krrit.gov.pl) carried out public consultation on the implementation of the Directive in Poland, which met with rather a lukewarm response. The only organisation representing groups of people with hearing or visual impairments to reply was audiodeskrypcja.pl, a portal on audio description run by two active blind people, appealing for AD to be included in television broadcasting. No deaf association has urged the Council to set a minimum percentage of SDH or SLI on television. This shows that Polish associations still need to learn how to act as pressure groups so that they can exert influence on legislation.

As a member of the United Nations, Poland is also obliged to follow *The Standard Rules on the Equalization of Opportunities for Persons with Disabilities* adopted by the United Nations General Assembly in 1993. Rule 5 on accessibility stipulates that:

> Appropriate technologies should be used to provide access to spoken information for persons with auditory impairments or comprehension difficulties;
> States should encourage the media, especially television, radio and newspapers, to make their services accessible.

National law also imposes legal obligations on Polish state television to carry out public mission, as set forth in the Broadcasting Act of 29 December 1992 (*Ustawa o radiofonii i telewizji*). Under this Act, TVP is obligated to:

> The transmission of teletext services (Article 21 section 1a.4);
> the dissemination of knowledge of Polish language (Article 21.1a.8);
> paying due regard to the needs of national and ethnic minorities and communities speaking regional languages, including broadcasting news programmes in the languages of national and ethnic minorities and in regional languages (Article 8a).

Another binding law for public television is the Licence Fees Act of 21 April 2005, which enables TVP to conduct its mission. Under Article 4 the following groups are exempted from paying the licence fee:[4]

> Deaf persons with ascertained anacusis or ambilateral hearing loss (measured on 2,000 Hz frequency of volume from 80 dB up);
> the blind whose visual acuity does not exceed 15%;
> senior citizens aged over 75.

Some Deaf people have suggested (www.deaf.pl) that they would be willing to pay the licence fee if it was to cover the cost of producing SDH. In this way, viewers would also be in a position to demand something for their money and become more active in the public arena. However, the whole discussion on licence fees may soon become pointless as the Polish government is preparing to do away with them altogether.

Last but not least, Poland has not yet officially recognised Polish Sign Language as a minority language unlike a number of other European countries (Table 1). The work on legislation to recognise PSL as a minority language is still underway.

Countries which recognise their national SL on constitutional level	Countries which recognise their national SL by other legal measures	Countries which have not yet recognised their national SL
Austria	Belgium	Bulgaria
Czech Republic	Denmark	Croatia
Finland	Estonia	Cyprus

Portugal	France	Hungary
Slovakia	German	Lithuania
Spain	Greece	Luxembourg
	Iceland	Malta
	Ireland	*Poland*
	Italy	Romania
	Latvia	Serbia and Montenegro
	Netherlands	Slovenia
	Norway	Switzerland
	Sweden	
	United Kingdom	

Table 1: Status of Sign Language in Europe (EUD, n.d.)

It seems that, unless appropriate equality legislation is passed, explicitly stating minimum benchmarks for both public and private broadcasters, Poles with hearing impairments are not likely to see any increase in current SDH or SLI provision levels at TVP or the commencement of SDH or SLI services on private channels.

9. Subtitling war

When discussing the legal situation, it would be impossible not to mention the events that took place in Poland in 2007 with regard to the free distribution of subtitles on the internet. A stormy debate on copyright issues ensued and the whole episode was dubbed a 'subtitling war' by the media.

The rise of the internet has undoubtedly contributed to the distribution of information in different forms, with legal regulations lagging behind actual practice. One such practice is known as *fansubbing/fansubs* (Díaz Cintas, 2005:5; Díaz Cintas and Remael, 2007:26) or *amateur subtitling* (Bogucki, 2009), which is said to have originated in the 1980s with subtitles produced by fans of Japanese *manga* and *anime*. Here is how Díaz Cintas and Remael (2007:26) explain the idea behind this type of subtitling: "Despite the questionable legality of this activity as far as the copyright of programmes is concerned, the philosophy underlying this type of subtitling is the free distribution over the internet of audiovisual programmes with subtitles done by fans".

In Poland there were a number of websites offering amateur subtitles free of charge to anybody who wished to download them: www.napisy.org, www.napisy.info, and www.napisy.com. In 2006 Díaz Cintas and Muñoz Sánchez (2006:44) wrote that until then there had not been any confrontation between copyright holders and translators. However, in 2007 the Polish police in cooperation with the *Fundacja Ochrony Twórczości Audiowizualnej* [Audiovisual Work Protection Foundation] arrested nine people (eight translators and one administrator) and charged them with the illegal distribution of their own translations of dialogue lists via the portal www.napisy.org and the possession of pirated software and films. In response to the police action, the translators published an open letter on the internet (www.napisy.org), in which they stated that their main goal was to help those who did not know a foreign language to watch foreign productions as well as deaf and partially sighted people. According to the police, under Polish law anybody who translates a dialogue list must have obtained consent from the copyright holder to make such a translation available.

10. Conclusion

We now live in an information society. With the rapid development of information and communication technologies, more and more people with hearing impairments, especially the elderly, are threatened with information exclusion. In his book *Seeing Voices*, Sacks (1990:51) borrows Furth's (1966) term 'information deprivation' to talk about a problem experienced by deaf people as they are less exposed to incidental acquisition of information, which in the case of hearers takes place, for instance, when watching television. The European Commission (2009) states that: "the Information Society must share its benefits with the whole society, including people who find it more difficult to use new technologies, such as those with a disability and the elderly". It seems that legal requirements obliging media companies to make their services more accessible could pave the way for the widespread use of SDH (and a wider use of SLI) in Poland, empowering the deaf and the hard-of-hearing to become fully enabled citizens. The Deaf community itself must also take an active stand by voicing their demands and lobbying for more accessibility services and public awareness.

Notes

1. Interestingly, the films with SDH have been prepared so far by the staff working for TVP (as there were no other professionals available), who did not indicate dialogues in the cinema-like fashion, i.e. with dashes, but using an empty line as in teletext.
2. Signed Polish is known in Polish as *system językowo-migowy* (SJM). It has two varieties: full (*wariant pełny*) and functional (*wariant użytkowy*). The full version is an exact representation of the oral Polish language, including finger-spelt inflectional endings, which results in the slower pace of signing (around 30% slower than normal extemporaneous speech). Its purpose is purely educational (Szczepankowski, 1998:140). The functional variety

consists in simultaneous speaking and signing, without indicating any inflectional endings. It is the functional variety that is used on television.
3. The survey is still in progress (www.ankietka.pl/ankieta/19013/napisy.html). So far 52 participants have taken part, of whom 70% are Deaf and 30% hard-of-hearing. Nearly 60% of respondents belong to the 25-39 age group and 35% are aged 15-24.
4. The English version of the Acts comes from the KRRIT website: www.krrit.gov.pl.

References

Bogucki, Łukasz (2004) "The constraint of relevance in subtitling". *The Journal of Specialised Translation* 1: 69-85.

Bogucki, Łukasz (2009) "Amateur subtitling on the internet", in Jorge Díaz Cintas and Gunilla Anderman (eds) *Audiovisual Translation: Language Transfer on Screen*. Basingstoke: Palgrave Macmillan, 49-57.

Conrad, Ruben (1977) "The reading ability of deaf school-leavers". *British Journal of Education Psychology* 47:138-48.

Díaz Cintas, Jorge (2005) "Audiovisual translation today. A question of accessibility for all". *Translating Today* 4: 3-5.

Díaz Cintas, Jorge and Pablo Muñoz Sánchez (2006) "Fansubs: audiovisual translation in an amateur environment". *The Journal of Specialised Translation* 6: 37-52.

Díaz Cintas, Jorge and Aline Remael (2007) *Audiovisual Translation: Subtitling*. Manchester: St Jerome.

Dries, Josephine (1995) "Breaking Eastern European Barriers". *Sequentia* 2(4): 6.
www.obs.coe.int/oea_publ/sequentia4.pdf.en

EFHOH (2005) *Newsletter of the European Federation of Hard of Hearing People*. September:
www.efhoh.org/mp/db/file_library/x/IMG/30512/file/2005EFHOHNews LetterSep.pdf

EUD (n.d.) *EUD Sign Language*. European Union of the Deaf:
www.eud.eu/EUD_Sign_Language-i-229.html

European Commission (2009) *eAccessibility – Opening up the Information Society*. Europe's Information Society, Thematic Portal:
http://ec.europa.eu/information_society/activities/einclusion/policy/accessibility/index_en.htm

Furth, Hans (1966) *Thinking without Language: Psychological Implications of Deafness*. New York: Free Press.

Gambier, Yves (2003) "Screen transadaptation: perception and reception". *The Translator* 9(2): 171-89.

Garcarz, Michał (2007) *Przekład slangu w filmie. Telewizyjne przekłady filmów amerykańskich na język polski* [*Translating slang in film. Television translations of American films into Polish*]. Kraków: Tertium.

Gottlieb, Henrik (1998) "Subtitling", in Mona Baker (ed.) *Routledge Encyclopaedia of Translation Studies*. London and New York: Routledge, 244-8.

Jelinek Lewis, Margaret S. and Dorothy W. Jackson (2001) "Television literacy: comprehension of program content using closed captions for the Deaf". *Journal of Deaf Studies and Deaf Education* 6(1): 43-53.

Jensema, Carl (1998) "Viewer reaction to different television captioning speeds". *American Annals of the Deaf* 143(4): 318-24.

de Linde, Zoé and Neil Kay (1999) *The Semiotics of Subtitling*. Manchester: St. Jerome.

Neves, Josélia (2005) *Audiovisual Translation: Subtitling for the Deaf and Hard-of-Hearing*. London: Rohampton University. PhD Thesis: http://roehampton.openrepository.com/roehampton/handle/10142/12580

Neves, Josélia (2007a) "Of pride and prejudice. The divide between subtitling and sign language interpreting on television". *The Sign Language Translator and Interpreter* 1(2): 251-74.

Neves, Josélia (2007b) "A world of change in a changing world", in Jorge Díaz Cintas, Pilar Orero and Aline Remael (eds) *Media for All. Subtitling for the Deaf, Audio Description and Sign Language.* Amsterdam: Rodopi, 89-98.

Neves, Josélia (2008) "10 fallacies about Subtitling for the d/Deaf and the hard of hearing". *The Journal of Specialised Translation* 10: 128-43. www.jostrans.org/issue10/art_neves.pdf

Padden, Carol and Tom Humphries (1988) *Deaf in America: Voices from a Culture*, Cambridge, Mass.: Harvard University Press.

Remael, Aline (2007) "Sampling subtitling for the deaf and the hard of hearing in Europe", in Jorge Díaz Cintas, Pilar Orero and Aline Remael (eds) *Media for All. Subtitling for the Deaf, Audio Description and Sign Language.* Amsterdam: Rodopi, 23-52.

Sacks, Oliver (1990) *Seeing Voices. A Journey into the World of the Deaf* [Polish translation: *Zobaczyć głos. Podróż do świata ciszy*]. Poznań: Zysk i Spółka.

Stone, Christopher (2007) "Deaf access for Deaf people: the translation of the television news from English into British Sign Language", in Jorge Díaz Cintas, Pilar Orero and Aline Remael (eds) *Media for All. Subtitling for the Deaf, Audio Description and Sign Language.* Amsterdam: Rodopi, 71-88.

Subbotko, Donata (2008) "Kapitulacja BBC Prime" [Capitulation of BBC Prime]. *Gazeta Wyborcza,* 11 January.

http://wyborcza.pl/1,76842,4827095.html

Szczepankowski, Bogdan (1998) *Wyrównywanie szans osób niesłyszących* [The Equalisation of Opportunities of Deaf Persons]. Siedlce: Wydawnictwo Wyższej Szkoły Rolniczo-Pedagogicznej.

Woźniak, Olga (2007) "Mówienie o kolorach" [Talking about colours]. *Przekrój* no. 48/3258, 29 November: 84-5.

Bridging the gap between Deaf Studies and AVT for Deaf children

Soledad Zárate

Imperial College, London, UK

Abstract
The production of appropriate subtitles for the deaf and the hard-of-hearing (SDH) requires a clear understanding of who the target audience is. The main British national channels have reached in 2009 a subtitling target of 80% to 100% of the programmes broadcast, and base their subtitling practices on the ITC *Guidance on Standards for Subtitling* (1999), which resulted from research mainly carried out in the early 1980s. Very little research has been conducted on subtitling for deaf children in the UK – or elsewhere for that matter –, it is clearly outdated and it does not consider the full potential of digital technology. Although more extensive research on the reading characteristics of deaf children has been conducted within Deaf Studies, the two disciplines – i.e. Audiovisual Translation (AVT) and Deaf Studies – have developed independently from each other. This paper bridges the gap between AVT and Deaf Studies in an attempt to gain a comprehensive picture of deaf children's reading characteristics and abilities.

1. Introduction

Subtitling for deaf children should be placed within the wider context of subtitling for the deaf and the hard-of-hearing (SDH). The research specifically focussed on this audience from a subtitling angle is very limited, hence the need to widen the scope of this study and place it within the more extensive research that has been carried out on the reading characteristics of deaf children within Deaf Studies. Traditionally, research in Deaf Studies and Audiovisual Translation (AVT) have developed independently. This paper takes an interdisciplinary approach and attempts to bridge the gap between the two fields in order to gain an understanding of how deaf children read. The word 'deaf' is here used as a general term to indicate children affected by any range of hearing loss, in line with the National Deaf Children Society (NDCS, 2009) and the Royal National Institute for Deaf People (RNID, 2009).

An estimated 840 babies are born deaf in the UK each year (NDCS, 2003; RNID, 2008), and one in 1,000 are deaf at the age of 3. There are some 20,000 deaf children aged 0-15 years, of which 12,000 are born deaf.

An interesting study into the process of acquiring language is the one carried out by Gregory (1976:8) with deaf children aged 2 to 5 years. She found that 57% communicated with their mothers exclusively through gestures, in the forms of miming and pointing rather than signing, suggesting that deaf children naturally choose to communicate through a visual modality.

However, only 5-10% of deaf children have deaf parents and acquire British Sign Language (BSL) as their first language (BBC, 2009); the rest learn it at school or while in contact with other deaf children (Kyle *et al.*, 2005:7). Children born to families who use sign language acquire BSL at the same rate as hearing children do when acquiring English (Conrad, 1979:317). There is almost no information on the sign competence of deaf children, and, according to Powers *et al.* (1998), this is partly due to the lack of suitable measures. However, statistics show that 80% of deaf children are educated in mainstream schools, where different types of inclusion programmes (i.e. individual, resource base, and unit) are in place (NDCS, 2003). The individual inclusion programme consists of additional support from a specialist, for example a visiting teacher for the deaf or a teaching assistant. The resource based programme is generally in place for larger numbers of deaf children, where specialist teachers – e.g. teachers of the deaf or communication support workers – and resources are specifically arranged for deaf students. Finally, some schools have a unit, where part of the school is set aside for teaching deaf children. This data clearly suggests that most deaf children are somehow in contact with the spoken language.

The real situation is that deaf children may have BSL as a first or second language. As BSL is a visual-gestural language, it is perceived visually and is produced using gestures of the hands, body and face (Deuchar, 1984:1). Space and movement are used to convey semantic and syntactic information. It has a structure, which is however different from that of English, and is as flexible and inventive as any spoken language (Musselman, 2000:21). Laborit (1993:9) sums up what sign language represents for deaf people: "Signing, this dance of words in the space, is my sensibility, my poetry, my inner-self, my true style" (my translation).

2. SDH research

The research carried out with British deaf children within the AVT field is rather limited. Other countries have done even less than Britain or nothing at all. The seminal *Handbook for Television Subtitlers* (Baker *et al.*, 1984) is of a general nature and only includes one short section on subtitling for deaf children. The investigations focussed on the effectiveness of subtitling strategies with children in secondary schools for the deaf, whose comprehension was tested at various language levels and reading speeds. The recommendations put forward by the authors include the suggestion that the reading speed should be set at a rate of 60 words per minute (wpm). On editing style, Baker *et al.* (*ibid.*) refer with due reservations to guidelines adopted by WGBH, a US public television channel. It is suggested that new words should be sensibly introduced, by allowing additional reading time and by highlighting the new word with colours or upper case. Furthermore, Teletext information pages should be used to provide simple definitions of unusual vocabulary and to contextualise the programme.

The most recent study in the UK was carried out by Gregory and Sancho-Aldridge (1996), who conducted a research project aimed at assessing deaf children's comprehension of subtitled television programmes. They considered three age groups (5-7, 8-11 and 12-16) and presented them with subtitled material at three levels of complexity (complex/broadcast, simple/simplified and basic). The simplified level was the one that provided children with the greatest source of information. Complex or broadcast subtitles proved to be suitable for the oldest group only, since the youngest group had difficulties in following the subtitles and could only pick up isolated words. It was noted that exposing the youngest group to subtitles on a regular basis helped them improve their use of subtitles as well as develop their reading skills. The use of subtitles to develop reading abilities, hence literacy, was advanced by the researchers.

As part of a study on subtitling for deaf children on British television (Zárate, 2008), I conducted interviews with professionals working for subtitling companies which provide subtitles for children to the major British broadcasters. They all state that the subtitling companies adhere to the *ITC Guidance on Standards for Subtitling* (Ofcom, 1999), although they also have their own in-house guidelines. The guidance relies almost entirely on premises and details from the *Handbook for Television Subtitlers* (Baker *et al.*, 1984*)*; hence on research conducted over twenty years ago, and, like this book, includes one section specifically devoted to children. The guidance has been more recently reviewed by the Office of Communications (Ofcom, 2006) but no major changes have been implemented. The main recommendations in the children's section are: to ensure synchronicity between voice and subtitles; to opt for the omission of words rather than reformulation of sentences; to use simplified grammatical structures; to introduce difficult words in a sensible way; and to set reading speeds at a rate of 70-80 words per minute. Reading speed is one of the aspects tackled by Baker *et al.* (1984) and it has certainly changed over the last twenty years as lifestyles have. The increased exposure to television, computers, mobiles and other audiovisual devices may have affected reading speed and other reading abilities. Also, over the last two decades, education for deaf children has changed. In particular, a larger number of deaf children are educated in mainstream schools that have in place some sort of inclusion programme, as previously discussed. These changes may also have affected the way deaf children develop their reading abilities, although there is no explicit evidence (ADPS, 2006) and further research would be most welcome.

Subtitling companies in the UK agree that young audiences have specific needs and this is normally reflected in the use of lower reading speeds, a major degree of textual editing, and sometimes a preference given to the description of sound effects in onomatopoeic forms rather than the use of descriptive labels. Nevertheless, some of these strategies seem to owe more to intuition than to factual information, and a lack of a solid knowledge and awareness of deaf children's reading abilities and needs is manifest. In response to the review of the guidance (Ofcom, 2006), the NDCS (2006) and the RNID (2006) requested a greater understanding of deaf children's needs. In conducting my own research, I have found that subtitlers in the UK and in some other European countries are interested in reading about deaf children, as they generally find themselves working for deaf children without really knowing what their needs are. The practitioners I have been in touch with are not specialists in SDH for children. In fact the current trend – at least in the UK, where subtitling for broadcasting is exclusively intralingual and tailored for deaf audiences – is the training and recruitment of a 'versatile subtitler' who can translate pre-recorded programmes for children, pre-recorded programmes for adults, and live programmes (such as news and sports events) through respeaking. The benefits of this trend are probably reflected in the considerable increase of broadcast subtitling targets reached in 2008 – 80% to 100% – by the main national channels, but it is necessary to bear in mind that there might be some drawbacks concerning the quality of the subtitles.

3. A Deaf Studies perspective

Extensive research on the reading characteristics of deaf children has been carried out in Deaf Studies in the last thirty years (Powers *et al.*, 1998). The results produced by this research activity outline a few general patterns that characterise the reading abilities of deaf learners: they lag considerably behind hearing learners in their reading achievements; have limited vocabulary acquisition and knowledge of multiple meanings; have poor knowledge of semantics and syntax, and a delayed knowledge of grammatical rules.

However, most research only takes into consideration older children and tends to be focussed on socio-cultural aspects that are not closely connected to this paper, such as ethnicity, gender and parental support.

Another crucial point is that most of these studies have been carried out on conventional reading – i.e. text on paper –, which is a different task altogether from reading subtitles on screen. The differences go beyond reading speed to include the disappearance of the immediate linguistic context, the communicative value of images and, in more general terms, the nature of the medium.

Watching a subtitled programme, unlike reading a book, requires the ability to read at a certain pace without the possibility of stopping or going back to previous information. Hence the importance of having clear guidelines on reading speed rather than approximate recommendations. Of course deaf children's reading rates would vary according to their reading abilities and age, therefore the subtitling practice would benefit from empirical studies on different age groups, aimed at setting reading speeds and, differentiating at least between preschool children's programmes, school children's programmes and young teenagers' programmes. The importance of conducting reading speed studies with actual subtitled programmes is further emphasised, owing to the very peculiar nature of the audiovisual product, where the visual stimuli consist of textual information accompanied by images. Reading subtitles, unlike reading a book, is a complementary task that children perform in order to understand the audiovisual product.

According to research carried out from an educational and psychological perspective (Castles and Coltheart, 2004), children need to associate letters with sound in order to be successful readers, an argument which is obviously not promising for deaf children given their hearing impairment. More timely are the conclusions reached by Harris and Beech (1998), who conducted a study on a group of twenty-four severely and profoundly prelingually deaf children aged five and a group of hearing controls (a matched sample of hearing participants). The four best readers, that is the four children with the highest reading scores, had two rather different profiles: two were non-signers with good spoken English, good implicit phonological awareness and good language comprehension;[1] and two were native signers with poor implicit phonological awareness but still good language comprehension. These results suggest that deaf children may become successful readers by more than one route.

Research conducted by Marschark and Harris (1996) encourages exposure to both oral language and signing as deaf children develop an understanding of sounds through oral language and a secure language base through signing. In a previous work, Marschark (1993) claims that deaf children develop their reading skills at a lower pace than their hearing peers, and their condition seems to be reflected in the knowledge they have of the world. Marschark *et al.* (2002) seemingly speak of 'the language of their world', meaning sign language. I would like to raise a correlated question:

would not deaf children develop their knowledge of the world similarly to hearing children if they were given access to 'the language of their world'? And would not that knowledge of the world acquired through signing facilitate their reading? That knowledge of the world would probably provide them with a solid base that could prove most beneficial to their comprehension of the new words and unfamiliar expressions they encounter while reading.

Although, as already discussed, reading subtitles on screen is for many reasons a different activity from reading text on paper, I still consider the research on reading comprehension, mainly carried out within Deaf Studies, valuable and relevant to understanding my audience. It is imperative that research on SDH is carried out within AVT, but since that research has been very limited to date and since another discipline, Deaf Studies, has produced fruitful evidence on one aspect that relates well to this study – namely reading comprehension –, bridging the gap between the two is a worthwhile first step.

4. Reading comprehension

In this section I will consider some of the variables that are most problematic for deaf children, namely vocabulary (Paul and Quigley, 1984:117) and syntax. As discussed later, the development of vocabulary is the only subskill that seems to profit from watching subtitled programmes (Koolstra *et al.*, 1997). On the other hand, syntax poses a major challenge for SDH since it has been observed that deaf students are more likely to comprehend syntactic structures in a discourse of several sentences rather than at the level of single sentences, as in the first case intersentence redundancies may allow them to revise falsely interpreted sentences (Gormley and Franzen, 1978). I share Gormley and Franzen's (*ibid.*) view on the fact that research has mainly focussed on syntax and this is possibly due to the substantial syntactic differences between spoken and signed languages. In their words (*ibid.*:544): "Unfortunately, nearly all research with the deaf has centered on the recognition of syntax in written language to the exclusion of semantic understanding". What has probably been underestimated is that deaf children may still comprehend the text by ignoring syntax and moving to meaning. Deaf children might apply a top down reading model (LaSasso, 1993; Simpson *et al.*, 1992), where they bring meaning to the text through their knowledge of the world, rather than a bottom up model (Adams, 1990; Padden and Ramsey, 1998), where they extract meaning from the text. However, understanding the syntactic problems that deaf children encounter is relevant to this paper and, more specifically, to the production of subtitles.

4.1 Vocabulary

According to Stern (2001), deaf children starting school at the age of four or five have, on average, 500 words as part of their vocabulary as opposed to the 3,000-5,000 words known by hearing children. This reduced knowledge of vocabulary is a consideration to be borne in mind when producing subtitles. The position of subtitlers is, however, a difficult one since it is not always immediately self-evident whether or not deaf children are familiar with the vocabulary used, so subtitlers need to assess which words are unknown and which new, and apply a suitable strategy. One of the most extensive studies on vocabulary was conducted by Silverman-Dresner and Guilfoyle (1970, 1972), based on children aged 7 to 17. Two reports containing descriptive data on the reading vocabulary of deaf children were produced. These are unfortunately quite outdated, and where more recent data is not available – as seems to be the case – subtitlers will often need to use their own judgement.

Research on language acquisition and development tends to be based on conventional reading (i.e. printed text). DeVilliers and Pomerantz (1992) conducted a study based on upper school and middle school students on how deaf students learn new words from a written context. A lack of interaction between making correct syntactic judgements about words and deriving meaning from them was noted, and the acquisition of new words proved to be more closely related to the students' overall reading comprehension.

An exception to research based on printed texts only is the study conducted by Neuman and Koskinen (1992), who examined how 'comprehensible input', as defined by Krashen (1985), in the form of subtitled television, influences incidental vocabulary second language (L2) learning. Krashen argues that children learn L2 incidentally, through exposure, by focussing on the meaning rather than the form or grammar of the message. Students stretch their knowledge when they are provided with and receive 'comprehensible input', i.e. information that goes slightly beyond their actual knowledge (Díaz Cintas and Fernández Cruz, 2008:203). Neuman and Koskinen (1992) recruited for their study Southeast Asian and Hispanic bilingual students, aged twelve and thirteen, enrolled in US schools. Four different versions of a children's television workshop science production, entitled *3-2-1 Contact*, were considered: subtitled television, television without subtitles, reading along and listening to text, and textbook. The results of the study indicated that students learned more words incidentally from subtitled television than from any of the other three versions. Moreover, the students in the subtitling group remembered more scientific information than the others. These findings seem to be in line with the suggestion by Díaz Cintas and Fernández Cruz (2008) that subtitled programmes can be used as a tool for language instruction, in particular for the acquisition of vocabulary and concepts.

These conclusions are supported by another very relevant study conducted by Koolstra *et al.* (1997) on the impact of television on (hearing) children's reading comprehension of foreign language subtitled programmes. Koolstra *et al.* (*ibid.*:132-3) observe that the learning and expansion of new vocabulary is the only subskill that benefits from watching subtitled programmes:

> Subtitles offer only short transcriptions of the dialogues in television programs, and, therefore, provide no practice in comprehending normal coherent texts. In addition, subtitles have to be read at a forced and fast pace, leaving little opportunity to reflect on the text. Therefore, it is doubtful that children's reading comprehension profits much from watching subtitled foreign language-programs. However, there is evidence that one subskill of reading comprehension, vocabulary, may profit from watching subtitled programs.

It was also suggested that the development of decoding skills may be promoted since reading subtitles provides an opportunity to practise word recognition. Having identified the new words, should they be introduced, highlighted, repeated and left on the screen for longer? In SDH the introduction of new words concerns not only verbal acoustic signs, i.e. dialogue exchanges, but also the description of nonverbal acoustic signs, i.e. sound effects and music. To describe animal noises, for instance, subtitlers can either use onomatopoeia, hence reproduce sounds phonetically (for a dog *arf arf*), or descriptive labels, where a statement is made (*dog barks*). While onomatopoeia may be more amusing, it is arguable whether deaf children are naturally able to associate it with sounds and understand it immediately. However, it is also true that children might become familiar with onomatopoeia while engaging in other forms of reading, namely comics. Also, sometimes onomatopoeia clearly suggests the sounds described – e.g. *moo* –, and is not simply a matter of phonetic transcription but representative of nouns and verbs. Should this last type be favoured?

The introduction of new words in subtitles is beneficial for the building up of deaf children's vocabularies. However, this is not always the strategy adopted on British television, where difficult words like *cholesterol* or *health conscious* may be replaced by simpler words like *fat* or *healthy*, though, in some cases, difficult words – *bamboozled* – seem to be accidentally introduced. The use of systematic and clear strategies, be it highlighting, repetition, or the use of lower reading speeds, is clearly needed.

In this section I have considered Deaf Studies research on conventional reading as well as AVT research conducted with hearing L2 learners. I regard this last approach as relevant because the foreign language in question is English and there is ample evidence that suggests that deaf children acquire English similarly to hearing children learning English as a second language (Charrow and Fletcher, 1974; Charrow, 1975). Moreover, Flagg *et al.* (1980), in their pilot study of subtitling conducted with partially deaf students, reached some conclusions that have later been corroborated by authors like Neuman and Koskinen (1992). They observed that eye fixations with complementary contexts were not affected, while comprehension was increased.

4.2 Syntax

Does syntax play a crucial role in reading comprehension? Views on this matter are quite conflicting. As previously seen, vocabulary can be considered singularly in an SDH context, since it has been identified as a component that is greatly improved by watching subtitled programmes (Koolstra *et al.*, 1997; Neuman and Koskinen, 1992). Kelly (1996) conducted a study on a group of deaf adolescents trained in oral school programmes, a second group schooled in total communication programmes, and a third group of students entering a postsecondary institution using total communication. The study examined the relationship between vocabulary and syntax, and the contribution that each of them makes separately to reading comprehension. The author found that vocabulary and syntactic knowledge did not function independently since the relationship between vocabulary and reading comprehension is dependent on syntactic abilities. Also, if syntactic abilities are limited, the reader may be unable to apply stored knowledge of vocabulary. This may be due either to the misinterpretation of syntactic relations that eventually confuses the processing of vocabulary, or to laborious syntactic analyses that neglect lexical processing. All in all, this view sharply contrasts with some of the research presented in the previous section – DeVilliers and Pomerantz (1992); Neuman and Koskinen (1992) – and more generally with constructivist theories. Gormley and Franzen (1978:546) elucidate further:

> from a constructivist's point of view the deaf can understand a printed message without explicit control over the syntactic structure. This does not deny the usefulness of written language in aiding comprehension, but merely points out that the deaf, particularly good deaf readers, may bypass the surface structure of syntax and process written information at the deep structure level of semantic information.

Gormley and Franzen (*ibid.*) observe that deaf students, particularly beginner readers, find syntactic structures difficult to understand at the level of individual sentences, while they are more likely to comprehend them within a discourse of several sentences, where intersentence redundancies may be available to allow them to reconsider wrongly interpreted sentences. This point is very relevant for SDH where subtitles tend to appear on screen in the form of single sentences. It follows that syntactic structures, particularly in subtitled programmes aimed at younger audiences, need to be as simple as possible.

5. From conventional to multimedia reading

Audiovisual materials require a multimedia as opposed to a conventional type of reading, which means that the focus cannot be on the text alone but needs also to be directed at the images, the subtitles and, to a certain extent in SDH, the soundtrack. In this respect, the recent research conducted by Gentry *et al.* (2005) has revealed that multimedia reading in the form of (1) print and pictures has more potential in terms of comprehension than other types of multimedia reading, namely, (2) print only, (3) print and digital video of sign language, and (4) print, pictures and digital video of sign language. The hearing-impaired children who took part in the study were aged 9 to 18 years and were mainly recruited from both integrated mainstream schools and residential non-integrated schools, while school programmes in which the students communicated orally were excluded. They were presented with multimedia stories on CD-ROM in the four different formats, and their comprehension was tested by story retelling using sign language. In this experiment, print as a constant modality and combined with other modalities and pictures proved to be the most effective complement, since it was concluded that the stories presented via print and pictures were most readily understood by the children. These findings prompt researchers to investigate further how subtitles – rather than print – and moving pictures – rather than static ones – place themselves in the context of reading comprehension.

Referring to the dual coding theory, which assumes the existence of two separate symbolic systems, one dealing with verbal information and the other with nonverbal information, Díaz Cintas and Fernández Cruz (1998:211) shed light on the potential of subtitled video materials, when they write that: "It could be argued that subtitled videos oblige learners to process the same message three times, hence the higher percentage of success in recalling words, spellings and phrases". In a foreign language learning context, these three inputs refer to pictures, soundtrack and subtitles. In an SDH context, this implies that children would process the (same) message twice, through nonverbal (images) and verbal (subtitles).

Another concept with a lot of potential in SDH is what Krashen's (1985, 1987) calls 'affective filter'; a defence mechanism that children may raise against failure with a negative effect on their performance. According to this scholar, the filter is lowered and the children become more positive when they are highly motivated and almost unaware of the hearing or reading processes enacted. This has prompted academics like Díaz Cintas and Fernández Cruz (1998) and Neuman and Koskinen (1996) to identify subtitled videos as potential deterrents against the affective filter. The creation of a friendly and relaxed situation in which the affective filter is low is perfectly feasible in an audiovisual context, since entertainment and educational content can be easily combined in this modality. Indeed, children are more likely to associate reading with a book than with a subtitled video.

To conclude, and in line with Ewoldt *et al.* (1992), I would like to reflect on the importance of presenting well-organised texts that make use of surface characteristics, such as underlining, italics and boldface type, in order to enhance reading comprehension. This approach, transposed to the specific area of subtitles, acquires vital importance since children have to cope with the reading rate of the subtitles, which convey not only speech, but also sound effects and music. Reading is not the main (or only) activity in question, as viewers also have to watch the images, and it then becomes a complementary task. The presentation of subtitles, in terms of segmentation and the functional use of typographical features – e.g. typeface, colour, lower/upper case, etc. –, is not just an aesthetic matter but a factor that clearly affects readability. In the UK, subtitled television programmes make use of some of these features in a functional, although not always consistent, way and this is the main reason why further empirical research is urgently needed.

6. Conclusion

This paper takes an interdisciplinary approach to gaining an understanding of deaf children's reading comprehension to be ultimately applied to SDH. Reading subtitles on screen and reading text in a book or any other printed material are two very different tasks. There is very little research on the former, though patterns of children's reading comprehension of printed texts have been outlined within Deaf Studies. It is my contention that these findings can be a solid stepping stone from which to investigate further the issue of reading on screen, with some of these findings equally applicable to AVT. Some research that has been done on the use of subtitling for second language acquisition and that has focussed on aspects relevant to this paper – i.e. vocabulary and reading comprehension – has also been considered. And I have referred to the very limited research on SDH that has been conducted from within AVT, which is clearly outdated since it was mainly conducted in the eighties.

Yet another reason for the need to update this type of research is the fact that over the last two decades the educational system for deaf children as well as their lifestyles – particularly their exposure to television, computers, video games and other audiovisual devices – have certainly changed, and this may have in some way affected their reading abilities.

Another crucial point is that research has been based exclusively on Teletext and analogue technology. The switchover to digital television in the UK started in 2008 and is scheduled to be completed by 2012, with many other European countries bound to follow suit. The potential offered by digital television – which allows greater flexibility and interactivity as well as the use of a wider range of colours and a myriad of font styles – has never been studied from a subtitling perspective. The need for updated empirical research on SDH is therefore imperative, in particular in the following areas: reading speeds; editing (omission or reformulation); harmonization of the visual cues (bold, italics, underline, upper case) used to convey paralinguistic features (intonation, hesitation) and nonverbal signs (music, sound effects); the need for consistency or otherwise between conventional writing and subtitles in the use of typographical cues.

Empirical research focussed on any of the areas mentioned above would be of enormous benefit to deaf children. Combining SDH research with research conducted in other disciplines can only help researchers get a more comprehensive and thorough understanding of their audience and might, eventually, have a positive impact on the quality of the subtitles we watch on our screens.

Notes

1. Beech and Harris (1998) distinguish clearly between *implicit phonological awareness*, that is the ability to break down words into their constituent sounds at the level of the syllable or subsyllabic unit, and *explicit phonological awareness* or *phonemic awareness*, which is the ability to detect and manipulate phonemes within words. Implicit phonological awareness develops before the child learns to read, whereas explicit phonological awareness develops as a result of learning to read.

References

Adams, Marilyn J. (1990) *Beginning to Read: Thinking and Learning about Print.* Cambridge, MA: Massachusetts Institute of Technology.

ADPS (2006) *Welcome to ADPS.* Edinburgh: Achievements of Deaf Pupils in Scotland.
www.education.ed.ac.uk/adps

Baker, Robert G., Andrew D. Lambourne and Guy Rowston (1984) *Handbook for Television Subtitlers* (revised edition). Winchester: I.B.A. Engineering Division.

BBC (2009) *Your Voice: British Sign Language.*
www.bbc.co.uk/voices/multilingual/bsl_today.shtml

Castles, Anne and Max Coltheart (2004) "Is there a causal link from phonological awareness to success in learning to read?" *Cognition* 91(1), 77-111.

Charrow, Veda R. (1975) "A psycholinguistic analysis of Deaf English". *Sign Language Studies* 7, 139-50.

Charrow, Veda R. and John D. Fletcher (1974) "English as the second language of Deaf children". *Developmental Psychology* 10(4), 463-70.

Conrad, Rudi (1979) *The Deaf Schoolchild: Language and Cognitive Function.* London: Harper & Row.

Deuchar, Margaret (1984) *British Sign Language.* London: Routledge & Kegan Paul.

De Villiers, Peter A. and Sarah B. Pomerantz (1992) "Hearing-impaired students learning new words from written context". *Applied Psycholinguistics* 13: 409-31.

Díaz Cintas, Jorge and Marco Fernández Cruz (2008) "Using subtitled video materials for foreign language instruction", in Jorge Díaz Cintas (ed.) *The Didactics of Audiovisual Translation.* Amsterdam and Philadelphia: John Benjamins, 201-14.

Ewoldt, Carolyn K., Neita K. Israelite and Ron Dodds (1992) "The ability of Deaf students to understand text. A comparison of the perceptions of teachers and students". *American Annals of the Deaf* 137, 351-61.

Flagg, B., F. Carrozza and R. Jenkins (1980) *Perception and Comprehension of Captioned Television: A Pilot Study.* Cambridge, Mass.: Centre for Research in Children's Television, Harvard University.

Gentry, Mary M., Kathleen M. Chinn and Robert D. Moulton (2004/2005) "Effectiveness of multimedia reading materials when used with children who are Deaf". *American Annals of the Deaf* 149(5), 394-403.

Gormley, Kathleen A. and Anne McGill Franzen (1978) "Why can't the Deaf read? Comments on asking the wrong question". *American Annals of the Deaf* 123(5), 542–47.

Gregory, Susan (1976) *The Deaf Child and His Family.* London: Allen and Unwin.

Gregory, Susan and Jane Sancho-Aldridge (1996) *Dial 888: Subtitling for Deaf Children.* London: ITC.

Harris, Margaret and John R. Beech (1998) "Implicit phonological awareness and early reading development in pre-lingually deaf children". *Journal of Deaf Studies and Deaf Education* 3, 205-16.

Kelly, Leonard P. (1996) "The interaction of syntactic competence and vocabulary during reading by deaf students". *Journal for Deaf Studies and Deaf Education* 1, 75-90.

Kyle, Jim, Anne Marie Reilly, Lorna Allsop, Monica Clark and Alexy Dury (2005) *Investigation of Access to Public Services in Scotland Using British Sign Language.* Edinburgh: Scottish Executive Social Research. www.scotland.gov.uk/Resource/Doc/930/0012107.pdf

Koolstra, Cees M., Tom H.A. Van der Voort and Leo J.Th. Van der Kamp (1997) "Television's impact on children's reading comprehension and decoding skills: a 3-year panel study". *Reading Research Quarterly* 32(2), 128-52.

Krashen, Stephen D. (1985) *The Input Hypothesis: Issues and Implications.* New York: Longman.

Krashen, Stephen D. (1987) *Principles and Practice in Second Language Acquisition.* London: Prentice-Hall International.

Laborit, Emmanuelle (1993) *Le Cri de la Moquette.* Paris: Robert Laffont.

LaSasso, Carol J. (1993) "Reading comprehension of deaf readers: the impact of too many or too few questions". *American Annals of the Deaf* 138, 435-41.

Marschark, Marc (1993) *Psychological Development of Deaf Children.* New York: Oxford University Press.

Marschark, Marc and Margaret Harris (1996) "Success and failure in learning to read: the special (?) case of deaf children", in Cesare Cornoldi and Jane Oakhill (eds) *Reading Comprehension Difficulties: Processes and Intervention.* Hillsdale, NJ: Erlbaum, 279-300.

Marschark, Marc, Harry G. Lang and John A. Albertini (2002) *Educating Deaf Students: From Research to Practice.* New York: Oxford University Press.

Musselman, Carol (2000) "How do children who can't hear learn to read an alphabetic script? A review of the literature on reading and deafness". *Journal of Deaf Studies and Deaf Education* 5(1), 9-31. http://jdsde.oxfordjournals.org/cgi/content/abstract/5/1/9

Neuman, Susan B., and Patricia Koskinen (1992) "Captioned television as comprehensible input: effects on incidental word learning from context for language minority students. *Reading Research Quarterly* 27(1), 95-106.

NDCS (2003) *Statistics on Childhood Deafness in the UK.* London: The National Deaf Children's Society.

www.ndcs.org.uk/applications/site_search/search.rm?term=statistics&sea
rchreferer_id=2&submit.x=0&submit.y=0

NDCS (2006) *Response to "Television Access Services: Review of the Code and Guidance"*. London: The National Deaf Children's Society.
www.ofcom.org.uk/consult/condocs/accessservs/responses/NDCS.pdf

NDCS (2009) *Deafness*. London: The National Deaf Children's Society.
www.ndcs.org.uk/family_support/glossary/deafness.html

Ofcom (1999) *ITC Guidance on Standards for Subtitling*. London: Office of Communications.
www.ofcom.org.uk/static/archive/itc/itc_publications/codes_guidance/sta
ndards_for_subtitling/index.asp.html

Ofcom (2006) *Television Access Services. Review of the Code and Guidance.* London: Office of Communications.
www.ofcom.org.uk/consult/condocs/accessservs/access.pdf

Padden, Carol and Claire Ramsey (1998) "Reading ability in signing Deaf children". *Topics in Language Disorders* 18(4), 30-46.

Paul, Peter V. and Stephen P. Quigley (1984) *Language and Deafness.* San Diego: College-Hill Press.

Powers, Stephen, Susan Gregory and Ernst D. Thoutenhoofd (1998) *The Educational Achievements of Deaf Children.* London: DfEE

RNID (2006) *Response to "Television Access Services: Review of the Code and Guidance"*. London: Royal National Institute for the Deaf.
www.ofcom.org.uk/consult/condocs/accessservs/responses/rnid.pdf

RNID (2008) *Statistics.* London: Royal National Institute for the Deaf.
www.rnid.org.uk/information_resources/aboutdeafness/statistics/?ciid=21
4722

RNID (2009) *Deaf and Hard of Hearing People.* London: Royal National Institute for the Deaf.
www.rnid.org.uk/information_resources/factsheets/deaf_awareness/factsh
eets_leaflets/deaf_and_hard_of_hearing_people.htm

Silverman-Dresner, Toby and George R. Guilfoyle (1970) *The Deaf Child's Knowledge of Words: Volume I and II, Alphabetical List of Test Items. Final Report.* Washington, DC.
http://eric.ed.gov/ERICDocs/data/ericdocs2sql/content_storage_01/00000
19b/80/37/18/4c.pdf

Silverman-Dresner, Toby and George R. Guilfoyle (1972) *Vocabulary Norms for Deaf Children: The Lexington School for Deaf Education Series, Book VII.* Washington, DC: Alexander Graham Bell Association for the Deaf.

Simpson, Paul A., David R. Harrison, Arabella Stuart (1992) "The reading abilities of a population of hearing-impaired children". *Journal of the British Association of Teachers of the Deaf* 16, 47-53.

Stern, Abram (2001) "Deafness and reading". *Literacy Today* 27.

www.literacytrust.org.uk/Pubs/stern.htm

Zárate, Soledad (2008) "Subtitling for deaf children on British television". *The Sign Language Translator and Interpreter* 2(1), 15-34.

Standing on quicksand: hearing viewers' comprehension and reading patterns of respoken subtitles for the news[1]

Pablo Romero-Fresco

Roehampton University, London, UK

Abstract

Although the interest regarding live subtitles is shifting from quantity to quality, given that broadcasters such as the BBC already subtitle 100% of their programmes, hardly any research has been carried out on how viewers receive this type of subtitle. The aim of this article is to cast some light on this issue by means of two experiments focussing on comprehension and viewing patterns of subtitled news. The results obtained in the first experiment suggest that some of the current subtitles provided for the news in the UK prevent viewers from being able to focus on both the images and the subtitles, which results in an overall poor comprehension of the programme. In order to ascertain whether this is due to the speed of the subtitles or to other factors, a second experiment is also included. In this case, an eye-tracker has been used to record the participants' viewing patterns. The results show that the word-for-word display mode of live subtitles results in viewers spending 90% of their time looking at the subtitles and only 10% looking at the images, which affects overall comprehension.

1. Introduction

In recent years, respeaking has established itself as the most cost-effective method of subtitling live events such as news, debates and sports for the deaf and hard-of-hearing. In this technique, a subtitler listens to the original soundtrack of a live programme and respeaks it – repeats it or reformulates it, depending on whether it is possible to keep up with the original speech rate, including punctuation marks – to a speech recognition software program, which turns the recognised utterances into subtitles displayed on the screen with minimum delay. Although respeaking has been used for over eight years now by broadcasters such as the BBC, little is known about respoken subtitles and virtually nothing about their reception. The pressure imposed by European and national legislation in EU member states has often forced broadcasters to focus on the quantity of live subtitling rather than on assessing its reception, which is crucial given the importance for the viewers of programmes such as news bulletins, whether deaf or not. The aim of this article is precisely to investigate the reception of respoken subtitles in news programmes by focussing on a) how much information viewers obtain from these subtitles when displayed at different speeds and b) how these subtitles are actually read, with the help of eye-tracking technology.[2]

With regard to the first objective, attention will be turned firstly to the speed of respoken subtitles, which lies at the root of the old debate between verbatim and edited subtitles. Verbatim subtitles are usually favoured by deaf associations, which regard them as the only way to provide deaf viewers with full access to the audiovisual content, and by subtitling companies, since they involve considerably less time (and fewer skills) than edited subtitles and are thus cheaper. Edited subtitles are often supported by academics, who believe verbatim subtitles are usually too fast to be read and comprehended by deaf viewers. The first experiment included in this article attempts to cast some more light on this issue by means of a reception study on the comprehension of respoken subtitles displayed at different speeds.

The second objective mentioned above, the analysis of how viewers actually read respoken subtitles, constitutes the second part of the present article. After an introduction to some of the research carried out so far regarding reading behaviour in subtitling, eye-tracking technology is used to ascertain some of the most salient patterns of how viewers perceive different types of respoken subtitles.

2. The comprehension of respoken subtitles depending on their speed

First of all, it is important to differentiate between at least three different types of speed: speech rate, rate of respoken subtitles and reading rate, all of which are influenced by numerous factors that make research on this issue particularly difficult.

2.1. Speech rate

Often measured in words per minute (wpm)[3], the speech rate may be regarded as the speed with which speech is produced. A further distinction is to be made between spontaneous speech and scripted speech. Although there are countless factors that can affect spontaneous speech rate, it is generally believed to be, at least in English, somewhere between 140 words per minute (wpm) and 160 wpm (Steinfield, 1999; Wingfield *et al.*, 2006). Scripted speech on TV, typically featuring fewer pauses and a faster delivery, is set by Uglova and Shevchenko (2005), at least in US news programmes, at 200 wpm, and even faster in weather forecasts. Recent research (Romero-Fresco, 2009), carried out on programmes broadcast by the BBC in the UK, points to the existence of different speeds for different genres. In sports, the speed would appear to range from 124 wpm to 182 wpm, with an average of 160 wpm. News programmes seem to be spoken faster, between 161 and 198 wpm, with an average of 180 wpm, and interviews and weather reports even faster, between 211 wpm and 245 wpm with an average of 230 wpm.

2.2. Rate of respoken subtitles

The little research carried out so far (Eugeni, 2009; Romero-Fresco, 2009) seems to indicate that the respeakers' speech rate (RSR) depends largely on the speech rate of the source text (original speech rate, OSR). According to this research, the respeaking speed may range from 106 wpm to 190 wpm and it is often lower than the speed of the original speaker. Indeed, respeakers lag 0-20 wpm behind original speakers who speak at up to 180 wpm and approximately 40 wpm behind speakers who speak faster. In other words, respeakers do not usually manage to produce verbatim subtitles, even though this is what they are encouraged to do. Even when respeaking a sports programme delivered at a slower speech rate than respeakers can produce, they often lag 20 wpm behind. The following chart (Romero-Fresco, 2009) includes a comparative analysis of the OSR in three sports programmes, three news programmes and four interviews/weather reports, indicated in the x axis, and the RSR, shown in wpm in the y axis:

Graph 1: Comparison of original speech rate and respeakers' speech rate

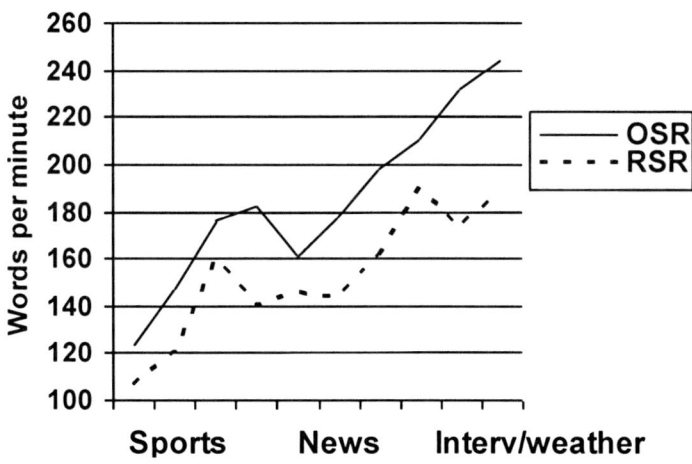

The reason for this may lie in the introduction of oral punctuation by respeakers when they are dictating to their speech recognition software. Indeed, the average number of full stops and commas introduced is very similar to the number of words respeakers lag behind original speakers. In other words, respeakers do adapt to the ST speech rate and, especially in speeds up to 180 wpm (sports and news), manage to say the same amount of words per minute as the original – if we include full stops and commas in this count. This would be the reason why respoken subtitles seem to be invariably edited. In order to produce verbatim subtitles, respeakers would have to speak faster than their original speakers (uttering all the ST plus punctuation marks), which is probably against the grain in this shadowing-like type of translation.

For the purpose of the present article, these data on respoken subtitles raise an important issue: given the widely held notion, especially among psychologists (Maiche Marini *et al.*, 2004), that an individual can usually hear and process acoustic information more quickly than they can read it, to what extent are respoken subtitles with a speed of up to 190 wpm (16 cps) readable for viewers? The first experiment included in this article will attempt to answer this question but, before that, the next section presents an overview of research carried out so far on this issue and some of the guidelines resulting from it.

2.3. Reading speed and guidelines

As is the case when dealing with speech rate, figures on reading speeds must be taken with a pinch of salt, given that an individual's reading rate may depend on a number of factors as varied as the reading level of the materials, the purpose of the reading, the conceptual context of the material and especially the accuracy or efficiency of comprehension (Carver, 1974), among many others. Besides, it is also essential to take into account the different types of reader/viewer, especially when dealing with subtitles for the deaf and hard-of-hearing (SDH):

> Even among groups of hearing subjects, one finds considerable differences in reading speeds. These differences, though, are particularly relevant within the deaf community, which is known to be very heterogeneous, with outlooks and needs so different that it is difficult to adequately meet them all together (de Linde and Kay, 1999:11).

Thus, despite the limited scope of this article, a distinction must be made at least in terms of readers (hearing/hard-of-hearing and deaf adults) and material (print/subtitles).

As far as hearing adults are concerned, the average reading speed of printed material seems to be about 300 wpm (Carver, 1976; D'Ydewalle and de Bruycker, 2007). As for subtitles, not many studies have been carried out on hearing adults' reading speed. Particularly relevant in this sense is the research conducted by D'Ydewalle *et al.* (1987), who used eye-tracking technology to test three different presentation times for subtitles: 192 wpm, 130 wpm and 96 wpm. The object of this study was to ascertain if the so-called six-second rule (a full two-line subtitle displayed on screen for 6 seconds and shorter subtitles scheduled proportionally, equivalent to 130 wpm), accepted as common practice in most subtitling countries, could be validated by empirical research on reading speeds. His results leave little room for doubt, the six-second rule being identified as setting the appropriate reading speed for the participants. In recent years, and based on the idea that regular exposure to subtitles may have increased the viewers' reading speed (Ofcom, 2005), this six-second rule has been applied to longer lines than the ones referred to by D'Ydewalle (78 characters instead of 64) which results in subtitling companies setting the recommended speed at 160 wpm and, in the case of DVDs, at up to 180 wpm. Further research is still needed to investigate the reception of such speeds on the part of hearing viewers.

As far as deaf and hard-of-hearing viewers are concerned, the first problem comes from the fact that it is impossible to regard them as one homogeneous group.[4] For those referred to as Deaf by Neves (2008:143), reading presents some additional difficulties to those faced by hearing people, given that they have less language-specific knowledge (semantic and syntactic), fewer oral skills necessary for reading (i.e. phonological processing) and poor encyclopaedic language knowledge necessary to understand texts (Torres Monreal and Santana Hernández, 2005). It is for this reason that, as shown by both Conrad (1977) and Torres Monreal and Santana Hernández (2005), the reading level of deaf high school students corresponds to that of hearing students who are seven years younger.

With regard to reading subtitles, although research is scarce, the most relevant study is probably the one carried out by Jensema (1998), who tested different subtitle speeds (96-200 wpm) with 205 deaf, 110 hard-of-hearing and 262 hearing participants. Results indicated that, for most viewers, 145 wpm was the preferred speed and that anything over 170 wpm was generally deemed as too fast.

The question is now whether, as was mentioned above regarding hearing viewers, ten years later reading speeds have increased. The subtitling industry seems to believe so, as is reflected in many of the subtitling guidelines available. In the UK, the standards for subtitling laid out by the Independent Television Commission (ITC) in 1999 set the reading speed for SDH at 140 wpm, very much following Jensema's (1998) findings. Yet, this recommendation was revisited in 2005 by the Office of Communications (Ofcom), which carried out a study presenting different subtitling speeds to 21 moderately deaf, 21 severely deaf and 22 profoundly deaf people. Although, as stated in this report (2005:4), almost 40% of the participants considered 180 wpm to be too fast and "the majority of deaf viewers would like the subtitle speed to stay the same", Ofcom's final recommendation ("subtitling speed should not normally exceed 180 wpm [15 cps]") effectively allows broadcasters to increase the previous recommended subtitling rate up to 40 wpm. Following this study and after extensive consultation with disability organisations, broadcasters and access service providers, the set of SDH guidelines drawn up by Ofcom in 2006 recommends 160-180 wpm given that it attracted "little adverse comment". Yet, important organisations such as Sense, Tag, the Royal National Institute for the Blind and the Royal National Institute for the Deaf regarded these speeds as too fast and likely to pose problems to some viewers.

In other words, 180 wpm (15 cps), the maximum SDH speed set by the UK guidelines, has been widely agreed upon by broadcasters, service providers and some deaf associations, but is seen as somewhat excessive by many viewers and most academics. In this sense, Neves (2005) warns that subtitles displayed at 180 wpm or faster, even if they are displayed in blocks, with careful line breaks and synchrony with the image, pose a great deal of difficulty for deaf (and even some hard-of-hearing) viewers.

What about respoken subtitles, overlooked by these guidelines and displayed at speeds of up to 190 wpm, word-for-word, without careful line breaks and with no synchrony with the image?

2.4. First experiment: viewers' comprehension of respoken subtitles for the news

As mentioned in the introduction, the research presented here is the first stage of a larger study on the reception of respoken subtitles included within the EU-funded project DTV4ALL. Following Jensema (1998), participants in DTV4ALL have been divided into three groups: hearing, hard-of-hearing and deaf viewers. The two experiments included in this article have been conducted with the first group of participants: hearing viewers.

The purpose of this first experiment is two-fold: to find out how much visual and verbal information is obtained through respoken subtitles in news programmes and to gather the participants' views on the speed of these subtitles. The material used for the experiment consisted of four clips from the Six O'Clock News broadcast on 4 July 2007 by BBC1. The participants chosen for the study were 30 hearing viewers, between the ages of 20 and 45, native or near native-speakers of English and very familiar with subtitling.

Half of them were postgraduate students currently doing an MA on Audiovisual Translation at Roehampton University and the other half was formed by lecturers and professional subtitlers. All viewers were proficient readers and habitual subtitle users.

During the experiment, participants were shown two clips with two news items and were asked to answer questions about one. Following Jensema's (1998) methodology, the clips had no sound and so viewers had to rely on the subtitles to retrieve the information. The clips were subtitled by respeaking at two different speeds: 180 wpm, which is, as explained above, the common speed for respoken news on the BBC, and 220 wpm, which allows for verbatim subtitling of most weather reports and interview programmes. The latter speed constitutes an increase of 40 wpm over the recommended speed for hearing viewers (180 wpm), exactly the same increase deaf and hard-of-hearing viewers are currently having to face (from the 140 wpm recommended by Jensema [1998] to the current 180 wpm).

In order to carry out a quantitative analysis of the amount of information retrieved by the viewers, the two news clips were notionally divided, drawing on Chafe's (1980) concept of *idea units*,[5] which has already been applied to respeaking (Eugeni, 2009; Romero-Fresco, 2009), into 14 semi-units: 8 verbal units and 6 visual units. In (very few) cases in which participants retrieved a semi-unit that was not included in these 14, the new unit was also factored in the analysis. For the purpose of the analysis of the findings, a simple division was made whereby any result between 0% and 25% is regarded as zero to poor information retrieval, 25%-50% goes from poor to sufficient, 50%-75% from sufficient to good and 75%-100% from very good to perfect information retrieval.

Finally, a further problem was posed by the absence of a yardstick with which to compare the results obtained by participants watching subtitled news. Can we indeed expect viewers under normal conditions (no subtitles) to obtain 100% of the visual and acoustic information of a news clip? In order to answer this question, a preliminary test was run with 14 other students (from the above-mentioned class at Roehampton University) who watched the same clips with sound but no subtitles and were asked the same questions. The following two sections include the findings obtained in the three tests (no subtitles, 180 wpm and 220 wpm) and a discussion of these findings.

2.4.1. Findings

Graph 2 shows the overall results, whereas tables 1, 2 and 3 use the above-mentioned rating (from *very good* to *very poor*) to assess the performance of the participants in the tests with no subtitles, 220 wpm and 180 wpm respectively. For the latter two, a comparison is drawn in these tables between the performance of the participants and their opinion on the speed of the subtitles:

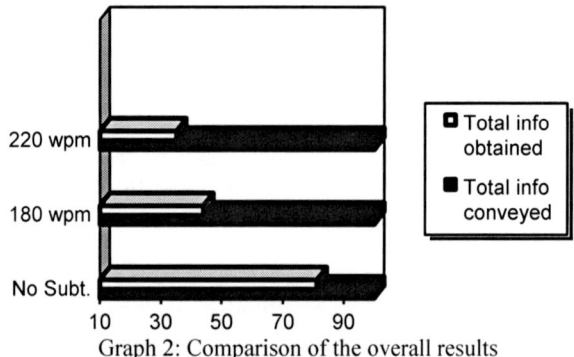

Graph 2: Comparison of the overall results

No subtitles	
Performance	
Very good	100%
Good	0%
Almost good	0%
Sufficient	0%
Less than sufficient	0%
Poor	0%
Very poor	0%

Table 1: Performance of the participants without subtitles

Subtitles at 220 wpm					
Opinion			Performance		
Slow	1%		Good	0%	
OK	23%	24%	Almost good	6%	20%
			Sufficient	13.3%	
Fast	76%	76%	Less than sufficient	20%	80%
			Poor	30%	
			Very poor	30%	

Table 2: Opinion and performance of the participants
with subtitles displayed at 220 wpm

Subtitles at 180 wpm					
Opinion			Performance		
Slow	13%	66%	Good	3%	49%
OK	53%		Almost good	6%	
			Sufficient	40%	
Fast	33%	33%	Less than sufficient	20%	51%
			Poor	21%	
			Very poor	10%	

Table 3: Opinion and performance of the participants
with subtitles displayed at 180 wpm

2.4.2. Discussion

In the no-subtitles condition, all participants achieved what was regarded as very good comprehension, particularly of the images (90.5%, as compared to 73.2% of the verbal information), which is normal considering that no subtitles were displayed.

As for the test with subtitles at 220 wpm, 80% of the participants did not obtain sufficient information, only 20% obtained sufficient information and none obtained good information. Besides, 60% could only remember a poor or very poor account of the news. Although not surprising, given the high subtitle speed, these results warn against the possibility of producing verbatim subtitles for certain programmes such as debates, interviews and weather reports, which are sometimes spoken at this rate. Indeed, most viewers (76%) considered these subtitles to be too fast. Many of them also added that it caused them 'stress' and 'headache' and pointed out that the images were too fast, which, although not true (they were as fast as in the other clips), goes to show how the speed of subtitles can affect the overall perception of an audiovisual programme.

The test with subtitles displayed at 180 wpm is more significant, as respoken subtitles are often displayed at this speed in some sports programmes and many news programmes, interviews and debates. In this case, most participants (66%) were happy with the speed of the subtitles and yet, more than half of them (51%) did not obtain sufficient information. This suggests that viewers may be unaware of how much information they are losing due to the speed of respoken subtitles. Thus, although most of them regarded the speed as OK or even too slow, only 3% obtained good information and 31% got poor or very poor information. More worryingly, 1 out of 3 participants acquired incorrect information, believing, for example, to have seen the President of Nicaragua or Tony Blair, neither of whom appeared on the news.

3. How do we read respoken subtitles?

In order to ascertain whether the low scores obtained in the first experiment are due to the speed of subtitles or any other cause, such as their display mode, the experiment presented in this section resorts to eye-tracking technology to explore the viewing patterns of participants watching these respoken subtitles.

3.1. Eye-tracking and subtitling

Despite its obvious potential for the study of Audiovisual Translation and more specifically for that of subtitling, eye-tracking research in this area is still very scarce, with the exception of a few scholars such as Jensema *et al.* (2000) and D'Ydewalle *et al.* (1991, 2007). Looking precisely at how subtitles are read, Jensema *et al.* (2000:284) found a general tendency whereby viewers typically move their gaze to the beginning of a subtitle within a fraction of a second, then read the subtitle and finally glance at the images once they have finished reading. Yet, reading is far from being a smooth process. Rather than moving continuously across the page/screen, our eyes pause and focus on specific parts and then jump across words and images. The visual information necessary for reading is obtained during those pauses, known as fixations, which typically last about 200–250 ms (Liversedge and Findlay, 2000). The jumps between fixations are known as saccades, which take as little as 100 ms and are the fastest movement the human being is capable of making (Rayner and Pollatsek, 1989). During saccades, vision is suppressed and no useful information is obtained, which is known as the saccadic suppression (Wolverton and Zola, 1983). Yet, even though we cannot read during saccades, the eyes need not fixate on every word when reading a subtitle. As shown in Rayner (1998), the global perceptual span, the area from which useful information is obtained during a fixation in reading, extends from the beginning of the fixated word to 14 or 15 characters to the right of fixation. With the fovea (part of the eye responsible for sharp central vision) we determine the location of a fixation, the foveal area, which spans 6 to 8 characters around the fixation point. Then, the so-called parafoveal area extends up to 15 characters to the right of fixation (Häikiö *et al.*, 2009). Needless to say, the fact that there is no need to fixate on every word allows for faster reading. This seems to apply to print and even block subtitles, but what happens when we are reading subtitles that are displayed word-for-word on the screen?

Although not exactly applied to subtitles, the news coming from the field of psychology in this regard is discouraging. Experiments conducted by Rayner *et al.* (2006:321) demonstrate "the importance of the continued presence of the word to the right of fixation [...] in order for fluent reading to occur". It would seem that when our eyes are fixated on the foveal word (n), we have enough preview benefit of the next word, the parafoveal word (n+1), to pre-process it, which is crucial to maintaining normal patterns of reading behaviour. Needless to say, in scrolling subtitles, this word to the right of the fixation, the n+1 word, is often unavailable for viewers, as words are displayed one at a time. In Rayner *et al.*'s (2006) study, the absence of this word causes regressions (the eye moves back to previous words already read) and considerable disruption to reading, slowing down the reading speed significantly. The following study aims to ascertain whether this disruption is also produced by the word-for-word display of respoken subtitles in the news.

3.2. Description of the experiment

Conceived as a tentative initial application of eye-tracking to research in respeaking, the present experiment was conducted with 5 participants, all of them, as was the case in the previous study, hearing lecturers on subtitling or professional subtitlers, proficient readers of English and habitual subtitle users. The aim was to find out how viewers read respoken, word-for-word subtitles as opposed to block subtitles. Participants were shown two news clips from the Six O'Clock News (4 July 2004) subtitled by respeaking. The first clip was subtitled in scrolling mode (word-for-word); the second, in blocks. Eye movements were monitored via a non-intrusive tracker, which was used to determine a) the number of fixations per subtitled line and b) the amount of time spent on images as opposed to the time spent on subtitles. The equipment used was Tobii 50 series eyetracker (Tobii 1750), at a frame rate of 50Hz and a 35 ms latency. Viewing was binocular and the images were presented on a 17" monitor at a viewing distance of 60 cm. The computer kept a complete record of the duration, sequence, and location of each eye fixation, and Tobii Studio was used to analyse all data recorded.

3.2.1. Findings

Graphs 3 and 4 show the group results for the number of fixations (y axis) of all participants on each of the 24 subtitled lines (x axis) displayed in scrolling mode and in blocks respectively:

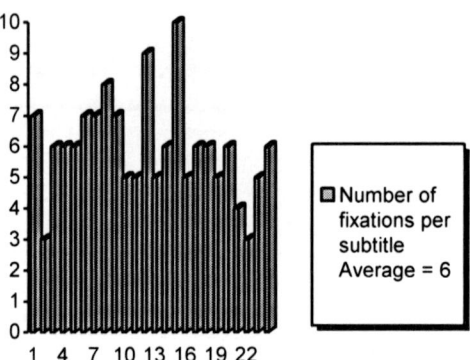

Graph 3: Word-for-word – Fixations (y) on each scrolling subtitle (x)

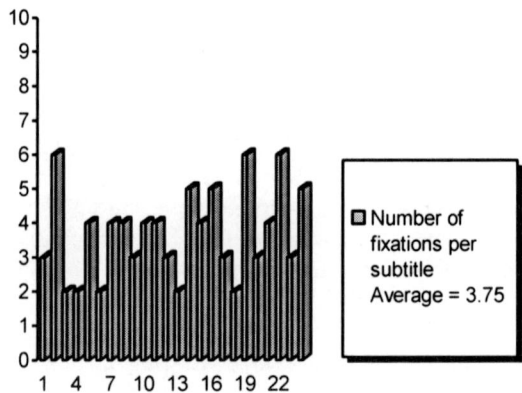

Graph 4: Blocks – Fixations (y) on each block subtitle (x)

Graphs 5 and 6 show the amount of time spent by all participants on the images and the subtitles of the clips respoken in scrolling mode and in blocks respectively:

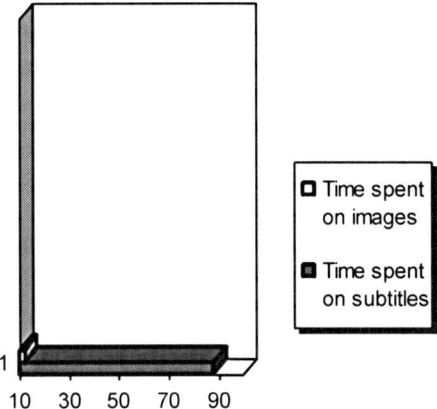

Graph 5: Word-for-word – Time spent on images and the subtitles (scrolling)

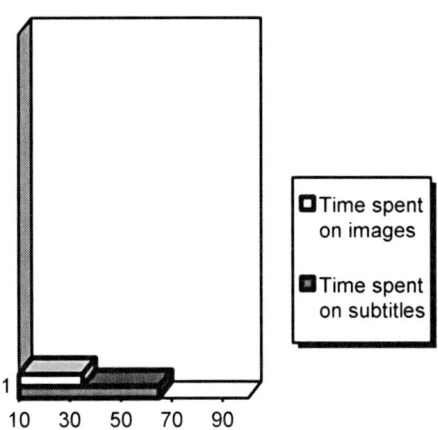

Graph 6: Blocks – Time spent on images and subtitles (block mode)

As can be seen in these results, word-for-word subtitles cause almost twice as many fixations as block subtitles. In the scrolling mode, the number of fixations per subtitled line ranges from 3 to 10, with an average of 6. Given that the average number of words per line in the clips analysed is 6, it would seem that viewers fixate on every word of every scrolling subtitle. In block subtitles, the number of fixations ranges from 2 to 6, with an average of 3.75. In other words, viewers skip almost every other word of the subtitle when reading it. Consequently, viewers of the scrolling mode spend most of their time reading the subtitles (88.3% vs 11.7% spent on the images), whereas viewers of block subtitles have more time to focus on the images (66.6% on the subtitles, 33.3% on the images).

3.2.2. Discussion

As anticipated by Rayner *et al.* (2006), most viewers seemed to have problems with the absence of the word to the right of the fixation in scrolling, word-for-word subtitles, often casting their eyes on gaps where no word had been displayed yet. In the following example, four out of five attempts of the viewer to read the line 'at least one is in the operating room' fall into this gap. Instead of finding solid ground (a word or a whole line) the viewer's gaze falls on a sort of quicksand, which results in the loss of precious time (a whole second here, that is, 0.250 ms per each of the four astray fixations) in his/her reading process:

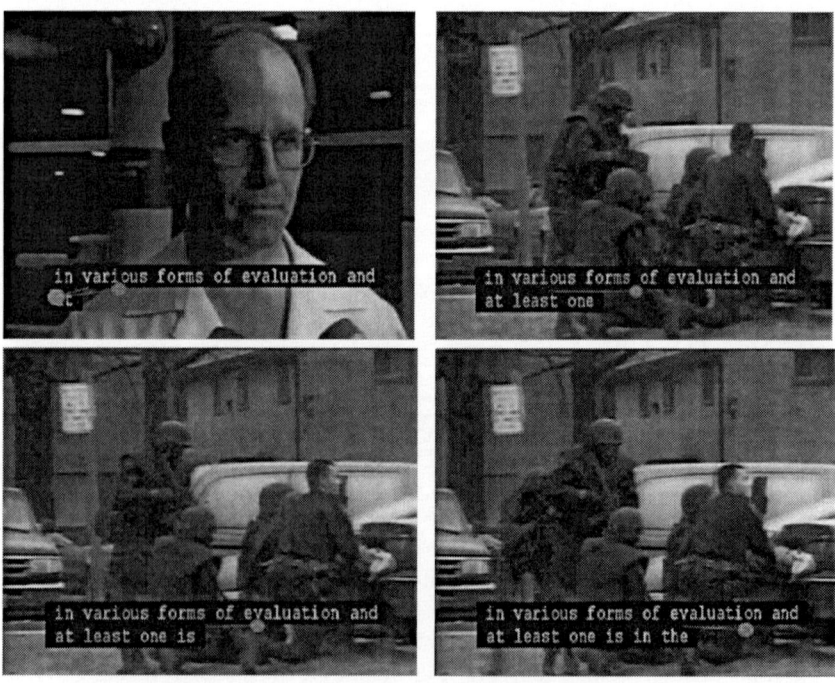

Screenshots 1-4: The 'quicksand' effect reading scrolling subtitles

Very often, this 'quicksand effect' causes the viewer to go back (the regressions pointed out by Rayner *et al.* [2006]) and fixate on previous words, thus wasting further reading time. In the following example ('we've got several patients that are'), having fixated on a gap after 'several', the viewer goes back to 'we've' and 'got', then skips 'several' (already read) and focusses on 'patients', only to fall on quicksand again:

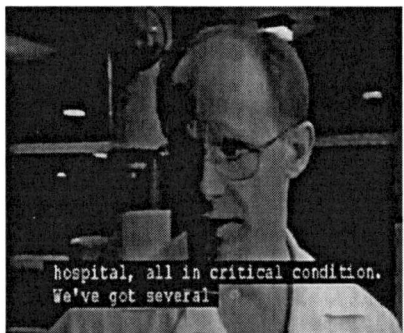 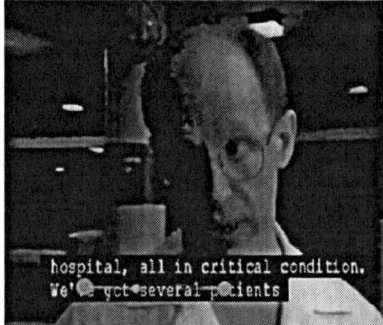

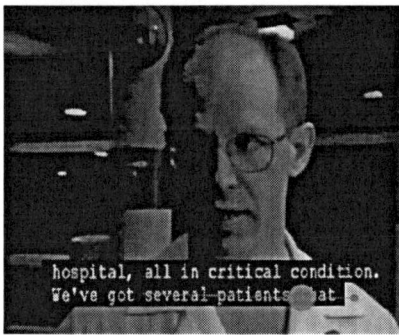

Screenshots 5-7: Regressions and chaotic patterns reading scrolling subtitles

In contrast, the reading pattern of block subtitles seems faster and less chaotic. Corroborating Jensema *et al.*'s (2000) observations, the viewers' gaze turns quickly to the subtitles, where this time they find firm ground on which to cast their eyes before looking up to the images. Thus, the same line as before ('we've got several patients that are') displayed in a block is read by this viewer in only four fixations (on 'we've', 'several', 'patients' and 'that'). There is no need to read all the words and considerably less time is spent on the subtitle, which allows more time to focus on the image:

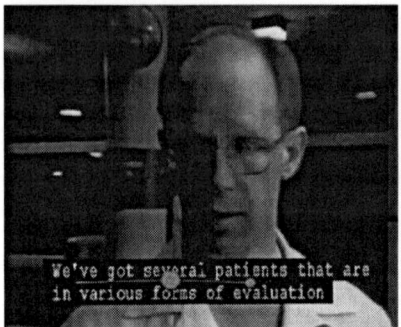 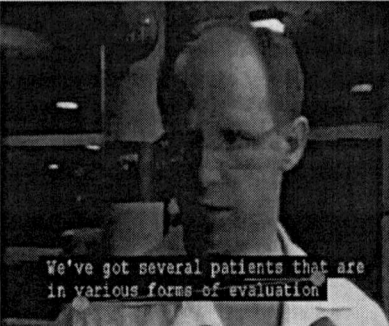

Screenshots 8-9: Reading patterns with block subtitles

4. Conclusions

As pointed out above, many scholars believe that verbatim subtitles displayed at 180 wpm and above, often favoured by subtitling companies and deaf associations, are too fast to guarantee full comprehension on the part of the viewers, even if these subtitles are displayed in blocks, with careful line breaks and in synchrony with the images. How does the audience receive the respoken subtitles, displayed at up to 190 wpm, in word-for-word mode, without careful line breaks and with little synchrony with the images?

The first experiment included in this article attempts to answer this question in relation to hearing viewers (as a first step which will be followed by studies with deaf and hard-of-hearing viewers) watching news subtitled by respeaking. The results obtained suggest that most viewers struggle to obtain sufficient (verbal and visual) information from respoken subtitles with no sound. Whereas, without subtitles, viewers obtain an average of 80% of the content, the average with subtitles at 180 wpm (as they are often shown on TV) decreases to 44%. Only 3% of the participants obtain what may be described as good information and 31% percent obtain poor or very poor information. Furthermore, 1 out of 3 obtains wrong information. Interestingly, viewers do not seem to notice this issue, as they see no problem with the speed of the subtitles. With subtitles displayed at 220 wpm, however, the speed is deemed too fast and results are lower, which warns against the provision of verbatim subtitles for interviews and other programmes spoken at fast rates.

It should be noted that two of the conditions of this first experiment were artificial. Firstly, participants were not completely ignorant about it and knew beforehand that they were going to be asked about the visual and verbal content of the news clips. In this case, findings could be regarded as all the more relevant, as participants might be expected to make a bigger effort than usual to retain information. Secondly, it might be argued that hearing (and even hard-of-hearing) viewers would not normally have to rely on subtitles to watch the news. Pending the application of this experiment to deaf viewers, the low comprehension obtained by the hearing group, proficient readers and habitual subtitle users, sends a worrying message, given the reading difficulties often observed in deaf viewers.

A possible solution to the problem posed by the low comprehension of the respoken subtitles used in this experiment could lie in editing. As shown in Romero-Fresco (2009), respeakers can often edit up to 17% of a programme, subtitling it at 160 wpm and missing only 8% of the relevant information. Therefore, when possible, it would appear sensible to respeak at a lower speed with edited subtitles, losing 8% of the content rather than 56% of the comprehension on the part of the viewers.

Yet, as is suggested by the second experiment included in this article, speed may not be the only problem. Indeed, the application of eye-tracking research to the analysis of reading patterns of viewers watching respoken subtitles shows a significant difference depending on whether subtitles are displayed in blocks or in scrolling mode. In block display, viewers seem to use the subtitle as a solid ground from which to obtain all the verbal information without fixating on every word, and from which they manage to look up at the images and complete the meaning of a shot. In word-for-word mode, this is not possible. Words are displayed one at a time, which causes viewers to fixate on every word, thus spending most of their time (almost 90%) on the subtitles and very little (10%) on the images. In these subtitles, words are not even displayed with a regular rhythm, which makes it impossible to predict their appearance and accounts for a very chaotic reading pattern. Added to this is the 'quicksand effect', whereby viewers often jump the gun and fixate on gaps where no words have been shown yet, thus wasting considerable time. This effect causes viewers to go back to re-read previous words (regression), wasting even more time that cannot then be devoted to the images. The fact that, as recently found by Rayner *et al.* (2009), images take considerably longer to encode than words, only makes these results more worrying.

Yet, the fact that this article has focussed on the problems that respoken subtitles pose for viewers should not detract from what is surely the most important aspect, namely that respeaking (for instance as carried out by Red Bee Media for the BBC) has finally met the challenge of providing high quality accessibility to live TV. In this sense, the only improvement that may be suggested here is to slow down the speed of the respeaker with heavier editing and perhaps to strive for a more regular display of the words shown in scrolling mode. Time, and especially further research in different fields, will tell whether it is possible finally to produce block subtitles with little delay (which seems possible with Dragon 10) and whether the results obtained in the present article are representative of a one-off situation or indicative of a more stable pattern.

Notes

1. This article has been written in the framework of the research project "Subtitling for the Deaf and Hard-of-Hearing and Audio Description: objective tests and future plans" (FFI2009-08027), funded by the Spanish Ministerio de Ciencia e Innovación.
2. The analysis presented in this article is the first stage of a larger study on the reception of respoken subtitles included within the EU-funded project DTV4ALL (www.psp-dtv4all.org).
3. As explained by Ofcom (2005), words per minute (wpm) may not be the most appropriate means to evaluate subtitling speeds, which are often preferred in characters per second (cps). Yet, given that the present study also deals with speech and reading rates, which are typically given in wpm, this is the unit that will be used throughout this article. When necessary, however, the equivalent in cps will be provided. This will apply mainly to the English language, where the average word is considered to have five characters (Díaz Cintas, 2008:97).
4. As pointed out by Neves (2008:143), an important distinction is to be made between the deaf, that is, "people who are deaf but who belong to the social context of the hearing majority and relate to the oral language as their mother tongue", and the Deaf, "a social and linguistic minority, who use a sign language as their mother tongue and read the national language as a second language". Given that the focus of this article is on the subtitles and not on the audience, the term deaf will be applied to both groups and distinctions between the two groups will only be made explicit when necessary.
5. Chafe (1985:106) defines idea units as "units of intonational and semantic closure", which can be identified because they are spoken with a single coherent intonation contour, preceded and followed by some kind of hesitation, made up of a one verb phrase along with whatever noun, prepositional or adverb phrase are appropriate, usually consist of seven words and take about two seconds to produce.

References

Carver, Ronald (1974) "Improving reading comprehension: measuring readability". *American Institute for Research, Final Report*, R742.

Carver, Ronald (1976) "Word length, prose difficulty, and reading rates". *Journal of Reading Behavior* 8: 193-203.

Chafe, Wallace (1980) "The deployment of consciousness in the production of a narrative", in Wallace Chafe (ed.) *The Pear Stories: Cognitive, Cultural and Linguistic Aspects of Narrative Production*. Norwood, N. J.: Ablex Publishing Corp, 9-50.

Chafe, Wallace (1985) "Linguistic differences produced by differences between speaking and writing", in David Olson, Nancy Torrance and Angela Hildyard (eds) *Literacy, Language, and Learning: The Nature and Consequences of Reading and Writing*. Cambridge: Cambridge University Press, 105-22.

Conrad, Richard (1977) "The reading ability of deaf school-leavers". *British Journal of Education Psychology* 47:138-48.

Díaz Cintas, Jorge (2008) "Teaching and learning to subtitle in an academic environment", in Jorge Díaz Cintas (ed.) *The Didactics of Audiovisual Translation*. Amsterdam and Philadelphia: John Benjamins, 89-103.

D'Ydewalle, Géry, Johan Van Rensbergen and Joris Pollet (1987) "Reading a message when the same message is available auditorily in another language: the case of subtitling", in J. K. O'Reagan and A. Lévy-Schoen (eds) *Eye Movements: From Physiology to Cognition*. Amsterdam and New York: Elsevier Science Publishers, 313-21.

D'Ydewalle, Géry, Caroline Praet, Karl Verfaillie and Johan Van Rensbergen (1991) "Watching subtitled television: Automatic reading behaviour". *Communication Research* 18(5): 650-66.

D'Ydewalle, Géry and Wim De Bruycker (2007) "Eye movements of children and adults while reading television subtitles". *European Psychologist* 12(3): 196-205.

Eugeni, Carlo (2009) "Respeaking the BBC news: A strategic analysis of respeaking on the BBC". *The Sign Language Translator and Interpreter* 3(1): 29-68.

Häikiö, Tuomo, Raymond Bertram, Jukka Hyönä and Pekka Niemi (2009) "Development of the letter identity span in reading: evidence from the eye movement moving window paradigm". *Journal of Experimental Child Psychology* 102:167-81.

ITC (1999) *ITC Guidance on Standards for Subtitling*. London: Independent Television Commission.

Jensema, Carl (1998) "Viewer reaction to different television captioning speeds". *American Annals of the Deaf* 143(4): 318-24.

Jensema, Carl, Sameh El Sharkawy, Ramalinga S.Danturthi, Robert Burch and David Hsu (2000) "Eye movement patterns of captioned television viewers". *American Annals of the Deaf* 145(3): 275-85.

Liversedge, Simon P. and John M. Findlay (2000) "Saccadic eye movements and cognition". *Trends in Cognitive Science* 4: 6-14.

de Linde, Zoé and Neil Kay (1999) *The Semiotics of Subtitling*. Manchester: St. Jerome.

Maiche Marini, Alejandro, Jordi Fauquet Ars, Santiago Estaún Ferrer and Claude Bonnet (2004) "Tiempo de reacción: del cronoscopio a la teoría de ondas". *Psicothema* 16(1): 149-55.

Neves, Josélia (2005) *Audiovisual Translation: Subtitling for the Deaf and Hard-of-Hearing*. London: Roehampton University. PhD Thesis.
http://roehampton.openrepository.com/roehampton/handle/10142/12580

Neves, Josélia (2008) "10 fallacies about subtitling for the d/Deaf and the hard of hearing". *The Journal of Specialised Translation* 10: 128-43.
www.jostrans.org/issue10/art_neves.pdf

Ofcom (2005) *Subtitling – An Issue of Speed?* London: Office of Communications.

Ofcom (2006) *Television Access Services – Review of the Code and guidance*. London: Office of Communications.

Rayner, Keith (1998) "Eye movements in reading and information processing: 20 years of research". *Psychological Bulletin* 124: 372-422.

Rayner, Keith and Alexander Pollatsek (1989) *The Psychology of Reading*. Broadway (US): Lawrence Erlbaum Associates.

Rayner, Keith, Simon P. Liversedge and Sarah J. White (2006) "Eye movements when reading disappearing text: the importance of the word to the right of fixation". *Vision Research* 46: 310-23.

Rayner, Keith, Tim J. Smith, George L. Malcolm and John M. Henderson (2009) "Eye movements and visual encoding during scene perception". *Psychological Science* 20(1): 6-10.

Romero-Fresco, Pablo (2009) "More haste less speed – edited versus verbatim respoken subtitles". *VIAL (Vigo International Journal of Applied Linguistic)* 6:109-33.

Steinfield, Aaron (1999) *The Benefit to the Deaf of Real-time Captions in a Mainstream Classroom Environment*. Ann Arbor: University of Michigan. PhD Thesis.

Torres Monreal, Santiago and Rafael Santana Hernández (2005) "Reading levels of Spanish deaf students". *American Annals of the Deaf* 150(4): 379-87.

Uglova, Natalia and Tatiana Shevchenko (2005) "Not so fast please: temporal features in TV speech". Paper presented at the meeting of the Acoustical Society of America, Vancouver, BC.

Wingfield, Arthur, Sandra L.McCoy, Jonathan E. Peelle, Patricia A. Tun and L. Clarke Cox, (2006) "Effects of adult aging and hearing loss on comprehension of rapid speech varying in syntactic complexity". *Journal of the American Academy of Audiology* 17: 487-97.

Wolverton, Gary S. and David Zola (1983) "The temporal characteristics of visual information extraction during reading", in Keith Rayner (ed.) *Eye Movements in Reading: Perceptual and Language Processes*. New York: Academic Press, 41-52.

Audio description as a complex translation process: a protocol

Gala Rodríguez Posadas

Universidad de Granada, Spain

Abstract
The aim of this paper is to analyse the production protocol of an actual audio description assignment for the US film *Memoirs of a Geisha* (2004). In doing so, I shall examine the translation process in which the audio describer is involved, covering each stage from the first contact with the client for the acceptance of the assignment to the narration and recording of the script produced. I will focus particularly on the production stages in order to deal with the question of problem-solving from a functional perspective. To achieve the proposed objective, the line of argument will be supported by a protocol of translation stages postulated by Risku (1998).

1. Introduction

The aim of this paper is to analyse the production protocol of an actual audio description assignment for the US film *Memoirs of a Geisha* (Rob Marshall, 2004). In doing so, I shall examine the translation process in which the audio describer is involved, covering each stage from the first contact with the client for the acceptance of the assignment, to the narration and recording of the script produced. I will focus particularly on the production stages in order to deal with the question of problem-solving from a functional perspective. To achieve the proposed objective, the line of argument will be supported by a protocol of translation stages postulated by Risku (1998).

2. Audio description, a new translation mode

Adopting a semiotic point of view, Jakobson (1959:429) distinguishes between three different types of translation:

1. Intralingual translation or rewording is an interpretation of verbal signs by means of other signs of the same language.
2. Interlingual translation or translation proper is an interpretation of verbal signs by means of some other language.
3. Intersemiotic translation or transmutation is an interpretation of verbal signs by means of signs of nonverbal sign systems.

As discussed by Díaz Cintas (2007), audio description (AD), which as a translation type is within the scope of Audiovisual Translation (AVT), constitutes a novel dimension in intersemiotic translation, namely a translation of the moving images of a film into words that support the storyline. Due to some technical constraints, the translation process of AD is doubly subordinated. On the one hand, it is subordinated to the silences that the original film script leaves free in order to introduce the AD commentary, and on the other hand, to the audio cues of the film. Accordingly, audio describers face a very special type of translation brief. As will be seen below, they must have certain competences developed to a similar level as for the conventional translator or the professional working between two purely linguistic codes. These competences include source text problem identification, transfer of cultural references, explicitation of what is implicit and *vice versa*, and task prioritisation.

According to Nida (1964), the main goal for the translator is to provoke a similar reaction in the target audience as the source text provokes in the original audience. This prime objective can and should also correspond to the main purpose of the audio describer, i.e. to have a similar effect on the blind person, through the soundtrack and the audio description script (ADS), as the film has on the sighted person by means of soundtrack and moving images. This intersemiotic translation is carried out through the replacement of images by words, in an attempt to achieve levels of drama, aesthetics or suspense similar to those in the original film.

As mentioned above, AD may be said to be a new translation mode constrained by the techincal dimension in a similar way to subtitling, dubbing or software localization. In the sections that follow, the AD practice is tackled from different perspectives: linguistic, semiotic, translational and cultural.

3. Translation as a complex cognitive activity

According to Risku (1998:142), translation is a problem-solving process in which the translator carries out an autodidactic activity based on a method of trial and error. For this reason, professional audio describers may refer to their own translation experience rather than to general or isolated cases. Translators take decisions and act in a flexible manner when confronting different problems or situations encountered in different films and film genres. This is the reason why, to an audio describer, transforming the images of a film into words means to translate, or in other words, to describe the fictionalised reality.

Taking into account these considerations, it can be concluded that the practice of AD requires great flexibility and a capacity for adaptation on a technical and practical level. It is not a question of the indiscriminate application of a general and universal methodology, but rather the research, application, checking and approval of solutions relative to specific and real problems. As Risku puts it (*ibid*:142):

> The goals and methodology of translation cannot exclusively depend on specific previously described problems. Translation competence is neither based on rules nor innate, but depends completely on experience. It is impossible to provide a single goal for every intercultural communicative situation, or a universal translation method (My translation).

Through experience and a method of trial and error, AD scriptwriters will draw their own conclusions which, while not being universal translation strategies, may be applied to similar situations in the future. This approach may in turn feed future translation strategies which may be put into practice on the particular script on which the audio describer is working.

Before covering the production stages, some questions regarding how AD is understood professionally should be addressed. During the preparation process of the ADS, the film is regarded as the source text (ST) whereas the ADS, which is eventually recorded over the film's soundtrack, makes up the target text (TT).

In order to correlate the stages of the translation process with those of the ADS preparation, I shall draw on the translation stages protocol designed by Risku (1998). In Table 1, Risku's stages appear alongside the professional AD stages proposed by the author of the present article, which will be explained in detail later on.

Risku's (1998) translation stages	Proposed AD stages
1. Contacting the client	1. Contacting the client
1.1 Defining the brief	1.1 Defining the brief
1.2 Deontology	1.2 Deontology
2. Reception stages	2. Reception and viewing stages: problem
2.1 Information research	identification and documentation
3. Production stages	3. Production stages
3.1 Establishing a goal	3.1 Establishing goals
3.2 Building a model	3.2 Predictions and extrapolations
3.3 Predictions and extrapolations	3.3 Planning the tasks
3.4 Planning the actions	3.4 Problem solving and decision making
3.5 Problem identification	3.5 Building strategies
3.6 Building strategies	3.6 Implementing the tasks
3.7 Decision making	
3.8 Implementing the actions	
4. Review and control stages	4. Review and control stages
4.1 Reviewing strategies and effect control	4.1 Reception of corrected text
	4.2 Error assessment
	5. Recording stage

Table 1: Translation and AD stages

As can be observed in Table 1, the problem-identification stage, which is positioned 3.5 in Risku's list, has been brought forward to the second stage in the case of AD. This is because, from the moment audio describers begin to watch the film they are working on, they start identifying problems that will need to be solved in the production stage. At the same time, the identification of problems in the film will guide audio describers in the research stage, since this stage is aimed at solving such problems. Furthermore, a series of changes can be appreciated with regard to Risku's reception stage, due to the fact that audio describers are looking for information both before and after the viewing. Additionally, a series of tasks in the pre-production stage also presents slight changes.

I will now proceed to enumerate each stage that the audio describer must cover until the script is recorded, highlighting the differences with regard to Risku's stages. In order to do this, I will base the explanation on my experience acquired with the AD of the film *Memoirs of a Geisha*.

3.1. Contacting the client

As in every translation process, the first step is to establish contact with the client and become familiarised with the task that is going to be carried out.

For the AD of *Memoirs of a Geisha*, I took into account on the one hand, the company's interest in making the film accessible, contracting certain responsibilities, a deadline and mode of delivery. On the other hand, I considered the final receivers of the AD, the non-sighted audience of the TT. The company decided to commission the assignment of preparing the ADS for the film, of 139 minutes.

Once the commission was accepted, I received a digital copy of the film – in this case it was already dubbed into Spanish – with the time code reader (TCR) engraved on the upper part of the image. This is the copy used by every person involved in the process: the audio describer, the reviser, the voice talent and the sound engineer.

The overall methodology undertaken consisted of supporting the storyline of *Memoirs of a Geisha* with my descriptions in order to enable the final receiver to understand the film in a way similar to a sighted person, making sure that no part of the storyline was left unresolved.

3.1.1. Defining the brief

Based on the silences present in the film, the audio describer's tasks are to note the in and out times at which every piece of description will be inserted, and to describe the images in such a way that the film can be understood without them.

3.1.2. Deontology

Despite the apparent simplicity of the brief, the fact that audio describers have to work with all kinds of topics and genres must be taken into account, as well as the need to acquire a specialist knowledge and vocabulary to deal with sometimes rather obscure references. This is why the documentation stage prior to the production and problem solving stages has such an enormous importance.

3.2. Reception and viewing stages: problem identification and documentation

During this stage, the focus is on a close viewing of the film and and the audio describer must detect the problems that will later trigger a decision making process. An example of this may be the appearance on screen of an implicit cultural reference, which will have to be researched so that it can be made explicit, if possible, in the image-to-word transfer. During this viewing, the audio describer should take notes of all the difficulties and nuances that will have to be considered during the production stage. These two phases are inseparable because, as mentioned earlier, if the describer fails to identify the issues, the information necessary to solve them cannot be researched.

Before viewing the film, and ideally before accepting the assignment, basic information about the film like the director, cast, awards received and year of production should be researched by visiting online resources such as the multilingual movie browser Internet Movie Database. The information contained in this database may prove useful for taking decisions on problems regarding the characters for instance, since a list of actors is provided, with a photograph and a description of the character portrayed by each one.

These could be said to constitute parallel texts, texts that can help us to identify and deal with translation problems. For the compilation of such texts, certain criteria should be taken into account. For example, the texts included need to be representative and necessary, relevant and reliable, should present a common vocabulary, include keywords and so on. In my parallel text corpus for the audio description of *Memoirs of a Geisha,* it was useful to include the novel on which the film was based, as well as some data on geishas and other different elements in Japanese culture appearing in the ST, such as sumo wrestling and a cherry in blossom. Once we have detected all the areas that require documentation, the parallel texts that make up our small corpus should be saved in a text format, indicating the URL from which they were extracted.

3.3. Production stages

The actual production of the AD begins once the describer has completed research on the topic(s) of the film and has reflected on the possible strategies to be adopted. The main tool for carrying out the production of the ADS is a computer terminal equipped with a word processing utility in order to prepare the script, along with a DVD player on which the film is watched while the ADS is written, as shown in figure 1.

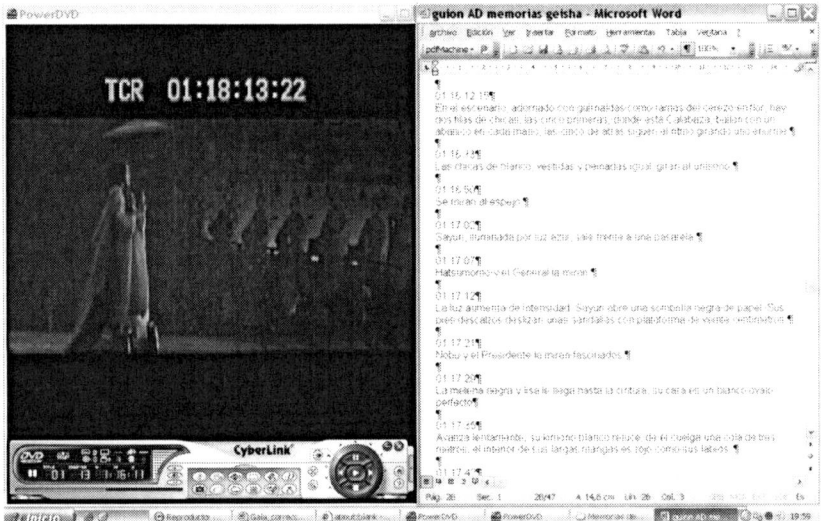

Figure 1: audio describing *Memoirs of a Geisha*

As supportive or accessory tools, the describer would also benefit from having the novel inspiring the film in electronic format, in case some research on the content is needed. In addition, terminological databases are useful for solving possible terminological problems.

3.3.1. Establishing goals

The main objective of audio describers is to make the film accesible to people with visual impairments and, consequently, the ADS should function as a support to the film's audiovisual storyline. As often occurs with translation assignments, AD assignments are also subject to time pressures and stringent delivery deadlines. Therefore, another objective is to establish the number of days in which the job should be completed satisfactorily and a viable remuneration rate for the audio describer.

3.3.2. Predictions and extrapolations

Here, Risku's (1998) "modelling construction" phase may be omitted in this AD protocol, because audiodescribers should know the model followed by most AD scripts and the methodology that should be applied to their assignment. The objective and methodology are gleaned by following the guidelines and norms drawn up in scripts they have previously translated, from AD training and from the format that they have previously applied to other AD scripts.

So, when faced with a new translation task, audiodescribers resort to their previous knowledge, the problems they have solved, the formats they have used, the documents they have consulted etc, which assist them throughout the process of translating the new ST. In other words, audiodescribers or 'image translators' anticipate any potential translation problems to be encountered in the new translation commission. Hence, before producing the new text, they will already be mindful of helpful strategies.

3.3.3. Planning the tasks

During production, and thanks to the preliminary viewing of the film, a plan of action can be drawn up, and more careful consideration given to the scenes to be audio described, the time available for the descriptions and the scenes presenting particular difficulties.

3.3.4. Problem solving and decision making

During the viewing, the problems presented by the film should have been identified and now, during the production stage, the describer is required to take specific decisions and to implement particular strategies. But first, it may be helpful to classify the most interesting challenges of *Memoirs of a Geisha* as follows:

1. Naming the characters
2. Clarifying off-screen voices
3. Describing flashbacks and flashforwards
4. Tackling cultural references

Risku (1998) compares the translation production stage with chess, where a player physically moves a piece, but cognitively is continually moving backwards and forwards until s/he achieves the objective. The same analogy can be applied to writing an ADS, where the audio describer goes continually back and forth to solve the problems, which are normally interrelated. I will now go through the points listed above in an attempt to illustrate the solutions to some of these problems in *Memoirs of a Geisha.*

Naming the characters

In the first minutes of the movie, the father of two girls sells them to a man who takes them to a far-off city. The man leaves the younger girl in the *okiya* (geisha boarding house) and continues on his way with the older sister. It is not until the end of this presentation, in which the five characters appearing in the first part are introduced, that the naming of characters can be undertaken. The audiodescriber waits for the main characters to be introduced in the film before mentioning them in the ADS in order to maximise coherence and in the hope that the blind audience will recognise the characters' voices as the protagonists of the movie.

It is in minute nine that the name of the main character, Chiyo, appears for the first time in the ADS. Until that point, reference to her was achieved through resorting to noun substitution, that is, naming her as 'the girl' or 'the little one'. Before that, we have already heard the names of the other characters in the dialogue: Mother, Pumpkin, Hatsumomo and Auntie, whom I only designated by name after having described her twice as 'the one with the stick'. A clarifying description was then added: 'Auntie, the woman using a walking stick, rubs Chiyo's feet'. This description is mentioned on 00:09:28:00 and solves the character-naming problem, since by this point all the characters have been named without needing to resort to substitutions.

Clarifying off-screen voices

At certain moments in the film, the off-screen voice of the main character is heard, narrating her own life story. On these occasions, I decided to warn the receivers that the diegetic voice they were going to hear was off-screen, and to describe the images that were being shown simultaneously with the off-screen narration.

> 00:03:38:00 → The main character's off-screen voice narrates the story while the train advances through lush green mountains.

In the example above, the strategy applied involves presenting the information before the actual image (the lush green mountains) has been shown, as happens many times in AD. This decision has been taken because the describer is aware that receivers only perceive the acoustic information of the film, and one possible solution is thus to provide the audio described information just before the sound of the action actually occurs.

Describing flashbacks and flashforwards

In the fragment described below, there is a time leap from the main character's childhood to adulthood. She suddenly appears with an adult body for the first time, while in the previous scene she was a girl. There is little time available to clarify this change, since it coincides with the diegetic sound of the radio broadcasting about the Second World War, which is also relevant for the storyline and, immediately afterwards, there is a series of continuous dialogue exchanges and sounds. Therefore, as soon as the image shows somebody closing a window, and despite not being able to distinguish the character, the AD mentions that she is a young woman. Later, a brief silence is exploited in order to specify that Chiyo is now a teenager and that her companion, Pumpkin, is a young *maiko* (a geisha-to-be):

> 00:39:44:00 → The city is covered by a thick blanket of snow. In the okiya a young woman closes the windows.

> 00:40:03:00 → Pumpkin is a young maiko.

> 00:40:19:22 → Chiyo is a teenager.

Tackling cultural references

Although I do not intend to pursue a study about cultural references in this article, and it would be a mistake to add too many details on this topic due to its complexity, in this particular movie it is a crucial issue, given the fundamental role played by Japanese culture in the narrative of the ST. It is for this reason that the describer needs to have a thorough knowledge of the culture portrayed in the film, and must also know how to designate and incorporate typical elements of the original culture – i.e. cultural references – into the target one, where they are perhaps less well known or indeed totally unknown. Here we understand cultural references as "[c]ategories, in which cultures take off from each other and that build the special profile of a given culture through their structured totality" (Maletzke 1996:42, my own translation). This author classifies cultural references according to the following categories: national character, perception, time and space experience, thought, language, nonverbal communication, value orientation, and behavioural patterns – the latter comprising customs, rules, roles, social groups, and social relationships. These elements are not to be considered in isolation but as "[e]lements functionally linked to each other, that find their place in connection with the totality within its structure" (*ibid.*, my own translation). This type of information is often difficult to translate or to introduce into the target culture and the describers' strategies will be conditioned by:

> • Their knowledge of the cultural setting of the film;
> • Their acceptance of this culture and the acceptance of the target audience;

• The status that describers think that culture has in relation to their own culture.

Audio describers may resort to strategies like transcription or transcription with explicitation, oriented towards the film's source culture; or, alternatively, move closer to their own language or that of the target culture, through the use of paraphrase or adaptation.

In view of the enormous variety of cultural references found in *Memoirs of a Geisha*, as much in the dialogue as in the staging of the film itself, the adoption of a foreignising approach from the beginning was thought to be the most appropriate solution, a strategy defined by Venuti (1995:20) as "[a]n ethnodeviant pressure on those [target] values to register the linguistic and cultural difference of the foreign text, sending the reader abroad". Though in our case, the *reader* becomes the film's *receiver*.

This foreignising strategy therefore promotes the inclusion of foreign cultural elements in the TT. Since our film is the vehicle for differences as marked as those inherent in the Japanese culture, it lends itself to the appearance of many cultural signs. In *Memoirs of a Geisha*, Japanese culture is omnipresent through the portrayal of ritualised social acts which are central to the geishas' customs, and hence it is vital to include such cultural manifestations in the AD.

This foreignising approach may prove controversial for some, who might think that including foreign terms in the AD could confuse the receiver of the storyline. I would argue, however, that in AD we should always try to provide as much cultural enrichment as possible through our text. I also defend the idea that using a word that can be perfectly understood from the context or the dialogue does not distract the receivers from the storyline; on the contrary, it will bring them closer to it. For example, in the AD description 'Mother, followed by Pumpkin, brings a pair of thong sandals, a pair of tabi and a kimono', the word *tabi* refers to socks with a seam for the big toe, widely used in Japanese culture where showing bare feet, especially in women, is considered a social taboo. The dialogue exchange that follows the description is: 'Outside you wear these, inside these. We don't display our naked feet like monkeys'; so that the term is mentioned in the movie dialogue prior to its appearance in the ADS, making it clear that *tabi* are some kind of footwear. Besides, it would be unfair to those familiar with the term to call them simply 'socks' in the ADS, since, apart from being culturally incomplete, it would seem to patronise and underestimate the audience.

AD should always make use of specific vocabulary, which is why the documentation phase is so important. Thus, in the present AD I used the original term *rickshaw* for the carts drawn by one person and used as a mode of transport; *samisen* for the stringed instrument they play; *okiya* for house; *hanamachi* for neighbourhood; *obi* for the long sash that the geishas tie round their backs; and *dohjo* for the elevated surface where the sumo wrestlers fight. Most of these terms are also used in the English screenplay, so their inclusion in the Spanish ADS is a question of loyalty and coherence with the film text. In fact, all these words can be found in any of the Spanish parallel texts selected in our comparable corpus, especially in the eponymous novel.

A cultural reference in *Memoirs of a Geisha* that should not be overlooked by the describer is the recurrent appearance of the cherry in blossom, which evokes the passing of time and is a well-known symbolic referent in the Japanese culture. Thus, every time a cherry in blossom appears on screen, a description is provided for it:

> 00:35:30:00 → It is daytime. Chiyo leans over the bridge with a far-away look. There is a cherry in blossom behind her.
>
> 01:06:04:00 → She places the cutting under the handkerchief in a make-up box. Sayuri walks along the street past a cherry in blossom. She goes into Mameha's house.
>
> 01:23:25:00 → They walk past a cherry in blossom.

The receiver is also alerted even when the reference is symbolic or figurative:

> 01:16:12:15 → On a stage, behind a curtain of garlands resembling the branches of a cherry in blossom, girls with fans dance in two lines. Pumpkin is among them.

Other cultural references that require careful treatment are the geishas' make-up, hairstyle and clothes. These women wear the *obi* tied with the bow at the back, which differentiates them from prostitutes, who tie it at the front. Thus, the first time the geisha Hatsumomo appears, I specifically mention this detail. Later, when Chiyo finds her sister, the AD specifies that the *obi* is tied with the bow at the front, to stress what the dialogue reveals, that she has been sold to a brothel.

The AD attempts to make full use of information which was researched in the documentation phase. Thus, given that geishas are more discreet than *maikos*, use less make-up, wear fewer adornments, and their kimonos are less colourful, with a predominance of pastel shades, I decided to offer descriptions of their make-up, the colour and prints of their kimonos and the adornments for their hair. The following descriptions try to capture these details:

00:05:27:00 → They get down. Behind the iron gate, the little one sees an attractive young woman with white make-up on her face, red lips and black hair perfectly put up. She wears a dark kimono with a floral print.

00:55:22:00 → Surprised, she looks at herself from head to foot. An ornamental comb with white flowers falling over her face embellishes a black bun, and contrasts with her pale face with a little rouge on her cheeks. Her eyes and eyebrows are traced in black.

3.3.5. Building strategies

During the problem-solving and decision-making stages, strategies are designed and implemented in order to provide coherence to the ADS and make it acceptable to the audience. So far, I have looked at strategies such as repetition, foreignising, anticipation, omission, cohesion between the film text and the audio described text, and suitability to film genre.

As seen before when dealing with character designation, a repetition strategy was applied, and once a character is named in the screenplay, his or her name is repeated in the ADS. This also constitutes a strategy of coherence and cohesion between the film text and the AD. The audio describer's specification of the diegetic off-screen voice is equivalent to an anticipating strategy, since the description clarifies whose voice it is before the voice is actually heard. In order to describe time leaps, two strategies can be resorted to: omission and anticipation. The first consists of leaving out visual aspects that are not relevant for the action going on at a given moment, while the second provides the AD commentary a little earlier than the change actually occurs. For dealing with cultural references in *Memoirs of a Geisha*, I have proposed a foreignising strategy in order to bring the ST culture closer to the TT, which in turn involves specification, repetition, and lexical adaptation.

Without a doubt, one of the most important strategies in the preparation of an ADS is the constant revision that the audio describer must carry out while writing the script. On detecting a silence in the film, the audio describer using a computer equipped with a word processing utility to prepare the script, along with a DVD player, writes the passage describing the image and, by reading it aloud, checks that the description fits the time available. Once describers have gained some experience, they can make an educated guess as to what will fit into a certain period of time. They also learn that a line written with Arial font 11 normally takes about five seconds to be narrated in Spanish. It is important to have some knowledge of voicing scripts, since there is a considerable difference between normal reading and narrating. If a description is too long for the time available, less important elements need to be left out or shorter terms have to be found. However, when using specific AD software, it is not necessary to check by reading the description aloud since these programmes have a feature, also common to subtitling programmes, that warns describers when they have reached the time limit available for the text.

A valuable revision strategy consists of starting a new describing session by reading the last minutes of the ADS written in the previous session. For instance, if after a day working on a film the describer reaches time code 00:38:20:00, it will be convenient to start checking the script from time code 00:30:00:00 the following day. Otherwise, the first descriptions in the new session might lack coherence, especially in relation to the style of the earlier descriptions.

3.3.6. Implementing the tasks

By solving problems through a variety of decision-making processes, the audio describer carries out appropriate tasks throughout the production of the ADS. As seen above, the tasks did not lead in one direction only, but were recurrent throughout all the stages of the commission.

3.4. Review and control stages

Once the ADS is finished, the text file is sent via email to the client, i.e. the person who commissioned the AD, for a general evaluation of the text. The client normally sends back a corrected Word document in which elements that need to be eliminated are highlighted, and others are added, as shown in Figure 2:

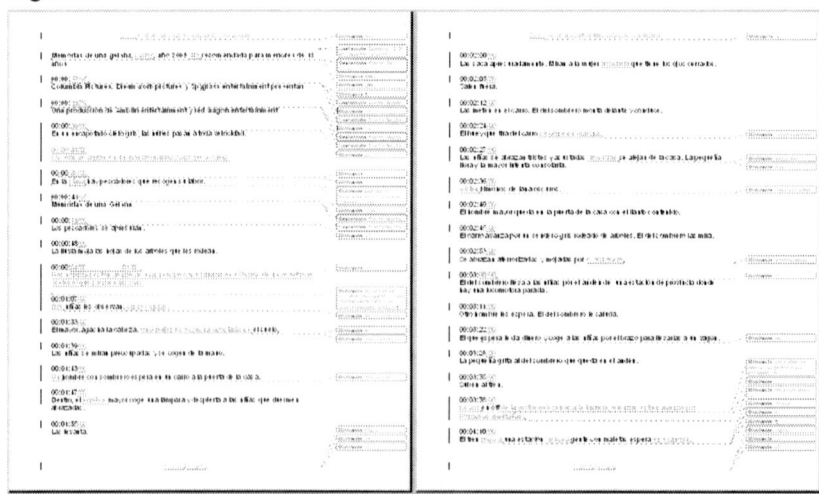

Figure 2: Corrected ADS of *Memoirs of a Geisha*

3.4.1. Reception of corrected text

Revising the corrected ADS is a relevant and useful task for audio describers, since it helps to reinforce their technique through a process of trial and error, so that they reflect on their mistakes as well as their successes. In the same way, revision enables describers to monitor their progress in AD practice and to apply the knowledge acquired to the creation of other AD scripts.

3.4.2. Error assessment

On revising the corrected ADS, audio describers should classify the various types of error, from minor to more serious: word and sentence order, time code synchronisation, lexical choice and information errors. The latter are often the most serious and arise when describers introduce unnecessary or irrelevant information, provide details which are less important for the storyline than other omitted pieces of information, or interpret the signs on the screen in an improper way. For example, in the description 'The older one lowers his head. There is an ill woman on the floor', an information error was committed, since the fact that the woman is ill is not yet established at this point in the film. Therefore, the commentary was replaced by 'The older one lowers his head. A woman lying on the floor listens to them'.

It is possible to improve our AD skills considerably by paying attention to, and learning from, these different kinds of error. We can also polish our technique and make a mental or possibly an electronic inventory of strategies to be applied in similar situations. Experience will make us faster and more precise audio describers.

3.5. Recording stage

This stage should also form part of the training of audio describers, since the visit to an audio recording studio is a great opportunity to assess ways by which to avoid inelegant or awkward sound combinations. Additionally, by paying attention to the reading of a professional voice talent, describers may want to read in a similar way when revising their ADS, and so reduce errors of time code synchronisation.

Usually, two professionals participate in the recording sessions: the sound engineer and the voice talent, who is not normally involved in the production stage. In the case of *Memoirs of a Geisha* a female voice was used. Occasionally, audio describers are also required to be present in the studio to provide advice to the voice talent on issues such as the pronunciation of certain foreign nouns. Frequently, especially if they do not attend the recording sessions, describers are instructed to indicate this information in the script. It is also useful for describers to be in the studio in case typing errors or misprints appear in the script, so that the description may be amended there and then.

4. Conclusions

I have emphasised parallels between AD and other translation modes in order to portray it as an innovative type of translation which offers promising professional opportunities. AD may be considered a rather special type of translation because it is not directed at a different linguistic community but rather at a specific social group. Nonetheless, I would like to argue that it is still a case of translation, with which it shares many similar tasks: research, the need for extensive lexical resources, use of parallel texts, etc.

In addition to a consideration of these aspects, the study has also explored the competences required of audio describers, discussing the AD process within a proposed framework based on Risku's (1998) translation model, but adapted to the particular needs of the ADS production (time constraints, multimedia nature of the ST). Along the way, I have remarked on similarities and parallels with the translation process and its strategies. But, above all, I hope this article has highlighted the very close relation which should exist between professional practice and research. Without this link, it would not be possible to theorise or to deepen the knowledge of the emergent and exciting new subject area provided by audio description.

Acknowledgements

I want to thank Antonio J. Chica, Juan Pedro Luque Hernández, Julian Bourne and Caroline Rees for the English translation and proofreading of this article. The preparation of this paper has been possible thanks to funding by the TRACCE project: *Evaluación y gestión de los recursos de accesibilidad para discapacitados sensoriales a través de la traducción audiovisual: La audiodescripción para ciegos. Protocolo para formar a formadores. Código: SEJ2006-01829/PSIC.*

References

Díaz Cintas, Jorge (2007) "Traducción audiovisual y accesibilidad", in Catalina Jiménez Hurtado (ed.) *Traducción y accesibilidad. Subtitulación para sordos y audiodescripción para ciegos: nuevas modalidades de Traducción Audiovisual*. Frankfurt am Main: Peter Lang, 9-23.

Jakobson, Roman (1959) *On Linguistic Aspects of Translation. Selected Writings 2. Word and Language.* Paris: Mouton.

Maletzke, Gerhard (1996) *Interkulturelle Kommunikation: zur Interaktion zwischen Menschen verschiedener Kulturen.* Opladen: Westdeutscher Verlag.

Nida, Eugene (1964) *Toward a Science of Translating.* Leiden: E. J. Brill.

Risku, Hanna (1998) *Translatorische Kompetenz. Kognitive Grundlagen des Übersetzens als Expertentätigkeit.* Tübingen: Stauffenburg.

Venuti, Lawrence (1995) *The Translator's Invisibility.* London and New York: Routledge.

The benefits of audio description for blind children

Alicia Palomo López

Universitat Jaume I, Castellón, Spain

Abstract
The aim of this paper is to shed some light on the as yet 'unknown' field of audio description (AD) for children by presenting a contrasting analysis of an empirical corpus formed by two audio descriptions (one in English and one in Spanish) of the same Disney film: *Lady and the Tramp* (1955). It is vital to consider AD for children as a different type, with its own particular features and requirements. Both ADs are analysed to see whether any differences or similarities can be found between them, and a discussion follows on the application of the various guidelines, norms and recommendations available to date. These results highlight the fact that visually impaired children have needs different from the general public, as they are more likely to have delayed language than other children because of the gaps in their experience. The main impetus behind this research is to learn about how these children can acquire and develop language skills with the use of audio described programmes or films via what is known as 'echolalia'.

1. Introduction

The aim of this paper is to shed some light on the as yet 'unknown' field of audio description (AD) for children by presenting a contrasting analysis of an empirical corpus formed by two ADs (one in English and one in Spanish) of the same Disney film: *Lady and the Tramp* (Geronimi and Jackson, 1955). I shall argue for the need to consider AD for children as a different type of AD, with its own particular features and requirements. It is vital that the audio describer takes into consideration that visually impaired or blind children have different needs from fully-sighted children as they are more likely to have delayed language because of gaps in their experience (RNIB, n.d.). Both ADs are analysed to ascertain whether any differences or similarities can be found between them. After examining different examples, I shall discuss the extent to which the guidelines proposed by the Office of Communication (Ofcom, 2000 and 2006) and the recommendations by the Royal National Institute for the Blind (RNIB, n.d.) for the audio description of children's programmes in the UK have been taken into consideration in the AD of the film under analysis. I shall also discuss the Spanish norm *UNE 153020*, written by the Asociación Española de Normalización y Certificación (AENOR, 2005), where AD for children is not specifically mentioned.

The main impetus behind this research is to learn about how blind and visually impaired (BVI) children can acquire and develop their language skills with the use of audio described programmes or films via what is known as 'echolalia' (Palomo López, 2008a and 2008b). To do so, I shall examine some of the main challenges in AD for children and illustrate them with examples concerning the amount of description and the type of language used, the treatment of songs and music, the sound effects and the tone and delivery of the narration.

2. The audience of children's films and programmes with AD

As regards the specific audience of children's films, the challenge lies firstly in determining the age group of this audience as there is not a universal definition of 'children', regardless of their visual impairment. For instance, Bazalgette and Staples (1995:92) define children as "people under the age of about twelve". For the RNIB (n.d.), the majority of their audio described videos for children are Walt Disney classic animations aimed at BVI children from the age of two upwards, of whom a significant proportion are also likely to have additional physical or learning disabilities due to congenital or neo natal problems which may make AD inaccessible for them. When referring to 'BVI children' in these pages, the term comprises children from two to twelve years of age, regardless of their level of visual impairment and whether this impairment is from birth or not.

Although the chosen corpus is a Disney film and children are the main audience of these productions, adults can also enjoy this type of film. If the programme is audio described, people without impairments – listening to audio described films while driving (García Crespo, 2007) –, blind or visually impaired, with perceptive cognitive problems, or simply part of the increasing ageing population (RNIB, 2007; Portlock *et al.*, 2006) can all benefit from this access service. However, when producing AD scripts for Disney animations, audio describers must ensure that the main audience for these products, i.e. children, is fully accounted for. The end product must address their specific needs if it is to captivate its target audience.

3. Language learning and language development in BVI children

The RNIB maintains that audio described videos for children can help with language development in several ways, in particular with the use of 'echolalia' (RNIB, n.d.). According to the *Developmental Journal for Babies and Children with Visual Impairment* (DfES, 2006:18), "repeating or echoing what other people say is a stage of development that all young children go through [as] a way of practising speech and learning about language and communication". Besides it is often a prominent feature in children with very limited vision who get rather 'stuck' in the echoing stage, that is, when frequent echoing of immediate phrases or delayed language continues longer than would be expected in typical development. This is what is known as 'echolalia' or 'echoing' and it can involve sounds or sound combinations, single words or whole phrases (*ibid*).

By taking this into consideration, the audio describer can produce a more effective AD script that may also contribute to the language development of the young BVI viewer. This way, AD may be used not only for accessibility purposes, i.e. to improve children's understanding and enjoyment of the film, but also with a secondary aim, as a means of language learning for BVI children (Palomo López, 2008a and 2008b).

The RNIB (n.d.) states that, as regards children's language development, AD has so far proved to be very popular among small children as they often use 'echolalia' as a precursor to meaningful speech. This is a very important phase in phonetic development for children whose language is delayed and is something that speech therapists encourage. Speech therapists also agree that audio described videos for children contribute to their linguistic development in many different ways. Firstly, the songs, rhymes, and process of listening to the video several times can help children develop echolalia speech as when, for instance, they repeat a story or a song word by word, often mimicking the same intonation as in the original. This is essentially a form of entertainment and, as such, can be considered a substitute for imaginary play. Secondly, AD can also help with language development because it reinforces the semantics of words by means of signposting objects and events during the description. It is vital that children can hear significant sound effects or noises because they add meaning to words such as 'train', 'barking', etc. (Palomo López, 2008a).

Cortical or cerebral visual impairment – which is often caused by brain damage around the time of birth – is now viewed as the most common cause of visual impairment in children and is a matter of international concern (RNIB, n.d.). For children who suffer from this condition, there may be nothing wrong with the eyes or optic nerves, but the problem lies in the brain, which is unable to interpret visual information. Brain damage may similarly lead to problems with hearing or motor functions. Hence, when producing an AD script, the describer should bear in mind this group of visually impaired children who also have cognitive problems, hearing problems or have difficulty concentrating on the television. This is why I would like to argue for a particular type of AD for children, different from the AD produced for the general public and able to take into account this specific audience so that they can benefit from it.

At an early age, children, with or without any special needs or visual impairment, tend to watch the same video many times over without really understanding the plot at first; however, it is evident that they appreciate the video for the songs, the larger-than-life characters and the sound effects. For BVI children, AD signposts events, objects and characters and, as they grow older and watch the film again, they start to follow the plot and the AD helps them to derive full enjoyment from the story. Thus, it is clear that one AD soundtrack needs to achieve two aims: on one hand, to provide 'signposting' for some children and, on the other hand, to convey important information concerning the plot for others (RNIB, n.d.).

4. Main challenges of audio describing children's programmes.

In this section I shall discuss some of the specific factors to be considered when audio describing children's films, using concrete examples from my corpus as illustrations. For the purpose of this study I have chosen the 2006 English DVD of *Lady and the Tramp* audio described by the British Independent Television Facilities Centre (itfc) and narrated by David Flaw and the 1997 video of *La dama y el vagabundo*, audio described by the Organización Nacional de Ciegos Españoles (ONCE) and narrated by Antonio Vázquez (Table 1):

Table 1. Corpus material

Source Text	Producer	Distributor	AD script writer	AD narrator
Lady and the Tramp (2006 [1955])	Walt Disney Pictures	Buena Vista Distributions	itfc: Peter Whigham	itfc: David Flaw
La dama y el vagabundo (1997)	Walt Disney Pictures	Buena Vista Distributions	ONCE: Antonio Muñoz	ONCE: Antonio Vázquez

The aspects that are particularly relevant to the analysis are: the amount of description provided, the nature of the language used, the treatment of music and songs, the description or otherwise of the sound effects, the tone and the actual delivery of the narration.

4.1. The amount of description and the language complexity

As regards the amount of description provided, there are significant differences between the two films. A word count taken in both AD scripts shows that the English AD script has approximately 4,800 words, whilst the Spanish has considerably more with over 6,000 words.

The RNIB (n.d.:online) guidelines on AD for children advise that "descriptions should not be too wordy, but should be punchy and to the point" since "young children have short attention spans and find it difficult to absorb huge amounts of verbal information". They go on to state that "the main emphasis should be on conveying the story rather than trying to offer children information about everything that they might miss" (*ibid.*).

On the other hand, the Spanish norm *UNE 153020* states that the audio describer must avoid exhausting the listener or visually impaired public, by providing too much or too little information in their AD script (AENOR, 2005:6). Despite this recommendation, a vast and very detailed description full of complex subordinate clauses is a prominent feature in the Spanish AD script.

As for language use, the *Developmental Journal for Babies and Children with Visual Impairment* (DfES, 2006) encourages parents to simplify their language input for their child as they may have difficulties understanding words or phrases. Therefore, it is strongly advised that short sentences and clear, simple language should be used in the AD scripts. This is indeed what we find in the English AD script: short, precise and clear narration.

Major differences between both AD scripts become apparent when comparing an extract from the beginning of the film, as shown in example 1 below:[1]

Example 1

English AD script	Spanish AD script
[01:58] On a dark night, lights glow from the houses of a little town onto the snow outside. More snow drifts down from the sky. [02:01] / ♪ / [02:57]	[03:11] Con su incesante caída los copos de nieve cubren las calles de <u>una pequeña ciudad de principios de siglo</u>. [03:16] / ♪ / [03:20] Es la víspera de Navidad. Los techos de los caserones están cubiertos de nieve y el humo de las chimeneas <u>asciende solemne</u> en la estrellada noche. [03:26] / ♪ / [03:34] Un elegante caballo tira de un trineo cruzando un pequeño puente. [03:38] / ♪ / [03:43] Una hilera de árboles caducos <u>se yerguen</u> a ambos lados de la tranquila avenida de un barrio residencial. [03:47] / ♪ / [03:50] Las ventanas encendidas y la dorada llama de las farolas iluminan la urbanización <u>como un ejército de luciérnagas haciendo guardia en los laterales de las calles nevadas</u>. / En el centro de la ancha avenida se levanta hermoso <u>un palaciego caserón de aviesos tejados puntiagudos y góticas vidrieras</u> a través de las cuales vemos en su interior el típico árbol de Navidad. [04:08] / ♪ / [04:13] [With its incessant fall, the snow flakes cover the streets of a small town from the beginning of the century. It is Christmas eve. The manor houses' roofs are covered in snow and the smoke from the chimneys ascends solemnly in the starry night. An elegant horse pulls a sleigh crossing a small bridge. A row of deciduous trees is erected at both sides of the tranquil avenue of a residential area. The lit windows and the golden flame emerging from the streetlamps lighten up the estate like an army of glow-worms standing guard by the sides of the snow-covered streets. In the middle of the wide avenue rises splendidly a palace-like manor house with wicked pointed roofs and gothic stained-glass windows through which we can see inside the traditional Christmas tree.]

It is evident that the Spanish AD offers a more detailed description using long and complex sentences, which are even incomprehensible at times, and which children might find difficult to follow. According to Ofcom and AENOR, the register should be suited to the age group at which the film is aimed and to the genre and context of the programme. However, this does not seem always to be the case in the Spanish version as can be seen in the previous example where the narrator uses some flowery language, archaic vocabulary and over-the-top metaphors, all of them underlined. The use of difficult words, complex vocabulary or syntactical structures could lead not only to the lack of understanding of the passage but also to the child's frustration and consequent loss of the plot, in turn resulting in loss of interest or attention.

Ofcom, the RNIB and AENOR all agree that too much description can be exhausting and even irritating to the viewer. This is why there should be occasional breathing spaces in the programme, allowing the soundtrack and atmosphere to be absorbed. Whilst this tends to be the norm in the English AD, the Spanish tends to fill in every gap with description so that children might lose concentration as a result.

4.2. Songs and music

One of the main features of AD for children is the treatment of songs and music. Disney films are known to be full of catchy and appealing songs in order to capture the children's attention, irrespective of their age. Disney films might be the first contact with television that very little children have and, despite not understanding the plot, they still enjoy watching the film for the musical animations and songs. As is pointed out by the RNIB (n.d.:online): "Some visually impaired children with complex needs or very young children may have difficulty grasping the story, but may nevertheless enjoy the songs. For these reasons it is important that, whenever possible, the songs remain intact without description over them". Ofcom (2000:28) states that there is evidence that "speech and music are processed by different centres of the brain; and therefore, children with damaged speech centres may, nevertheless, be able to process verse and melody".

When vital information needs to be conveyed, it should be presented after the first verse has been sung, during repetitions in the song or during instrumental passages (Ofcom 2000; RNIB, n.d.). What really matters is that children are given the opportunity to learn the tune and the words, and to enjoy the song (RNIB, *ibid.*).

When it comes to professional practice, a different approach is taken in both films concerning the description when songs occur. The English AD keeps songs free of description at all times, giving priority to the children's enjoyment and ignoring the description of the on screen information, as is shown in example 2, where a Christmas carol is sung in the background:

Example 2

English AD script	Spanish AD script
Opening credits read by the ADR: [00:08] Distributed by Buena Vista Film Distribution, Co., Inc. Walt Disney presents *Lady and the Tramp* from a story by Ward Greene. [00:19] / ♪ / [01:39]	[01:27] Walt Disney presenta... / *La dama y el vagabundo*. [01:34] / ♪ / [01:41] Basada en la historia de Ward Greene. [01:44] / ♪ / [01:46] Los títulos se impresionan sobre estáticos dibujos representando distintas escenas de la película. [01:51] / ♪ / [01:54] Canciones de Peggy Lee y Sonny Burke. [01:56] / ♪ / [02:00] Música de Oliver Wallace. [02:02] / ♪ / [02:05] Orquestación Edgard Pluma y Sydney Fine. Arreglos vocales John Rarig. [02:09] / ♪ / [02:13] Historia Erdman Penner y Joe Rinaldi. Película fotografiada en Cinemascope. [02:18] / ♪ / [02:21] Dirección y animadores Milt Kahl, Frank Thomas y Ollie Johnston. [02:26] / ♪ / [02:28] Productor Asociado Ermard Benneck. [02:30] / ♪ / [02:34] Dirigida por Hamilton Luske, Clyde Geronimi y Wilfred Jackson. [02:38] / ♪ / [02:43] Sobre la pantalla aparece una cita que dice: [02:46] / ♪ / [02:54]

[Walt Disney presents... *Lady and the Tramp*. Based on a story by Ward Greene. Titles are printed over static pictures representing different scenes of the film. Songs by Peggy Lee and Sonny Burke. Music by Oliver Wallace. Orchestration by Edgard Pluma and Sydney Fine. Vocal arrangements by John Rarig. Story by Erdman Penner and Joe Rinaldi. Film shot in Cinemascope. Management and entertainers Milt Kahl, Frank Thomas and Ollie Johnston. Associate producer Ermard Benneck. Directed by Hamilton Luske, Clyde Geronimi and Wilfred Jackson. Over the screen a quotation appears saying.] |

The Christmas carol that can be heard is not what we would call a 'Disney song', nor is it a song whose lyrics contribute to the storyline. However, the English audio describer has still decided to keep it free of narration, perhaps so that the public can enjoy the song and get into the Christmas spirit. Another feature of the English AD is that the opening titles are not read when they appear on screen. Instead, the audio describer has chosen to read them earlier so that the music is not interrupted. In fact, he clearly prefers to remain silent during the first song, ignoring most of the credits. For this very same reason, he has probably decided not to describe the background images under the credits – sketches of the story of the film – and waits until the music ends to start talking again. The Spanish AD, on the contrary, adopts a completely opposite approach whereby songs are inundated by narration that provides information about the opening credits as well as an over-detailed and flowery description of the images we see on screen.

Another strategy taken when dealing with songs is the use of intermittent AD over the songs. That is, whilst the song is being sung, the narration is also provided, interspersed with pauses during which parts the song can be clearly heard, as in example 3 below:

Example 3

English AD script	Spanish AD script
[28:02] Lady creeps to the baby's room and peeks in. Darling is walking up and down the bedroom holding a white bundle in her arms. [28:10] / ♪ / [29:30] Jim lifts Lady up to look at the baby. She wags her tail and they both scratch her ear. [29:36]	[29:14] Reina mira por la rendija de la puerta y ve a Linda meciendo al bebé en sus brazos cantándole una nana. [29:20] ♪ // [29:37] ♪* Reina entra al dormitorio conmovida. [29:39] ♪* // [29:54] ♪ Se acerca a la cuna enternecida. [00:41] ♪ // [30:12] Jaime alza en brazos a Reina mostrándole el bebé. [30:14] ♪ // [30:22] Linda lo destapa un poco. [30:24] ♪ [30:48] [Lady looks under the door gap and sees Darling rocking the baby on her arms, singing him a lullaby. Lady enters the bedroom overwhelmed. She approaches the cradle, touched. Jim lifts Lady up showing her the baby. Darling uncovers the baby a little.]

This approach risks causing some frustration, confusion and disorientation in the audience and it would probably have been better to respect the song without adding any AD when the action on screen is not vital. However, if the audio describer considers that the action must be described so that the audience can follow the storyline then, in that case, it would be better to audio describe it over the song.

4.3. Sound effects

As regards sound effects, it is worth emphasising that children with limited vision "are very aware of sounds in general and some may develop a particular awareness of certain sounds" (DfES, 2006:7). It is also suggested that "sounds, especially those that are tuneful, melodic and familiar, may be experienced as especially pleasant and positive, for example, music, songs, familiar themes on TV or tapes, and language" (*ibid.*). On the other hand, parents are encouraged always to prepare their children for noises that might frighten or overwhelm them. Bearing this in mind, audio describers should describe sounds and noises; in particular, loud sounds, or those that could be perceived as scary or frightening for children. Example 4 below illustrates how some noises like the chair banging the door, the steps upstairs, and the bell from the wall clock are described for the audience:

Example 4

English AD script	Spanish AD script
[05:07] *(S)* [05:24] Lady <u>looks at the ceiling</u>. [05:25] / [05:34] Lady looks up happily wagging her stumpy tail. [05:36] *(S)* [05:40] Jim's legs make dark shadows under the door. [05:42] *(S)* // [05:48] Lady scurries miserably back. [05:49] // [05:52] And scrambles into her basket. [05:54] / *(S)* [06:01] <u>A door bangs against the chair</u> in the hall pushing it away and Lady shoves her nose through the gap. [06:06]	[06:19] *(S)* [06:22] Triste y caprichosa, Reina <u>se echa a llorar</u>. [06:25] *(S)* [06:28] Desde su dormitorio en la planta superior, Jaime <u>golpea el suelo</u> irritado. [06:31] *(S)* // [06:35] Tozuda, Reina <u>aúlla más fuerte</u>. [06:37] *(S)* // [06:44] De pronto, la perrita escucha <u>pasos en la planta superior</u>. Jaime baja las escaleras. Reina <u>aúlla aún más</u> fingiendo estar triste. Jaime llega junto a la puerta. [06:52] *(S)* // [07:03] Reina vuelve al cesto con las orejas gachas. [07:05] *(S)* // [07:08] <u>Las campanadas del reloj de pared dan las dos de la madrugada</u>. Obstinada, Reina empuja la puerta con todas sus fuerzas <u>desplazando la silla</u> lo suficiente como para salir de la habitación. [07:17]
	[Sad and fussy, Lady starts crying. From his bedroom on the upper floor, Jim bangs the floor angrily. Stubborn, Lady barks even louder. Suddenly, the puppy hears steps on the top floor. Jim comes down the stairs. Lady barks even more pretending to be sad. Jim approaches the door. Lady goes back to her basket with her ears hanging down. The wall clock strikes two in the morning. Obstinate, Lady pushes the door with all her energy moving the chair enough to be able to leave the room.]

The describer should try not to talk over sound effects. However, "if they are part of the background atmosphere and there is important information to be described, the background level may be lowered to allow for the audio description" (Ofcom, 2000:19).

As far as Ofcom is concerned, the recommendation is to describe the sound effect, or the event leading up to it, just before it happens; however, sometimes a description may be more effective after the action. Describers may need to consider whether or not to specify a sound or noise before it can actually be heard, so that blind or partially sighted children can easily identify it when they hear it in the soundtrack. This technique, commonly used in AD, is called 'anticipation' and seems particularly necessary when describers refer to sudden loud noises which "need calm reassurance and explaining" (DfES, *ibid*). The opposite technique, that is, describing the sound or noise after it is heard in order to avoid anticipating important plot information or spoiling the suspense is known as 'signposting'. It is up to the audio describer to decide which of these two strategies is better suited to a particular situation.

Sound effects not only contribute to the action, especially in children's animations, but they can also be very entertaining as young children enjoy listening to them and imitating them (RNIB, n.d.). Furthermore, sound effects can help with echolalic speech and, in conjunction with the description, can add meaning to concepts, such as the wall clock bell in the above example, which will help BVI children to associate the sound of the bell with the clock. This is why it is better to slot the description in around important sound effects than to describe over them.

4.4. The tone and delivery of the narration

In children's programmes the tone and the delivery of the narration are vital. For Ofcom (2000:29), "feature-length cartoon films, particularly from Disney, require a great deal of thought and sensitivity. The descriptions should reflect the 'cute' aspect of the animations where appropriate". As highlighted in the Spanish norm, it is not only important to choose the right type of voice (masculine or feminine, adult or teenage), but it is also vital that the narrator's voice is clear, neutral and presents the right diction (intonation, rhythm and appropriate vocalisation) (AENOR, 2005:9). In the case of children's programmes, the Spanish norm also recommends the use of an expressive intonation at particular moments during the programme (*ibid*). This last remark is also mentioned in the Ofcom (2000) guidelines, although it is expressly stated that this should be done without undue exaggeration on the narrator's behalf, a piece of advice that is not always followed in the Spanish AD where the description of some scenes is delivered with undue exaggeration. In this regard, both ADs resort to the following strategy throughout the film: changing the narrator's tone and the speed of the delivery and becoming more vivid when describing an exciting or dangerous adventure sequence.

5. Conclusions

I hope that this paper has highlighted the need for approaching AD for children in a way that is different from AD for the general BVI public. Understanding the needs that visually impaired children have is, in my opinion, a prerequisite of producing high quality audio description that children are more likely to enjoy. At the same time, this will contribute to their language development and give them a sense of inclusion.

When analysing the AD of *Lady and the Tramp*, it appears quite obvious that the English audio describer has indeed followed the suggestions mentioned in the Ofcom guidelines in relation to music, songs and sound effects, as well as to the amount of description provided and the nature of the language used. Worth mentioning is the use of very precise and specific descriptive adjectives, adverbs, nouns and verbs, without forgetting that the film is addressed to children, rather than adults, and therefore making use of simple syntactical structures too.

As for *La dama y el vagabundo*, the AD does not follow the Spanish guidelines, which is hardly surprising since it was carried out prior to the introduction of the norm in 2005. What is more of a surprise, however, is that the Spanish AD contradicts or goes against what AENOR states in this norm, examples of which are the syntax and the language used. This shows that the current Spanish norm does not reflect the trends that were in force in Spain before 2005, at least concerning this type of children's film audio described by ONCE.

As regards the treatment of songs and music, both ADs represent opposite approaches. Whilst the English AD prefers not to audio describe over songs so that the audience can enjoy them, the Spanish audio describer has chosen a more intrusive technique providing AD with intermittent pauses during which the songs can be heard, a strategy that can be very frustrating and disruptive for the audience.

Both ADs tackle sound effects in the same way by describing them, or the event leading up to them, just before they happen or right after they have happened. It is essential that sounds are described for the BVI audience, in particular children, who may not be familiar with some of them. This approach will help children to associate words with sounds and, since they enjoy imitating sounds, it can also help them with echolalic speech. Finally, both audio describers agree in the tone and delivery of the narration reflecting in their descriptions the 'cute' aspect of this type of animation, with the only difference being that the Spanish version is apt to deliver the descriptions in a slightly more exaggerated tone. Nonetheless, both present clear intonation, rhythm and vocalisation and make use of the speed of the delivery to create suspense.

Bearing in mind the issues highlighted above, it is obvious that the main challenge lies in producing audio description for children suitable to their age and abilities. In this sense, the Spanish norm seems to be rather brief in its discussion of AD for children, including little or no detail about how to proceed. If this norm is to have a positive effect on the quality of the Spanish ADs of children programmes it will certainly have to be more detailed.

Notes

1. In this article the following convention has been adopted: '♪' stands for music and songs, '♪*' means that the song is heard at the same time as the AD is voiced, '*(S)*' for sound effects, '/' indicates short pauses between the audio describer's utterances and '//' means longer pauses when a character's utterance takes place.

References

AENOR (2005) *Norma UNE 153020: Audiodescripción para personas con discapacidad visual. Requisitos para la audiodescripción y elaboración de audioguías.* Madrid: AENOR.

Bazalgette, Cary and Terry Staples (1995) "Unshrinking the kids: children's cinema and the family film", in Cary Bazalgette and David Buckingham (eds) *In Front of the Children: Screen Entertainment and Young Audiences.* London: British Film Institute Publishing, 92-108.

DfES (2006) *Getting Stuck?: More Ideas for You and Your Child.* Special Issue of *Developmental Journal for Babies and Children with Visual Impairment.* Nottingham: DfES publications. www.earlysupport.org.uk/modResourcesLibrary/StreamRenderer/VI%20journal%20Getting%20stuck.pdf

García Crespo, Ángel (2007) *Taller de subtitulado y audiodescripción.* Manuscript.

Ofcom (2000) *ITC Guidance on Standards for Audio Description.* London: Ofcom. www.ofcom.org.uk/tv/ifi/guidance/tv_access_serv/archive/audio_description_stnds

Palomo López, Alicia (2008a) *Audio Description for Children: The Art of Reading Images as Storytelling. A Contrastive Analysis of the British and Spanish Practices of Audio Describing Children Films.* London: Roehampton University. MA Dissertation.

Palomo López, Alicia (2008b) "Audio Description as language development and language learning for blind and visual impaired children", in Rebecca Hyde Parker and Karla Guadarrama García (eds) *Thinking Translation: Perspectives from Within and Without.* Florida: Brown Walker Press, 113-34.

Portlock, Stephen, Leen Petré and Dan Pescod (2006) *The Future of Access to Television for Blind and Partially Sighted People in Europe.* European Blind Union. www.euroblind.org/fichiersGB/access-TV.html#intro

RNIB (n. d.) *Audio Description for Children.* London: RNIB.

www.rnib.org.uk/xpedio/groups/public/documents/publicwebsite/public_
ADforchildren.doc

Filmography

La dama y el vagabundo. 1955/1997. Clyde Geronimi and Wilfred Jackson.
American. Released in VHS.
Lady and the Tramp. 1955/2006. Clyde Geronimi and Wilfred Jackson.
American. Released in DVD.

Opera audio description at Barcelona's Liceu theatre

Cristóbal Cabeza i Cáceres

Universitat Autònoma de Barcelona, Spain

Abstract
This paper discusses the challenges involved in implementing a new method of AD in Barcelona's Gran Teatre del Liceu through a case study: Giordano's *Andrea Chénier*. It first describes the main features of opera AD and looks at some of the approaches taken in the UK and Catalonia. Then, it explains a new AD approach proposed by researchers from the Universitat Autònoma de Barcelona. Finally, a general overview of the opera *Andrea Chénier* is offered discussing the most important challenges and restrictions posed by the genre and explaining how the AD script was drafted and delivered.

1. Introduction

While surtitling has now been widely established in most opera houses (Matamala and Orero, 2007b), there is very little research and training available on the audio description (AD) of opera. According to some guidelines, such as the Spanish AENOR (2005:7), the German Bayerischer Rundfunk (Benecke and Dosch, 2004:19) and the British ITC (2000:9), AD should only be offered during the silent intervals of an audiovisual programme or when only background music is available. However, opera as an audiovisual event has its own specific requirements and I believe that a new compromise has to be achieved in order to go beyond those guidelines and make opera more enjoyable for blind people.

This paper discusses the challenges of implementing a new method of AD in Barcelona's Gran Teatre del Liceu through a case study: Giordano's *Andrea Chénier,* the first opera audio described in the 2007/2008 season. It first describes the main features of opera AD and looks at some of the approaches taken in Europe, specifically in the UK and Catalonia as opposed to other approaches used in countries like the USA, which will not be analysed here. It then explains a new AD approach proposed by researchers from the Universitat Autònoma de Barcelona after interviews with some regular users of this facility. The following section offers a general overview of the opera *Andrea Chénier* and discusses the most important challenges and restrictions posed by the genre. The last part of this chapter explains how the AD script was drafted and delivered, before summing up the conclusions.

2. Opera audio description and the different European approaches

Opera, like any other audiovisual event, needs audio description so that visually impaired people can enjoy it fully. According to Matamala (2007), the difference between the audio description of opera – together with other performing arts – and other types of AD is that it is carried out live. It is a "live planned audio description" (*ibid.*:124), which means that, although delivered live, it has been prepared beforehand and the audio describer has to be alert and react to unforeseen events which may occur during the performance.

As Matamala points out (2005:9-11), the key issue when audio describing opera is bringing together in a synthetic narration all the different visual elements that are available to sighted people. In the particular case of Barcelona's Liceu theatre, these elements are threefold:

- Staging: what is seen on stage, such as movements, set design, costumes, props, facial expressions.
- Surtitling or subtitling: operas are performed in the original language with Catalan surtitles.
- Libretto and leaflet: sighted people can consult the libretto, which is available on the Liceu website, and can also read a leaflet with a summary of the plot.

This classification is very interesting from the perspective of accessibility, since it touches on all the visual elements that need to be conveyed to impaired users. However, from the audio describers' point of view it would seem better to use a classification related to opera as a whole that may help answer questions such as 'when should the audio description take place?' and 'what should be audio described?'.

According to opera scholars like Pahlen (1963) and Arregui and Vela (2007), opera is composed of four basic elements: (a) music, the human voice and the orchestra, (b) libretto, the actual words sung; the plot, (c) acting, the performance of singers and (d) scenography, i.e. the set design, the costumes and the props.

If we focus on the question of when to audio describe, Matamala and Orero (2007a:206-7) point out that there are two different methods used in Europe: audio introduction and comprehensive ADs overlapping the dialogue exchanges. These two opera AD techniques differ as far as the music is concerned:

> When it comes to audio description, similarly, some feel that music should not be troubled by description, and that the text should be subservient to the music, which has led to AD in the UK meaning the production and recording of a cassette which is sent – by request – and can be listened to

before the actual performance. [...] The Catalan AD approach is inclined to be a comprehensive description. Throughout the whole performance the describer – always male – speaks over the music and on some occasions over songs.

So while in the UK, some opera audio describers carry out their ADs as an audio introduction (York, 2007), in Catalonia, audio describers carry out their AD during the performance.

With regard to the question of what should be audio described, there are also some differences between the approaches followed in the UK and in Catalonia. In the UK, audio introductions "give a coherent account of the plot, and illustrate it with vivid descriptions of sets, costumes, characterisation and stage business" (York, 2007:215). Catalan opera ADs do the same, although they seem to be "biased to offer descriptions of the plot and the thoughts and feelings of the characters" (Matamala and Orero, 2007a:205). The main difference then between the ADs in the UK and those in Catalonia is not 'what' is described, but rather 'when' the AD takes place.

3. A new method for opera audio description

Up until the 2006/2007 season, ADs at Barcelona's opera house were carried out in Catalan by two different associations: the ONCE (*Organización Nacional de Ciegos Españoles* [Spanish National Organisation for the Blind]) and the ACCDV (*Associació Catalana de Cecs i Disminuïts Visuals* [Catalan Association for the Blind and Partially Sighted]). Since AD was a private service offered by each of these two associations to their members only, the end result was that the same opera was audio described twice in Catalan. Blind people attended on different days and heard different ADs depending on the association to which they belonged (Cabeza and Matamala, 2008).

However, in 2007, the Liceu asked researchers from the Universitat Autònoma de Barcelona to handle the opera ADs in order to offer a single service in Catalan and to make it a public service available to any blind person. To do so, the Liceu proposed a trial AD with a total of 16 people (eight members from each association) in order to find out the most suitable AD technique to use in future productions. After analysing the ADs that had been created by the ACCDV in previous seasons, the only ones available to researchers, they set themselves the aim of developing a new proposal which tried to marry up the advantages of both the British audio introductions and the Catalan comprehensive ADs which sometimes overlapped with the singers.

The trial AD was carried out in a real setting during a performance of *Andrea Chénier*. It consisted of the AD of the two first acts of the opera.

First, a complete audio introduction of the whole opera, lasting about fifteen minutes, was offered. Then, Act One was audio described in a comprehensive manner, avoiding any overlapping with the singers. Finally, the AD of Act Two was offered only as an audio introduction.

The 16 AD service users attended the opera, in two different locations, one for each association, as they had requested. After carrying out the trial AD, the two groups were interviewed separately. People in both groups stated that the general audio introduction was useful to them, as they were able to get an overall idea of the plot. However, they pointed out that it was too long and that it contained too much information for them to process. As for the comprehensive AD of the first act, ONCE members liked the fact that the AD did not overlap with the singing. In contrast, some of the ACCDV members said they would not have minded overlapping and that they felt they were missing out on information about what had been sung. This is understandable, since those people were actually used to overlapping during AD. Lastly, all the participants from both associations agreed that the audio introduction of the second act was insufficient and they requested a comprehensive AD during the whole opera.

After having taken on board these opinions and comments, the UAB researchers proposed a new approach for ADs, which the Liceu accepted. It consisted of a concise audio introduction (lasting eight to ten minutes) of the whole opera before curtain up, including a coherent account of the plot, overall descriptions of costumes, characterisation and scenography, with the suggestion that this audio introduction could be posted on the Liceu's website for consultation prior to the performance. Moreover, it was decided that, time permitting, a short audio introduction of each act would be offered and a comprehensive AD without overlapping with the singers would be delivered during the performance. The elements to be described would be: costumes, hairstyles, stage and props, sounds not included in the libretto, plot and crucial moments of drama.

4. Operas at the Liceu: *Andrea Chénier*

Operas at the Liceu are sung in their original language with surtitles in Catalan above the stage. In addition, seats are fitted with Thin Film Transistor screens in which the Spanish and English surtitled versions can be read. However, as pointed out earlier, the libretto is only one of the many elements of an opera. There is also the music, the acting and the scenography, which are all brought together into what makes a production. The music and the libretto are the non-variable elements of an opera, while the acting and the scenography change from one production to another, making a new AD necessary. As an example, a synopsis of *Andrea Chénier* is offered below.

After presenting the most important challenges and restrictions posed by this production, I will go on to explain the methodology.

Andrea Chénier (1896) is defined as a *dramma istorico* and the protagonist was indeed a real-life poet and a well-known figure in French literary history. He was guillotined at the end of the Terror on 25 July 1794 for denouncing the excesses of the Revolution, with which he had initially fully sympathised. References to the guillotine occur throughout the opera, such as the shape of the screen that opens and closes each act (Figure 1 and Figure 2):

Figure 1: Guillotine shaped screen opening an act

Figure 2: Guillotine shaped screen closing an act

The plot describes Chénier's noble, generous personality and his tragic end. It also seeks to create a realistic image of the atmosphere and the background of the final years of the French Revolution. To achieve this, the production resorts to different strategies such as the use of sloping elements representing the imbalance of the Revolution (Figure 3) or a rotating platform representing the passing of time and the succession of venues (Figure 4):

Figure 3: Jagged angles

Figure 4: Rotating platform

The two lead characters – the sensitive poet and Maddalena de Coigny, a delicate young noblewoman who loves him – express lofty feelings. The French people play a key role in the historical events narrated, brought to life by the chorus in patriotic and revolutionary songs. In order to enhance the importance of the people, each act is closed by *tableaux vivants* in the form of representations of famous pictures depicting the Revolution (Figure 5):

Figure 5: *Tableau vivant*

All these metaphoric elements, although difficult to describe, ought to be included in the AD, since they help the understanding of the plot and characterise this specific production. Whether to include them in the audio introduction or during the course of the performance is a question that must be taken into account when drafting the AD script.

5. The audio description script

From the experience of drafting the AD for *Andrea Chénier*, it can be said that the process of developing an AD script can be divided into four phases: documentation, attending the dress rehearsals, writing the AD and the live testing of the AD.

The first contact with the opera starts during the documentation phase, when the audio describers access online information offered by the Liceu on its website (www.liceubarcelona.com), including the cast, a summary of the plot, the libretto and a photographic collection, in Catalan, Spanish and English. The programme booklet is another valuable document and contains articles about the opera (the historical context, the characters, and the author), the production (scenography, symbolism, and metaphors), and the actors' biographies, as well as the original libretto and its Catalan and Spanish translations plus the English and French translations of the plot summary. The last phase of this documentation process is a visit to the costume department after attending the dress rehearsals. During that visit, the audio describer is provided with information about the fabrics used, the type and style of the dresses and the role they play within the scenography. This phase helps the audio describer to build up an initial impression of the opera and is also very helpful for understanding the production and for writing the AD script.

The second stage of the process involves attending the dress rehearsals prior to the première, which is the first real contact with the opera play. During this phase, the audio describer would have to understand the plot and actions, take notes, identify 'strange' sounds that would need to be described and get visual information on the scenography, the dresses and any stage changes that might occur. After the dress rehearsal, the audio describer would be given a DVD with the recording of the rehearsal and Catalan subtitles, which are the surtitles originally offered during the performance (Figure 6). With this material the writing of the AD script can go ahead.

Figure 6: DVD given to the audio describer

Before starting, though, the audio describer has to decide which elements must be provided in the audio introduction and which during the course of the performance. In the case of *Andrea Chénier,* general elements such as the jagged angles or the rotating platform were included in the audio introductions, while the more specific ones such as the references to the guillotine or the *tableaux vivants* were included during the course of the performance. After taking these decisions, the audio describer is able to create the audio introduction script, in which s/he includes broad facts about the opera, general features of the scenography, a summary of the plot, an introduction to the characters and some general notes on the costumes. Once the audio introduction is ready, a comprehensive AD is written for each act including a combination of all the elements briefly described in the audio introduction but emphasising the specific details of the scene: the libretto (plot), the acting (key moments), any changes in the scenography and props and the hairstyles and costumes of each character. The AD script is read aloud by the audio describer while the opera is played on the DVD in order to check that the AD does not overlap with the singers. Reference pointers (subtitles, sounds or actions) are written down on the script so that the describer knows when to start reading the AD. This is an example of the AD script:

Original AD script	English back translation
(...l'abat ve de París) [subtítol] La mare renya Maddalena perquè encara no s'ha vestit.	(the abbot comes from Paris) [subtitle] Maddalena's mother tells her off because she hasn't got dressed yet.
(Sospir) [so] Arriba Bersi, la serventa, amb un vestit i una perruca.	(Sigh) [sound] Bersi, the servant, arrives wearing a dress and a wig.
(S'emporten el sofà) [acció] Dos servents s'emporten el sofà on seu Maddalena i ella es queixa d'haver de vestir-se a la moda de l'època.	(The sofa is taken away) [action] Two servants take away the sofa where Maddalena was sitting and she complains about having to get dressed in the fashion of the times.
(...vas feta una bruixa) [subtítol] La pantalla s'obre totalment i apareix el jardí del castell preparat per a la festa.	(...you look like a witch) [subtitle] The screen opens fully and the castle's garden appears prepared for the party.

Finally, as the last phase, the audio describer attends one of the actual performances in order to live test the AD, taking notes of any changes that may have taken place between the dress rehearsal without an audience and the actual final performances.

6. Conclusion

In the 2007/2008 opera season, researchers from the Universitat Autònoma de Barcelona started carrying out the audio descriptions at Barcelona's Gran Teatre del Liceu. The first opera they audio described was *Andrea Chénier* and they tried combining the advantages of two opera AD techniques that had already been around for some time: audio introductions and comprehensive AD which sometimes overlapped with the singers. The researchers carried out a trial AD with 16 blind or partially sighted people who were then interviewed. There was a mostly positive reaction to this new approach – i.e. audio introductions plus comprehensive AD without overlapping –. This means that, although they may have been used to the previous method of audio describing opera, and habits are not always easily changed, the vast majority of users considered the new method to be an improvement on the method used previously at the Liceu.

This article, after briefly discussing the two previously existing techniques mentioned above, explains the new method proposed and implemented by UAB researchers at Barcelona's opera house, which also helped promote the conversion of the AD service from a private to a public service. After the positive reaction of participants during the trials of that new method, UAB researchers went on to audio describe five more operas at the Liceu in the 2007/2008 season and will continue to do so in 2008/2009. However, it is my belief that there are still things that could be improved at the Liceu in order to achieve a greater accessibility for the blind. Offering touch tours, like those often available in UK theatres, would be one such idea.

Note

This research has been carried out with the support of the Universitat Autònoma de Barcelona, Spain. It has been supported by a grant from the Spanish Ministry of Science and Innovation (FFI2009-08027, *Subtitling for the Deaf and Hard-of-Hearing and Audio Description: objective tests and future plans*), and by a grant from the Catalan Government (2009SGR700). All photos have been taken by Bofill and are courtesy of the Gran Teatre del Liceu.

References

AENOR (2005) UNE 153020. *Audiodescripción para personas con discapacidad visual. Requisitos para la audiodescripción y elaboración de audioguías.* Madrid: AENOR.

Arregui, Juan P. and Juan Ángel Vela del Campo (eds) (2007) *La ópera trascendiendo sus propios límites.* Valladolid: Universidad de Valladolid.

Benecke, Bernd and Elmar Dosch (2004) *Wenn aus Bildern Worte werden. Durch Audio-Description zum Hörfilm.* Munich: Bayerischer Rundfunk.

Cabeza, Cristóbal and Anna Matamala (2008) "La audiodescripción de ópera: una nueva propuesta", in Álvaro Pérez-Ugena and Ricardo Vizcaíno-Laorga (coord.) *ULISES: hacia el desarrollo de tecnologías comunicativas para la igualdad de oportunidades y la comunidad sorda.* Madrid: Observatorio de las Realidades Sociales y de la Comunicación, 95-106.

ITC (2000) *Guidance on Standards for Audio Description.* London: Ofcom. www.ofcom.org.uk/static/archive/itc/uploads/ITC_Guidance_On_Standards_for_Audio_Description.doc

Matamala, Anna (2005) "Live audio description in Catalonia". *Translating Today* 4, 9-11.

Matamala, Anna (2007) "La audiodescripción en directo", in Catalina Jiménez Hurtado (ed.) *Traducción y accesibilidad: subtitulación para sordos y la audiodescripción para ciegos.* Frankfurt am Main: Peter Lang, 121-32.

Matamala, Anna and Pilar Orero (2007a) "Accessible opera in Catalan: opera for all", in Jorge Díaz Cintas, Pilar Orero and Aline Remael (eds) *Media for All: Subtitling for the Deaf, Audio Description and Sign Language.* Amsterdam: Rodopi, 201-14.

Matamala, Anna and Pilar Orero (2007b) "Accessible opera: overcoming linguistic and sensorial barriers". *Perspectives: Studies in Translatology* 15(4): 262-77.

Pahlen, Kart (1963) *Qué es la ópera.* Buenos Aires: Columba.

York, Greg (2007) "Verdi made visible: audio introduction for opera and ballet", in Jorge Díaz Cintas, Pilar Orero and Aline Remael (eds) *Media for All: Subtitling for the Deaf, Audio Description and Sign Language.* Amsterdam: Rodopi, 215-29.

Section 3

Didactic applications of AVT

The importance of listening with one's eyes:[1] a case study of multimodality in simultaneous interpreting

Elena Zagar Galvão

Universidade do Porto, Portugal

Isabel Galhano Rodrigues

University of Porto, Portugal

Abstract
The article deals with nonverbal communication in simultaneous interpreting and addresses the main functions of gestures in the booth. Its main objective is to compare the relationship between nonverbal communication (especially hand gestures) and speech in speakers, trainee simultaneous interpreters and professional simultaneous interpreters using a multimedia corpus. The first part of the article explains how the multimedia corpus was collected and prepared for analysis; the second part provides a multimodal microanalysis of various 'miniclips' extracted from one of the speeches and their parallel interpretations, and the third and final part focusses on the preliminary conclusions that can be drawn at this stage of the project.

1. Introduction

The project described in this paper originated from a first case study by Rodrigues (2006), in which a speaker's natural speech and gestures were compared to his professional simultaneous interpreter's speech and gestures through a microanalysis of the verbal and nonverbal modalities observed (words, prosody, and body movements). This first analysis prompted several questions about the role played by nonverbal communication in simultaneous interpreting (SI):[2] what are the main functions of gestures in the booth? How are gesture phrases or gesture units organised in relation to speech phrases in interpreting? Is what is expressed in gesture in the booth related to what is simultaneously expressed in speech? Is gesturing by interpreters clearly cultural or simply idiosyncratic? Should nonverbal communication be part of the training of interpreters? To start answering some of these questions, we decided to film some trainee interpreters during a simultaneous interpreting training session as well as their respective speaker/trainer. Later on, the same speech was used for interpretation by professional conference interpreters in order to compare the use of nonverbal communication by the trainees and the professionals. Thus, the main objective of this study is to compare the relation between nonverbal communication (especially hand gestures) and speech in speakers, trainee simultaneous interpreters and professional simultaneous interpreters.

This paper is divided into three main sections. The first explains how we collected the multimedia corpus and how we prepared parts of it for analysis. The second provides a multimodal microanalysis of various 'miniclips' extracted from one of the speeches and their parallel interpretations. The third and final part focusses on the preliminary conclusions that can be drawn at this stage of the project.

2. Corpus collection and methodology

As Pöchhacker (2004:199) points out, one of the main stumbling blocks in empirical research in Interpreting Studies is the difficulty in gathering data to build corpora:

> the problem of access to data, 'subjects' and informants 'in the field', which has long been regarded as a critical bottleneck in conference interpreting research, may be resolved as the need for 'applied research', once accepted, leads various kinds of stakeholders to offer more support and cooperation.

Conference interpreters are notoriously reluctant to be filmed or have their voices recorded. This is why we thought it would be easier to film trainees in the specialisation course in conference interpreting at the Faculty of Arts of the University of Lisbon, a post-graduate programme coordinated by Dr Garry Mullender, who kindly agreed to let us film one of the training sessions. We gathered the first part of our corpus in April 2007, when we filmed a speaker delivering two speeches in British English (each speech given twice) and two trainees, a man and a woman, each interpreting the two speeches into continental Portuguese. This first corpus, therefore, contains four speeches and four simultaneous interpretations for a total footage of approximately a hundred and sixty minutes. Another part of the corpus was collected in February 2008 and consisted of recordings of four professional conference interpreters, two men and two women, interpreting one of the speeches recorded in April. This second part of the corpus, however, has not yet been analysed in depth and will not be discussed in this paper.

Besides viewing all the eight films in the corpus to get a general idea as to the nonverbal language used by the subjects and its relation to spoken language, we decided to apply the methodology used by Rodrigues (2007). Thus, we selected a segment from one of the speaker's speeches, which was particularly interesting and rich in terms of nonverbal communication, and we proceeded to dissect it as much as possible in terms of discourse structure, prosody and hand movements. Using Adobe Premiere, we then produced a video clip of about two minutes, which was itself cut into various shorter clips and could be analysed with Anvil (www.anvil-software.de), a software application to annotate nonverbal language (Kipp, 2001, 2004). We also made .wav files from the clips so as to be able to transcribe the speech and analyse prosodic features with the program Praat (www.praat.org). Using this method, it is possible to compare and contrast all the following aspects of each speech and its respective interpretation: transcription of the speaker's speech (words and prosodic features such as stress, pitch and rhythm) and gestures (hands, head and trunk), and transcription of the interpreter's speech and gestures.

3. From observation to microanalysis

We started with the very simple observation that many simultaneous interpreters move their hands (as well as head and trunk) in the booth while working, though they know they cannot be seen by anyone. Clearly, a lot of the gesturing may be cultural and, as many would argue, idiosyncratic and subjective, but the question remains as to the functions of gesturing in SI (Rodrigues, 2007).

As several interpreting studies scholars have noted, and as any professional conference interpreter will confirm, conference interpreters make a point of being able to maintain visual contact with the speaker they have to interpret and, ideally, also with the audience. If they cannot see the audience, which is increasingly the case with videoconferencing, they usually want to have a full view at least of the speaker (Viaggio, 1997:284; Weale, 1997:296). Consciously or unconsciously, therefore, simultaneous interpreters know that in order to convey the verbal message as accurately as possible, they must have access to the whole communication situation, to all the channels of communication used by the speaker, which is much more than the speaker's mere words and their accompanying prosody.

The people in the audience watch the speaker addressing them in a foreign language/culture (verbal and nonverbal modalities) while, through the headphones, they listen to the interpreter, whom they cannot usually see, since s/he is working from a soundproof booth generally removed from the audience. The audience thus builds meaning from the interpreter's verbal input and the speaker's nonverbal input (posture, gestures, facial expressions, etc.), which should therefore match or at least not contradict each other. In this situation of 'scrambled kinesics' (Weale, 1997:296) the interpreter's vital role is to reconcile verbal and nonverbal language by resorting to a whole array of prosodic tools in the target language: intonation, stress, rhythm, pitch, pauses, sound elongation, etc.

3.1 Analysis of prosody, discourse structure and gestures

As in a previous work by Rodrigues (2007), a prosody analysis was carried out using the principles of Interactional Linguistics (Selting and Couper-Kuhlen, 2001) whereas the analysis of nonverbal communication was done by resorting to nonverbal communication research developed in different areas of human sciences (Kendon, 2004; McNeill, 2000; Poggi, 2007). The terminology and conceptual framework employed to describe gestures, such as beat, deictic gesture, iconic gesture and gesture space is based on McNeill (1992) and Kendon (1980).

The first step in the analysis consisted in choosing a specific part from one of the speeches delivered by the speaker/trainer. The speech selected gives a general overview of the situation of the European textile industry in the past few decades. Since what was filmed is a training session which, nonetheless, seeks to simulate a real-life conference situation, the speaker talks at a realistic speech rate, with a clear delivery in standard British English. In the two minutes from this speech that were examined, the speaker, sitting down behind a large table facing the booths, talks about the increasing competition to the European textile industry coming from various parts of the world. In doing so, he builds a virtual map of the world in the space in front of him and identifies the geographical location of several regions on this map, namely South East Asia, China, the Mediterranean basin, and the USA. It is a very interesting example of the iconic use of gesture to illustrate the objects he is referring to in speech, i.e. countries on an imaginary map of the world. After this iconic function has been established by the speaker, many of the gestures that follow are deictic, pointing to the specific area in virtual space where a country or region of the world has already been located. For example China is always found to the speaker's right and the USA to the speaker's left.

3.2 Microanalysis[3]

Following the *Gesprächsanalytisches Transkriptionssystem* (Selting *et al.*, 1998), each line of prosodic transcription (identified with a letter and number) represents an intonational unit (Selting and Couper-Kuhlen 2001), which corresponds to Kendon's prosodic phrase (Rodrigues, 2007:162-5). After each transcription, there is a brief description of the gestures accompanying the transcribed speech.

Transcription 1

Speaker	Interpreter
s-001 there's in´crEA`sing ´com`pe´TI`tion; s-002 ´coming `from ´MAny `different -corners of the ´´WORld.	i-001 is´to `porque=HÁ- -maiOR `competitivi´DA´´DE:::; i-002 `pRO´vinda´´dos `VÁrios cantos ´DO`MUN´do;

The beat (a biphasic gesture that marks rhythm) has several iconic properties, being at the same time an iconic gesture and a gesture depicting features of referents, actions or states. The item 'increasing' is accompanied by an iconic beat which reinforces and focusses its meaning. Together with prosody, the iconic gesture with both hands open and a slight alternating movement – right hand to the right, left hand to the right, both slightly bent – reinforces the meaning of 'many' and 'different' and conveys the idea of 'world' (a map in front of the speaker) and its 'corners'.

      Throughout the exercise the trainee holds a pen in his right hand to jot down numbers or words, if necessary, and holds an MP3 in his left hand to record himself for self-assessment; his hands are busy but this does not prevent him from gesturing.

      The interpreter uses beats (opening gestures), prosody and slight head-movements to focus on some of the lexical items belonging to different lexical clusters. The gestures accompany the lexical items *isto* [this], *competitividade* [competition], and *vários cantos do mundo* [various corners of the world].

Transcription 2

Speaker	Interpreter
s-003 ´we tend `to eh´FO`CUS s-004 or <<all> at least> we ´HAVE `been `focussing s-005 –on –eh ´CHI`na;	i-003 (---) -TE`mos `pod ´POsto- ´´mAis=´ ÊNfa`se" i-004 ´ns=últimos=´´anos ´na ´CHINA?

The gesture accompanying 'or' performs a repair, i.e. it marks a point of articulation of speech with a proactive movement, introducing a paraphrase aimed at conveying the message more clearly and precisely. Together with the lexical item 'or', this gesture has the function of an interactive evaluation signal (Rodrigues, 1998:73-4). The most important item is accompanied by an opening gesture in Portuguese, a beat with opening/focussing features and the speaker's change of gaze orientation from his notes to the audience. In other words, *China* is an important topic in the speaker's speech and the interpreter stresses the lexical item *China* using similar modalities: through prosody (pitch and intensity) and a beat with an opening character: hand slightly to the side, movement similar to the one made by the speaker, though much less ample and precise.

Transcription 3

Speaker	Interpreter
s-006 but one ´HAS `to re´MEM`ber; s-007 eh ´EU`rope ´had VE`ry `little; s-008 eh:: co´mmER`cial eh ´com`tActs eh `with ´CHI`na. s-009 the ´world `was diVIded into- two´CAMPS `in ´those `days;	i-005 ´mas conVÉ::::M ´lem`´brAr´ i-006 ´que=`AN`tes ↓ ´dos `anos noven´´TA; i-007 (0,344) ↑´a=-EUropA=eh:::. i-008 (0,385) ´tI`nha::::; i-009 (0,753)`pou´co `con´TA`cto- ´´COmer`´cial -com ´a `CHI`na. i-010 o ´mundo dividia-se em duas ´FREN::`tes

In units s-006 an s-007, the beats accompanying the lexical items 'has' and 'Europe' have a focussing function, while the hand configuration accompanying the verbalisation of 'very little' (right hand slightly closed and coming towards the speaker) is clearly linked to the meaning of the words, thus performing an iconic function and depicting the meaning of 'very little'. In unit s-008, the hand configuration and the hand movements suggest the idea of contact and exchange. Finally, the item *China* is produced together with a deictic gesture locating *China* in the speaker's gesture space. The speaker thus visualizes a virtual map in his real gesture space, where *China* is located on the right. At s-009, the speaker's beats focus on the words 'world', 'divided' and 'two camps'.

In the Portuguese units, there are beats and head movements focussing on the important items and creating a certain rhythm. The interpreter's gesture accompanying the verbalisation of *pouco* [little] seems to imitate the speaker's gesture, with a slightly closed hand conveying the meaning of 'little'. By using beats and prosody, the interpreter focusses on the lexical items which correspond to those whose verbalisation the speaker accompanied with beats. The vowel elongation at *duas fren:: tes* [two fronts] together with the opening gesture, correspond to the item emphasised by the speaker. The frequent vowel elongations in this passage indicate the interpreter's cognitive effort in the simultaneous mode.

Transcription 4

Speaker	Interpreter
s-010 eh ´YET=eh: `the´TEx`tile ´IN`dustry´has been ´FAcing`chANge- eh- s-011 sInce ´WEll `befOre `the nineteen	i-011 (4,351) ´e=`a=in´DU- -e -a inDÚStria ´têxtil `tem VINdo i-012 a:::::´´a:::- -AL eh::: ´´a::. ↑-ser- i-013 (0,179)`tem vindo -Al-vo de::::

`NIneties: `SIn`ce the nineteen `SEven`ties- s-012 –AS=I´ve just´SAID`	i-014 <<all>tem vindo a ser>`alvo de mudanças' ↑!`ANTES!de mil novecetos e `noventa::::

In units s-010 to s-012, there is a beat/iconic sequence with space-orientation features, a cultural way of understanding and representing time, comprising faster and shorter biphasic up and down movements at 'facing change'. There is also a beat with a backwards movement, anticipating the idea of a moment in the past; and a beat with a forwards movement, accompanying the verbalisation of 'since + decade', reinforcing the idea of the progression of time from that moment onwards. The beat with both hands at 'as I've just said', is at the same time (a) an iconic gesture, focussing on this remark; (b) a conversational signal closing the preceding act (closing topographic conversational signal); and (c) a conversational signal qualifying what has just been said as a repetition (interactive conversational signal of re-evaluation) (Rodrigues 1998:73-4). These units are a clear illustration of how gesture is used according to speech organisation: the gestures that accompany different verbal clusters present slightly different features in terms of hands used and their movement orientation.

As shown in the prosodic transcription above, the interpreter has problems articulating the utterance, most likely because he is hesitating between two verbal forms: *tem sido* [has been] and *tem vindo a ser* [has come to be], which he seems to prefer as a more precise rendering of the progressive aspect of the English present perfect continuous 'has been facing'. This hesitation and difficulty in verbal articulation are accompanied by a beat sequence and culminate in the verbalisation of *antes* [before], which is uttered along with an iconic gesture meaning 'past': the right hand (open palm towards the interpreter) and forearm move up towards the right shoulder with a rather ample stroke. Thus, the speaker's emphasis on 'well before' is rendered by the interpreter through the use of prosody (ascending pitch and higher intensity) as well as gesture (ample stroke). Both speaker and interpreter reveal the same perception or comprehension of time through their gestures as they locate the past behind and the present right in front of them and draw a line with a forwards movement to indicate time progression.[4]

Transcription 5

Speaker	Interpreter
s-013 ´so `we ´HA`ve to ´LOOK `at –eh- ´cOm`pe´TItion `eh::: s-014 `eh::-that –europe faces's bEEN FA`cing ´Ever `since –the ´SE`venties;	i-014 -por=´isso`temos ¨que VER=Eh::::: i-015 `os ´dEsa´fl`Os `qUE:::::´a=Un`ião`euro´pEIa; i-016 `QUE=a=`euro`↑PEIA- que=a=eu´RO`pa`tem´vin` do=a=- enfren´TAR::::' i-017 (-)`´DES`de=os=`a´nos ´se`tENta.

The verbal English form 'look' is emphasised through prosody and gesture: a kind of iconic beat and a nod of the head. Then, the word 'competition' is accompanied by prosodic emphasis and a beat with the right hand. Next (unit s-013) there is a repair: the beat focusses on the part of speech that replaces the 'repairable', i.e. the part of speech to be repaired (Rodrigues, 2007:268; Schegloff *et al.*, 1977). Thus, different phrases correspond to different hands: beat (right hand - repair) + head nod + prosody ('–'s been facing'); beat (left hand, reinforcing the temporal meaning of 'ever since the seventies'). Once again, the Western notion of time as a horizontal line moving from the past to the future is conveyed by the left hand beat accompanying the verbalisation of the lexical cluster 'ever since the seventies'.

In the Portuguese interpreting, a right hand beat (mirroring the speaker?) accompanies *ver + desafios* [see + challenges]. Beats with the same hand configuration and nods of the head are produced at the time of hesitation and repair. The gesture accompanying the verbalisation of *enfrentar* [confront] has similar features to the gesture used by the speaker. The interpreter, just like the speaker, depicts the idea of time through gesture: during the verbalisation of *desde os anos 70* [since the 70s], his right hand moves forwards from an imaginary point in space next to his body (representing the 1970s).

Transcription 6

Speaker	Interpreter
s-014 and ´that compe¨´TI´tion –has come ´from ´DI`fferent ´coun`tries s-015 it's ´come from- eh:::- ´sOUth`east ´ASIA? s-016 eh <<g>><all>i think you've all heard about> the::> ´southeast=`asian ´TIGERS- s-017 eh well' ´they´RE ´TIgers `in par´TI`cular `in the textile ´INdus`try.	i-019 ´IS`to:::: ´vem ´pr ´provÉM de - países de::::↑-LESte `eh::: ´asIÁ`tico::::. i-020 (1.587)´do`LES`te `eh `eh `eh i-021 <<all>´todA=A gente já ouviu↓´falar' de cer`teza> dos dos- ↑`TIgres ´da=Á`sia. i-022 (1,4) ´É ´estes `Eh::; `prepONdrantes -sobre↑tUdo `no – sectOR- -TÊX::↓´til-

The speaker's gestures represent the conceptual image of a map of the world. He locates the different regions and the elements belonging to these regions on different sides of his gesture space. On the right side, he locates 'South East Asia', the 'tigers' and the 'textile industry', a typically metaphoric gesture (Ekman and Friesen, 1969): a round container shaped with both hands on the right side. The item 'South East Asia' is accompanied by an iconic /deictic gesture with both hands while the utterance in unit s-016 is accompanied by an iconic gesture expressing uncertainty (oscillating movement). This adds information to what is being said, modifying the meaning of the expression 'I think' by making it more tentative. The expression 'in particular' is accompanied by a first phrase of a listing gesture-unit, thus isolating an important detail from a larger set of items. This gesture, therefore, performs a deictic/iconic function and not a listing one. The same forms with different functions are typical of lexical items such as 'well', used as an opening signal (Rodrigues, 1998) or discourse marker (Schiffrin, 1987) in conversation. This explains the need for analysing nonverbal modalities in relation to the whole communication context.

In Portuguese, the focus on the word *tigres* [tigers] (i-021) is also achieved through a kind of deictic gesture: the interpreter is not able to point because he is always holding a pen in his hand, but we can see that this meaning is nonetheless represented through gestures, as in the speaker's case. As for the location of *Asia* in his gesture space, there is a slight hand movement to the right.

Transcription 7

Speaker	Interpreter
s-018 -eh ´ther`is al´SO `eh ´com`pe´TItion'	i-022 ´e ´tam``BÉM -da::::::. ´cOmpetiçÃO'
s-019 `eh ´which hs ´come `frOm -eh !´medi`TE´RRANEAN! `countries.	i-023 `que tem ´vIN`do ´dos PAÍ`ses medite``RRÂ`neos.
s-020 -eh that=is ´to ´SAY'	i-024 (0,489) ou seja::- (1.202) ↑`Os - PAÍse::::s-
s-021 `eh´those on the ´SOUth- `and´east BANks `of the ´mediTERRA`nean;	i-025 `d ´do `SU´dESte `d da ba´CI`a ´medi´te`RÂnica.

Here the speaker makes a gesture depicting the position of the Mediterranean basin: his index finger points downwards and traces a semi-circle in the air; then, his whole hand rotates 180° from left to right.

The gesture accompanying the verbalisation in Portuguese of *países do sudeste da bacia mediterrânica* [countries from the South East of the Mediterranean basin] is slightly similar to the speaker's gesture: the interpreter's right hand (vertical position and fingers closed) traces a line (rather than a semicircle) from left to right.

Transcription 8

Speaker	Interpreter
s-022 <<g>countries>´like –TURkey' eh tuNIsia' And al`Geria; s-023 `eh which- eh ´have `eh ´fairly strong textile=Indus-tries ´as !WELL!'	i-026 ´turqUIA:::- - tuNÍsia e -al´GÉ`ria. i-027 (0.814)<<all>`são um exemplo destes↑`pAÍses; i-028 (1.431)`do ´sudOESte -da bacia do medite`´RRÂneo'

The speaker makes a listing gesture, counting the items *Turkey, Tunisia, Algeria* by touching (or rather slightly 'beating' on) his left-hand index, middle and ring finger with his right hand. In doing this, the right hand is open with palm down and the forearm moves up and down accompanying the listing of each item. In addition, the first and last items in the list are produced together with a nod of the head. It is also interesting to note the English interference when the interpreter says *Algéria* instead of *Argélia*, which is the correct Portuguese name for this country. The speaker's listing gesture is mirrored in the interpreter's right hand beats: three beats with opening sideward movements corresponding to the three items in the list.

4. Conclusion

With the data collected so far it is possible to start looking for answers to these main questions. Does nonverbal communication (gestures and prosody) by the trainee interpreter imitate the nonverbal communication of the speaker? Do they fulfil the same functions? Although it is evidently too early to draw any definitive conclusions at this stage of our research project, it is possible to note some interesting preliminary results. At the beginning, even after watching the microclips several times, the trainee interpreter appeared to move remarkably little; on a closer inspection, however, which was only possible through microanalysis (prosodic transcription and movement annotation with Praat and Anvil), it became clear that the trainee actually mirrored some of the gestures made by the speaker. This mirroring is not so evident at the beginning because the interpreter's gestures have almost always a lower degree of amplitude than the speaker's and they are hampered by the fact that he is holding objects in both hands. However, it is possible to say that there is a certain degree of mirroring, which consists mainly in reflecting some of the speaker's hand configurations as well as in organising virtual space in terms of geographical location of world regions in the same way. When the speaker's gestures focussing on words or phrases were not 'replicated' by the interpreter, then this focussing function was conveyed (and thus compensated for) through other modalities, such as prosody (pitch and intensity) and head movements.

Several important lessons can also be learnt as to the advantages and disadvantages of using Praat and Anvil to carry out a microanalysis of prosody and gesture. An obvious disadvantage is that it is time-consuming, so only a minute or two can be examined at a time. The great advantage, however, is that this type of analysis allows researchers to dissect gesture and speech down to the very finest detail and analyse their intimate relations. A very productive way of tapping the full potential of microanalysis could be to focus exclusively on the parts of speaker and interpreter corpora where there is a higher degree of 'gesture density' and study whether this phenomenon occurs on specific occasions such as, for example, when the speaker's delivery is very expressive and gestural or when the cognitive effort on the part of the interpreter is greater. This second hypothesis may occur for various reasons: the interpreter may be looking for a word or expression that is not readily retrievable from memory; the topic of the speech may involve concepts in an area of knowledge with which the interpreter is not familiar; the speaker's accent may be particularly hard to understand; or the interpreter may be experiencing a problem with delivery, i.e., a combination or sequence of words which are particularly difficult to say and the interpreter stumbles until finally the utterance is delivered with clarity. One such instance can be found in unit i-014, which is also one of the few times when the trainee interpreter makes an ampler gesture with his right arm and hand.

Another clear advantage that should be pointed out is the possible construction of small multimedia parallel corpora of English speeches and their respective simultaneous interpretations into Portuguese with full prosodic transcription as well as gesture annotation, which would constitute an invaluable tool for future research in applied interpreting studies as well as other disciplines. Such corpora would be very useful for training purposes, for studying patterns of language used in interpreted continental Portuguese, or for quality assessment in interpretation.

Notes

1. We are indebted to Sergio Viaggio (1997) for this wonderful synestethic metaphor.
2. The term simultaneous interpreting and its abbreviation SI will be used throughout this paper to mean "spoken-language interpreting with the use of simultaneous interpreting equipment in a sound-proof booth" (Pöchhacker, 2004:19). Simultaneous interpreter and conference interpreter will be used interchangeably to refer to the interpreter working in the simultaneous mode.

3. Due to space limitations, it was not possible to include the photographs illustrating the gestures described in the paper. Readers interested in obtaining these pictures should write to Elena Galvão at elenazagar@gmail.com.
4. Cf. Hall's idea (1990) of *hidden dimension*.

References

Ekman, Paul and Wallace V. Friesen (1969) "The repertoire of nonverbal behavior: categories, origins, usage and coding". *Semiotica* 1: 49-98.
Hall, Edward (1990/1969) *The Hidden Dimension*. New York: Anchor Books.
Kendon, Adam (1980) "Gesticulation and speech: two aspects of the process of utterance", in Mary Ritchie Key (ed.) *The Relationship of Verbal and Nonverbal Communication*. The Hague: Mouton, 208-27.
Kendon, Adam (2004) *Gesture. Visible Action as Utterance*. Cambridge: Cambridge University Press.
Kipp, Michael (2001) *ANVIL: A Generic Annotation Tool for Multimodal Dialogue*.
www.dfki.de/~kipp/public_archive/kipp2001-eurospeech.pdf
Kipp, Michael (2004) *Gesture Generation by Imitation – From Human Behavior to Computer Character Animation*. Boca Raton, Florida: Dissertation.com.
McNeill, David (1992) *Hand and Mind. What Gestures Reveal About Thought*. Chicago: University of Chicago Press.
McNeill, David (ed.) (2000) *Language and Gesture*. Cambridge: Cambridge University Press.
Pöchhacker, Franz (2004) *Introducing Interpreting Studies*. London and New York: Routledge.
Poggi, Isabella (2007) *Mind, Hands, Face and Body. A Goal and Belief View of Multimodal Communication*. Berlin: Weidler Buchverlag.
Rodrigues, Isabel Galhano (1998) *Os sinais conversacionais de alternância de vez*. Porto: Granito Editores e Livreiros.
Rodrigues, Isabel Galhano (2006) "Body in interpretation. Nonverbal communication of speaker and interpreter and its relation to words and prosody". Paper presented at *LICTRA VIII, Leipziger Internationale Konferenz zu Grundfragen der Translatologie*, Leipzig, 4–7 October.
Rodrigues, Isabel Galhano (2007) O *Corpo e a Fala. Comunicação verbal e não-verbal na interacção face a face*. Lisboa: Fundação C. Gulbenkian / Fundação para a Ciência e Tecnologia.

Schegloff, Emmanuel A., Gail Jefferson and Harvey Sachs (1977) "The preference for self correction in the organization of repair in conversation". *Language* 53: 361-82.

Schiffrin, Deborah (1987) *Discourse Markers.* Cambridge: Cambridge University Press.

Selting, Margret and Elizabeth Couper-Kuhlen (eds) (2001) *Studies in Interactional Linguistics.* Amsterdam and Philadelphia: John Benjamins.

Selting, Margret, Peter Auer, Birgit Barden, Jörg Bergman, Elisabeth Couper-Kuhlen, Susanne Günthner, Christoph Meier, Uta Quasthoff, Peter Schlobinski, Susanne Uhmann (1998) "Gesprächsanalytisches Transkriptionssystem (GAT)". *Linguistische Berichte* 173: 91-122.

Viaggio, Sergio (1997) "Kinesics and the simultaneous interpreter. The advantages of listening with one's eyes and speaking with one's body", in Fernando Poyatos (ed.) *Nonverbal Communication and Translation.* Amsterdam and Philadelphia: John Benjamins, 283-293.

Weale, Edna (1997) "From Babel to Brussels. Conference interpreting and the art of the impossible", in Fernando Poyatos (ed.) *Nonverbal Communication and Translation.* Amsterdam and Philadelphia: John Benjamins, 295-312.

Translation goes to the movies: a didactic approach

Maria José Veiga

Universidade de Aveiro, Portugal

Abstract
Designing an AVT module requires the development of both practical and theoretical approaches. Reflection on translation has taken place throughout the centuries, thus contributing to the shaping of a contemporary theoretical framework, and students must be made aware of these issues. However, it can be hard for translation teachers in general, and more particularly audiovisual translation (AVT) teachers, to approach translation issues with their students from a theoretical standpoint, particularly when the technical component of AVT courses seems so appealing when compared to reading texts. This article seeks to suggest some avenues for exploring scenes in films that relate directly to the discussion of some seminal texts on translation matters. The methodological approach posited here emphasises the use of films directly related to questions posed by the topic of translation: its aims, practices, limitations, and so forth. The main focus is on feature films, namely *Lost in Translation* (2003), *The Interpreter* (2005) and *Babel* (2006), so as to underline their potential grounds for theoretical reflection on translational dynamics, and to shed light on some methodological questions raised when approaching the complexity of (audiovisual) translation as a subject.

1. Introduction

Given the appropriate focus, the use of audiovisual material in the foreign language classroom has been widely disseminated as both a productive and successful pedagogical resource in the teaching and learning process (Díaz Cintas, 2008). It is my contention that translation courses constitute no exception to this. Actually, the use of a particular set of feature films in class may bring several advantages to courses on audiovisual translation (AVT) when they are the object of careful lesson planning. On the one hand, it is a common practice to exploit films as a basis for underlining or expanding linguistic and technical aspects, and, on the other hand, they can be used as a starting point for a discussion on subjects involving translation theory and practice.

Thus, I will attempt to shed some light on the possibility of making use of films in class in order to motivate students to carry out research on Translation Studies (TS). To this end, the examples provided are extracted from the following feature films: *Lost in Translation* (Sofia Coppola, 2003),

The Interpreter (Sydney Pollack, 2005) and *Babel* (Alejandro González Iñarritu, 2006). This means, however, that, although there could be ample room for a discussion on audiovisual translation modes (dubbing, subtitling, voiceover…), what is of paramount interest here is a close examination of the arguments and plots of these films so as to provide us with an overview of some issues closely connected with (Audiovisual) Translation Studies.

2. The choice of the feature films

Due to practical reasons, the chronological order of the actual year of release of the films will not be maintained and the order of discussion will be, first, *Babel*, then, *Lost in Translation*, and finally, *The Interpreter*. One question still remains: what reasons have prompted the selection of these films in particular? Indeed, this has not been made at random. The connotations inferred from the titles are in themselves almost self-explanatory for they can be easily associated to general themes within the field of TS: the need for translation in a multilingual and multicultural world, the significance of (mis)translation in human communication, and the importance of interpreters (and translators) in human interaction.

In addition to this, the three feature films follow a common thread: the continuous search by human beings to understand each other through language as well as the frustrating frailty and failure of language to establish communication. Being able to communicate implies that all parties should understand a common language in an attempt to create and convey a shared meaning that, in turn, will help them understand each other in interpersonal exchanges and relationships.

3. Films and Translation Issues: a symbiotic module

> Serious world problems of war, human rights, tropical rainforests and so on can be hard for language learners to connect with. Approaching global issues through movies is, therefore, a useful strategy, especially when the issues seem too difficult, too time-consuming or too remote from students' lives. The visual aspect of movies can help students understand both the language used and the issues portrayed. Further, movies speak to students' emotions as well as to their intellect, and allow them to enter an unknown world and experience its conflicts. Movies are authentic materials that bring real life into the classroom and provide a context in which language is effectively learned. (Fukunaga, 1998:online)

There are numerous bibliographical references on topics such as the teaching of (foreign) languages and culture, as well as written reflections on the teaching of languages through translation or film. Obviously, any courses on

AVT must also, by definition, incorporate films – and other audiovisual programmes – as their working source material. And yet, when it comes to reflecting on how to take advantage of these audiovisual materials to teach translation theory and concepts, the bibliographical references are rather scarce.

Thus this paper will propose a didactic approach that brings together the study of films and translation studies in order to focus on theoretical translation matters through the eyes of the three film directors mentioned above. Paraphrasing Fukunaga's sentence quoted above, I would argue that, *mutatis mutandis*, movies are indeed authentic materials that can bring virtual life into the classroom and provide a variety of contexts for research and reflection in which translation theories, techniques and practices can be effectively learnt.

In what follows, I shall refer to some of the main themes related to a proposed module on films and translation, with special emphasis on its aims and objectives, the teaching methods followed and the teaching materials and aids to be used. Even though components such as assessment, ECTS (European Credit Transfer and accumulation System), attendance, ICT and space facilities are of paramount importance in course design, their significance will be played down in this particular context which will be devoted to a discussion of specific methodological issues.

As for the aims and objectives, this module entitled Films and Translation Issues is intended to be primarily directed at undergraduate students, practising or future translators who wish to become acquainted with the principles of AVT or TS and to expand their knowledge in these particular academic fields. Language undergraduates might find it interesting to attend this module for some of the skills developed throughout the module can readily be transferred to include a variety of situations both at work and outside.

On the completion of this module, the students will have: (a) acquired a sound theoretical basis for Translation Studies, (b) developed critical awareness concerning ethical and professional issues in translating and interpreting in a multicultural world, and (c) enhanced and expanded their repertoire of skills and techniques involved in translation processes. Together with these general aims and objectives, learners will develop other transferable skills, namely: researching methods (to find and use data from several sources), note-taking skills, writing skills (organizing, revising, editing texts), public speaking skills (presentations in class), independence, working individually or/and as a part of a team and initiative.

As far as teaching methods are concerned, this section is based on the three tables discussed below (3.1, 3.2 and 3.3), which are then subdivided according to some of the didactic presuppositions that any basic unit or lesson plan should include: (a) aims and learning outcomes, (b) materials and aids, and (c) methodology and activities. In addition to these subdivisions, portfolio activities and further reading suggestions are provided, so as to offer not only additional preparation on the subjects dealt with in class, but also to increase the ability to reflect critically on translation as a subject which embodies both theoretical and practical elements.

As stated before, although an assessment of the planned units will not constitute one of the objectives of this study, this is implied through the consideration of portfolio organisation. Research-oriented modules are to be assessed either by written examination and coursework or a combination of both. It could also be furthered through oral examination and/or the quality of student participation in class.

It is estimated that the contents that correspond to each table should be roughly equivalent to ten to twelve-hour units, depending on the pace of the teaching and learning processes of the class. As a result, this module will consist of some 30 to 36 hours of face-to-face class teaching. If there is a preference for a combination of group lectures and tutorials, then between twelve to fifteen hours ought to be added so that the tutor would be able to monitor and assess the students' work, their strengths and weaknesses, closely. Given the nature of translation, tutorials could easily offer the opportunity for students to clarify ideas on translation issues and to explore others suggested by the tutor during group lectures.

Teachers should facilitate the comprehension and assimilation process of new contents. It would be disastrous if students were provided with a bibliographical list of relevant works and advised to read the items prior to a discussion in class without any prior preparation or suggestions on what to look for in the different works. My argument, however, is not that learners should not been given any reading material at all. On the contrary, they need guidelines to structure their reading competence as far as theoretical texts are concerned. Evidently, teachers are not supposed to do the thinking for their students. Rather, they should be the facilitators in the process of seeking and discovering new information, thus helping pupils to better acquire an epistemological framework. In a nutshell, and resorting to a rather hackneyed turn of phrase, teachers teach learners how to learn.

Moreover, it is the teacher's task to provide a learning environment conducive to equipping the students with the knowledge and skills required for them to demonstrate a full understanding of previous and recent approaches to translation, contemporary issues and potential future trends in TS. This might explain the reason why often teachers share remarkably similar preoccupations and concerns which repeatedly emerge before teaching a class: how to inspire students voluntarily to search for more information outside the classroom and to acquire greater knowledge on translation matters? How to provide students with translation metalanguage? How to introduce translation theory in graduate courses? How to introduce AVT issues into general translation classes? The content of the three tables below constitutes an attempt to offer some methodological paths and suggestions in order to provide some answers to the questions raised above.

3.1. *Babel*: the need for translation in a multilingual and multicultural world

After *Amores Perros* (2000) and *21 Grams* (2003), the multi-narrative *Babel* (2006) closes Alejandro González Iñárritu's 'death trilogy', where several separate dramas are interwoven to become irretrievably connected. Besides offering fertile grounds for debating cross-cultural relationships, *Babel* leads us back to fundamental thinking concerning Translation Studies as we know it today.

Table 3.1: *Babel* (Alejandro González Iñarritu, 2006)

Aims / Learning outcomes	Materials / Aids	Methodology / Activities
1. Understand the importance of the Christian theological narrative for the emergence of a theory of multiligualism	Images of paintings portraying the biblical passage of *Tower of Babel*, by Pieter Brueghel (the Elder c. 1525-1569) - *Tower of Babel* and the *Little Tower of Babel* (c. 1563) Biblical text (Genesis, chapter 11, verses 1-9; an authorized version)	Provide the students with images of the painting *Tower of Babel*, by Pieter Brueghel: offering information about the Tower of Babel and the emergence of languages Read the biblical text (Genesis, chapter 11, verses 1-9)
2. Acknowledge the distinction between biblical and scientific explanations on the origin of languages	Article: Ross (1997)	Show a language tree as proposed by Ross (1997), in contrast to the biblical account
3. Establish a relationship between the themes of feature film *Babel* and the message of the biblical and linguistic explanations on the multiplicity of language so as to	Film: *Babel*	Watch the film *Babel* Note-taking on any translation related topics Discussion of analogies between the film and the two previously presented texts: - the co-occurrence of many languages from five continents (in *Babel*:

develop a critical awareness of cultural diversity and its implications for translation		English, Spanish, Arabic, French, Japanese, Japanese Sign Language and Berber) - the failure to interact within one's own language/culture and its repercussions on human experience
4. Differentiate between intralingual, interlingual and intersemiotic translation	Articles: Jakobson (1959) Bachmann-Medick (1996)	Critical reading of Jakobson's article with reference to the film topics: - analysis of the characters' recurrent statement, "I don't understand", and question, "What did he say?" - need to translate Japanese Sign Language for the wider community - highlight the distinctive differences between *interlingual* and *intralingual* translation
5. Understand the interdisciplinary nature of translation	Articles: Holmes (1972) Gutt (1990)	Critical reading of the articles Debate the numerous scientific fields involved in Translation Studies

Portfolio activities:
1. Encourage students to search for information on the origins of world languages (online information; dictionaries of linguistics, etc.);
2. Collect material on: (a) the languages/cultures referred to in the film; (b) the European Union efforts to commit to multilingualism policies;
3. Familiarise learners with sign language interpreting and translation for the deaf and hard-of-hearing as AVT modes (Neves, 2005; de Linde and Kay, 1999).

Further reading:
Baker (2001); Gentzler (1993); Steiner (1975/1998); Toury (1995)

Translation will serve no communication purposes if cultural elements are not taken into account. This means that denotative meanings do not determine the effectiveness of a translation, as we shall see from the examples extracted from some of the scenes of the next feature film.

3.2. *Lost in Translation*: the significance of translation in human communication

For both characters, Bob and Charlotte, the city of Tokyo stands for sheer cultural and linguistic alienation. Tokyo is a reminder of how lonely and how silent we can get when isolated from the world we think we know. There is a specific scene which is the model for being literally 'lost in translation'. While on the set for filming a whisky commercial, Bob experiences the frustration of listening to very long verbal exchanges which the Japanese interpreter merely transfers into English as "Right side. And, uh, with intensity". Bemused by such linguistic economy, Bob retorts, not without sarcasm in his voice: "Is that everything? It seemed like he said quite a bit more than that". The non-Japanese speaking audience is also bewildered at the brief translation since the exchanges in Japanese are not subtitled either. The sense of loss when changing from one language into another, and the choices interpreters and translators make, is the main focus of analysis when presenting *Lost in Translation* in class.

Table 3.2: *Lost in Translation* (Sofia Coppola, 2003)

Aims / Learning outcomes	Materials / Aids	Methodology / Activities
1. Be aware of the significance of the phrase "lost in translation"	List of puns and idiomatic expressions in one or more languages Extracts from the poem *Lost in Translation* (Merrill, 1974) Selected passages from two different novels: *Lost in Translation* (Hoffman, 1989) and *Lost in Translation* (Mones, 1999)	Brainstorm exercise giving examples (puns, idiomatic expressions…) of linguistic or cultural phrases that lose their literal meaning in the process of translation Critical reading of the poem and of some of the passages from the two novels
2. Relate the topics presented in the film *Lost in Translation* to issues concerning translation theory	Film: *Lost in Translation* List the translation of the title *Lost in Translation* in several languages	Watch the film *Lost in Translation* Note-taking on any translation related topics Debate the possible reasons why the actual translation of the film's title has been 'lost in translation' in some languages (e.g. in European Portuguese *O Amor é um Lugar Estranho* [Love is a

		Strange Place]
3. Understand reduction strategies and other translation procedures, especially in audiovisual translation (and even more obviously, in subtitling)	Articles: Vinay and Darbelnet (1958) Livbjerg (1998) Vermeer (1989)	Critical reading of the articles Discussion of the methods or translation procedures: borrowing, calque, literal translation, transposition, modulation, equivalence, reduction, etc. Explore the notion of translation fallacy: essentially no word, phrase, text or utterance in language A can be unfailingly translated into language B without loss, addition or change of meaning Apply these concepts of translation procedures to the list of the translated titles of *Lost in Translation* into several languages Group work: taking into account the information from the articles and the exchange between Bob and the Japanese interpreter mentioned above, students should outline a debate on (un)translatability, translator's options, *skopos* theory, etc.

Portfolio activities:
1. Encourage students to search for (written or media) material containing examples of (un)translatability, translator's options, and relevance theory;
2. Collect (written or media) material so as to substantiate the relationship that can be established between language and identity of the self. Discuss how interlingual translation can be identified with the translation of the self;
3. Gather other examples of subtitled/dubbed material, which demonstrate the constraints of audiovisual translation;
4. Research on AVT modes of translation, especially on subtitling and subtitling for the deaf and the hard-of-hearing which are closely related to topics such as reduction, relevance, and media constraints.

Further reading:
Delabastita (1996, 1997); Gutt (1991); Sperber and Wilson (1986); Díaz Cintas (2008); Neves (2005)

In her analysis of the relationship established between language and the identity of the self, Oster (2003: 68) suggests that the title *Lost in Translation* successfully captures "that familiar term of frustration at the loss of nuance or beauty or rhythm or exactitude when we translate from one language into another". Indeed, some cultural references may lose their significance when dislocated from their linguistic and cultural contexts. And from this perspective, it could be argued that words have the potential for personifying cultural assumptions, as can also be inferred from some of the examples taken from *The Interpreter*.

3.3. *The Interpreter*: the importance of the translator in human interaction

Within the scope of this reflection, one of the most important verbal exchanges in *The Interpreter* is the example presented below:

Silvia Broome:	Do you think I'm making it up? Why would I report a threat I didn't hear?
Tobin Keller:	People do.
Silvia Broome:	I don't.
Tobin Keller:	Some people like attention.
Silvia Broome:	I don't!
Tobin Keller:	Maybe you don't want Zuwanie at the UN.
Silvia Broome:	I didn't make it up.
Tobin Keller:	How do you feel about him?
Silvia Broome:	I don't care for him.
Tobin Keller:	Wouldn't mind if he were dead?
Silvia Broome:	I wouldn't mind if he were gone.
Tobin Keller:	Same thing.
Silvia Broome:	No it isn't. If I interpreted gone as dead I'd be out of a job, if dead and gone were the same thing there'd be no UN.
Tobin Keller:	Your profession is playing with words Ms. Broome.
Silvia Broome:	I don't play with words.
Tobin Keller:	You're doing it right now.
Silvia Broome:	No you are. If I wanted him dead, I wouldn't have reported it. I would sit back and let it happen. That's not what I want, that's not why I'm here.

Although Silvia Broome speaks a make-believe language from a fictitious country, the portrayed situation is indeed real. As a result, vocabulary adequacy and precision can, as illustrated above, be a matter of life or death. Accountability issues are closely examined in this feature film, especially those relating to the interpreter's professionalism. This is an example of the kind of responsibilities for which a translator or interpreter can be held accountable.

Table 3.3: *The Interpreter* (Sydney Pollack, 2005)

Aims / Learning outcomes	Materials / Aids	Methodology / Activities
1. Equip the students with an overview of international organisations for translation services	Documentary film: *The Ultimate Movie Set: The United Nations* (Bonus of *The Interpreter*, DVD)	Presentation of the documentary film *The Ultimate Movie Set: The United Nations* Discussion of the socio-political dimension of the UN and its implications on the task of interpreters
2. Be acquainted with the functions of interpreters and their professional responsibilities	Film: *The Interpreter*	Watch the film *The Interpreter* Note-taking of elements connected with the interpreter's profession Discussion of issues facing professional interpreters and translators.
3. Raise awareness of explicit and implicit speech acts in translation, as a process and product	Documentary film: *A Day in the Life of a Real Interpreter* (Bonus of *The Interpreter*, DVD)	Debate the interpreter's diplomatic dimension for world communication: implications of consecutive interpreting (CI) for professionals
4. Be familiar with the implications of verbal choices in consecutive interpreting	Extract from the film: *The Interpreter* (exchange between Silvia Broome and Tobin Keller above) Books and articles: Austin (1962:14-6) Eco (2003) Nida (1964, 2001) Lewis (1985)	Relate the use of the words 'dead' and 'gone', uttered by Sylvia in the film, with Eco's (2003) notions of accuracy, adequacy and meaning negotiation. Discussion of the theoretical application of notions such as performative acts, communicative competence and pragmatics to Translation Studies
5. Understand consecutive interpreting idiosyncrasies	Article: Gile (1995a)	Discussion of Consecutive Interpreting (CI): - phases of CI: listening and analysis, memory, production

		- modes of speech in CI: impromptu, written to be read, (in)formal contexts - strategies of CI: summarising, generalising, note-taking... - linguistic specificities: terminology and genre-oriented texts - CI for the media
Portfolio activities: 1. Research on language policies: minority languages and languages which enjoy official status in international organisations, like the United Nations (UN) and the European Union (EU) (http://ec.europa.eu/education/languages/languages-of-europe/index_en.htm); 2. Find out reference material and terminological databases for translators and interpreters of large international organisations; 3. Research on minority languages and multilingual and multicultural policies in the EU; 4. Collect material on the languages and cultures referred to in the film; 5. Research work on (a) Special Broadcasting Service, which is "one of the world's larger subtilter organizations [providing] multilingual and multicultural radio and television services that inform, educate and entertain all Australians and, in doing so, reflect Australia's multicultural society" (http://en.wikipedia.org/wiki/Special_Broadcasting_Service); (b) media translation developments in the EU and their relation to multicultural policies. Further reading: Blakemore (1990); Cameron (2001); Gile (1995b); Hickey (1998); Hatim and Mason (1990); Nida (2001)		

All the pedagogical activities suggested in this module are aimed at achieving a critical understanding of translation, and in some instances interpreting, theories and concepts so as better to comprehend the dynamics of Translation Studies in their diversity and complexity.

4. Closing remarks

Neither the chosen examples nor the suggested texts are entirely innovative or exhaustive. They are merely intended to assist understanding of the multidisciplinary nature of TS and the wide range of themes yet to be explored and researched further, namely those closely associated with AVT.

Obviously, this presentation is open to debate and to improvement and should not be understood as an imposition of a series of inflexible suggestions. On the contrary, this module aims at offering a set of orientation points that should ideally be applied with the particular changes or adaptations suited to the specific needs of tutors, learners, course design, the articulation between the aims and contents of the syllabus and assessment criteria.

Above all, the main goal underlying the conception of this module is to ensure that theoretical translation issues can indeed be approached in the classroom assisted by the careful choice of appealing films and the promotion of a balanced selection of canonical texts and authors. As valuable pedagogical tools, films and texts in symbiotic relationship can help students and tutors to enhance, corroborate and expand on translation theories effectively.

References

Austin, John L. (1962) *How to Do Things With Words*. Oxford: Clarendon Press.

Bachmann-Medick, Doris (1996) "Cultural misunderstandings in translation: multicultural coexistence and multicultural concepts of world literature". *EESE* 7.
http://webdoc.sub.gwdg.de/edoc/ia/eese/artic96/bachmann/7_96.html

Baker, Mona (ed.) (2001) *Routledge Encyclopedia of Translation Studies.* 2nd Edition. London and New York: Routledge.

Blakemore, Diana (1990) *Understanding Utterances: The Pragmatics of Natural Language.* Oxford: Blackwell.

Cameron, Deborah (2001) *Working With Spoken Discourse.* London: Sage Publications, Ltd.

Delabastita, Dirk (ed.) (1996) *The Translator (Special Issue): Wordplay & Translation* 2(2). Manchester: St. Jerome Publishing.

Delabastita, Dirk (ed.) (1997) *Traductio: Essays on Punning and Translation.* Manchester and Namur: St. Jerome Publishing and Presses Universitaires de Namur.

Díaz Cintas, Jorge (2008) "Introduction: the didactics of audiovisual translation", in Jorge Díaz Cintas (ed.) *The Didactics of Audiovisual Translation.* Amsterdam and Philadelphia: John Benjamins, 1-18.

Eco, Umberto (2003) *Mouse or Rat? Translation as Negotiation.* London: Phoenix.

Fukunaga. Yasuyo (1998) "Teaching global issues through English movies". *Global Issues in Language Education* 30: 7-9.
http://jalt.org/global/30Mov.htm

Gentzler, Edwin (1993) *Contemporary Translation Theories.* London and New York: Routledge.

Gile, Daniel. 1995a. "Fidelity assessment in consecutive interpretation: an experiment". *Target* 7(1): 151-64.

Gile Daniel (1995b) *Basic Concepts and Models for Interpreter and Tanslator Training.* Amsterdam and Philadelphia: John Benjamins.

Gutt, Ernst-August (1990) "A theoretical account of translation – Without a translation theory". *Target* 2(2): 135-64.

Gutt, Ernst-August (1991) *Translation and Relevance: Cognition and Context.* Oxford: Basil Blackwell.

Hatim, Basil and Ian Mason (1990) *Discourse and the Translator.* London: Longman.

Hickey, Leo (ed.) (1998) *The Pragmatics of Translation.* Clevedon: Multilingual Matters.

Holmes, James S. (1972) "The name and nature of Translation Studies", in Lawrence Venuti (ed.) (2001) *The Translation Studies Reader.* London and New York: Routledge, 172-85.

Hoffman, Eva (1989) *Lost in Translation.* New York: Penguin.

Jakobson, Roman. (1959). "On linguistic aspects of translation", in Lawrence Venuti (ed.) (2001) *The Translation Studies Reader.* London and New York: Routledge, 138-44.

Lewis, Philip E. (1985) "The measure of translation effects", in Lawrence Venuti (ed.) (2001) *The Translation Studies Reader.* London and New York, 256-75.

de Linde, Zoe and Neil Kay (1999) *The Semiotics of Subtitling.* Manchester: St. Jerome.

Livbjerg, Inge (1998) "Teaching reduction strategies in translation". *Perspectives: Studies in Translatology* 6(1): 23-33.

Merrill, James (1974) *Lost in Translation.*
http://guccipiggy.objectis.net/poetry/merrill/lostintranslation
www.jeremygregg.com/quotes/jamesmerrill/lost%20in%20translation.ht
m

Mones, Nicole (1999) *Lost in Translation.* Bantam Dell Publishing Group.

Neves, Josélia (2005) *Audiovisual Translation: Subtitling for the Deaf and Hard-of-Hearing.* London: Roehampton University. PhD Thesis.
http://roehampton.openrepository.com/roehampton/handle/10142/12580

Nida, Eugene (1964) "Principles of correspondence", in Lawrence Venuti (ed.) (2001) *The Translation Studies Reader.* London and New York, 153-67.

Nida, Eugene (2001) *Contexts in Translation.* Amsterdam and Philadelphia: John Benjamins.

Oster, Judith (2003) *Crossing Cultures: Creating Identity in Chinese and Jewish American Literature.* Columbia: University of Missouri Press.

Rheingold, Howard (1988) *There's a Word for It…but It's Untranslatable.* London: Svern House.

Ross, Philipp (1997) "L'histoire du langage". *Dossier Pour la Science: Les Langues du Monde,* October: 20-7.

Sperber, Dan and Dreidre Wilson (1986) *Relevance: Communication and Cognition.* Oxford: Blackwell.

Steiner, George (1975/1998) *After Babel: Aspects of Language and Translation.* Oxford: Oxford University Press.

Toury, Gideon (1995) *Descriptive Translation Studies and Beyond.* Amsterdam and Philadelphia: John Benjamins.

Vermeer, Hans J. (1989) "Skopos and commission in translational action", in Lawrence Venuti (ed.) (2001) *The Translation Studies Reader.* London and New York: Routledge, 227-38.

Vinay, Jean-Paul and Jean Darbelnet (1958) "A methodology for translation", in Lawrence Venuti (ed.) (2001) *The Translation Studies Reader.* London and New York: Routledge, 128-37.

Filmography

Lost in Translation. 2003. Sofia Coppola. USA, Japan.
The Interpreter. 2005. Sydney Pollack. UK, USA, France.
Amores Perros. 2000. Alejandro González Iñarritu. Mexico.
21 Grams. 2003. Alejandro González Iñarritu. USA.
Babel. 2006. Alejandro González Iñarritu. Japan, Mexico, USA.

Text on screen and text on air: a useful tool for foreign language teachers and learners

Conceição Bravo

Universidade do Algarve, Faro, Portugal

Abstract
TV viewers and cinema-goers in Portugal have traditionally been exposed to a policy of subtitling, yet in spite of a high exposure to English-language audiovisual materials, secondary-school students' performance in English is poor and the majority claim to find EFL a difficult subject. A study was carried out on two groups of students to test the effect of subtitling exposure on their understanding of English. The results obtained allow for some reflection as to pedagogical settings, to raise learners' awareness of this learning resource, how they can adapt it to their own learning styles and pace, and how grammar and other language features can be explored without necessarily experiencing difficulties.

1. Introduction

TV viewers and cinema-goers in Portugal have traditionally been exposed to subtitling yet, in spite of the high exposure to English language audiovisual materials, high school students' performance in English is poor and the majority claim to find EFL a difficult subject. Screen translation has proved to be beneficial in other subtitling countries, like Belgium, the Netherlands, Canada and the Scandinavian countries. What then could be the problem in the Portuguese context?

A study was carried out on two groups of Portuguese state school students, aged 13-14, in their 5th year of learning English, to test the effect of subtitling exposure on their understanding of English and its pedagogical benefits. Aspects such as the vocabulary acquired by viewers, their understanding of idiomatic expressions and phrasal verbs were given particular scrutiny. The degree of vocabulary retention was also tested several weeks after the experiment had taken place, in the form of a consolidation test, and then again three months after the conclusion of the study. One group was exposed to the regular condition of English-audio and Portuguese-subtitles (FL+MT), while the other was exposed to English-audio and English-subtitles (FL+FL).

The results obtained for each group might serve as a tentative answer to the question at the outset. They allow for some reflection on pedagogical settings, and serve to raise learners' and teachers' awareness of this audiovisual learning resource, how they can adapt it to their own specific linguistic needs, styles and learning pace, and how grammar and other language features can be explored. Audiovisual translation (AVT) can promote autonomous language learning as a life-long process, as well as mediating linguistic, social and cultural issues between source and target communities.

2. Interlingual and intralingual subtitles as didactic aids in foreign language learning

The foreign language under study in this experiment is English for Portuguese native speakers, also referred to as L2. In trying to recognise and understand the type of variables which might facilitate the typical Portuguese EFL school learner, the study presented here seeks to assess which mode of television viewing – foreign programmes with standard subtitling or foreign programs with bimodal input – is most appropriate for foreign language learning.

2.1. The aim and the hypotheses

The aim of this study was to compare the usefulness of same-language subtitled viewing material (i.e. intralingual subtitling) versus mother-tongue subtitled material (i.e. interlingual subtitling) for foreign language learning (L2+L2 vs L2+L1). In other words, the aim was to investigate the acquisition of lexical elements of which the form and meaning were mostly unknown by the subjects. By usefulness I mean the pedagogical method which led learners to obtain better results in terms of foreign language comprehension of new lexical units such as idioms. I hoped to show how active viewing and participation reflected on students' performance in different vocabulary tests and overall comprehension. Finally, it also aimed at making learners aware that they could adapt this audiovisual learning resource to their own particular needs and styles.

The underlying question was: do two types of subtitling conditions have different effects upon the ability of intermediate-level school students in their understanding of content in general and on their performance in the post-viewing tasks? As an answer to this question, the following hypotheses were made:

i)   Portuguese students viewing English language audiovisual material with English intralingual subtitles reveal more difficulty in understanding content than those viewing audiovisual material with standard, interlingual subtitles in their mother tongue.

ii) Understanding and retaining English idioms in the audiovisual material depends on having a translated version into the students' L1.

2.2. The sample

I started with a pool of 77 intermediate school students, relatively homogenous with respect to age and record of academic achievement. The subjects were all aged 13 or 14. They were sorted into two groups, 1 and 2, and had to remain within their previously assigned classes. Group 1, the group of students who viewed English audio + Portuguese subtitles (L2+L1), had a maximum total of 39 students, although in 4 testing instances one student was absent. The average number was 38. Group 2, the subjects who viewed English audio + English subtitles (L2+L2), had a maximum number of 38 students, but in weeks 2, 3, 5 and 6 there was one student absent and in week 8 there were two students absent, the average being 37. Thus, group sizes were $N_1 = 38$ and $N_2 = 37$, as seen in Table 1:

Table 1: Subjects sample

1		Value Label	N
Condition	1	English + Portuguese	38
	2	English + English	37

So as not to concentrate the entire sample on participants from a single school setting, classes 1, 2 and 3 were taken from one intermediate school and class 4 from another intermediate school nearby. These schools encompass five years of schooling, between primary and high school (years 5-9). In Portugal, the grades in these schools are given on a scale of 1 to 5, with 1 and 2 representing 'failure' in the subject. Grade 3 is 'average' and 4 and 5 represent 'good' and 'excellent' respectively. I opted for 3 classes in one school as the English language teacher taught all these students and, based on her knowledge of them, suggested that they should be grouped in the following way: classes 1 and 2, based on their academic achievement of nine failures, twenty with grade 3 and nine with grades above 3, formed group 1.

Group 2 was composed of classes 3 and 4 (one class from each school). In terms of students' academic achievement in English in the previous year (8th grade), class 3 had ten students who scored grade 3; eight students with grades 4 and 5 and three students with grade 2. In class 4, eight students achieved grade 3 and nine students obtained grades 4 and 5, with no failures in the class. Based on their similarities, it was decided that classes 3 and 4 should be tested on performance under condition 2 (L2+L2, bimodal input) and classes 1 and 2 under condition 1 (L2+L1). Thus, this sample was truly representative of this population group in terms of its most important general characteristics: age, nationality, educational background, EFL learning background, academic capability, and socioeconomic status. According to the Common European Framework of Reference (CEFR) (Council of Europe, 2001), these students, in their final year of compulsory schooling (9th grade), were approximately at A2/B1 level of competence in English.

The decision at the start of this study was biased in that students with lower foreign language fluency were expected to be more dependent on their mother tongue for understanding foreign language audiovisual materials and for performing post-viewing language tasks, recognition and recall.

Within the sample there was a student who reported being neither a native English nor native Portuguese speaker. This student was from Bulgaria and spoke Portuguese at low-intermediate level and English at post-beginner level. Her initial reaction to viewing the episodes with English subtitles was negative, arguing that her English was weaker than her Portuguese and that she would benefit very little from such an experiment. I will refer to this student again in the results.

The course books used by both teachers in their respective schools were the same, thus conforming to agreed syllabus requirements and ability.

2.3. The setting

This was not a comparative study in the strict sense of the word, as all the independent variables in the teaching/learning situation would have had to have been controlled, which would have been practically impossible. The members of each group were asked to perform the same tasks under identical conditions in every respect except one: namely, that group 1 viewed the episodes with standard subtitles (L2+L1) and group 2 viewed them with bimodal input (L2+L2). The experiment was conducted in the normal foreign language scheduled classes, except for the presence of both the students' English language teacher and the researcher. Anonymity did not serve the purpose of this longitudinal investigation, as the respondents needed to be linked to the data scores in the weekly questionnaires. Hence, identity marking was necessary, whether in the form of their real names or a self-generated identification code, so long as they remembered and used the same code over the research interval. In either case, students were assured of their anonymity from the beginning and equally assured their participation and performance in the research would not affect their English language grade. In the end, the results of the study were presented to the individual classes and their respective teachers although test scores were never directly associated with names.

2.4. The materials

To explore the lexical method, the effects of learning expressions in context, and a variety of salient speech functions, the first season (of a total of six) of the popular US sitcom television series *The Fresh Prince of Bel-Air* was selected. It was released on DVD in 2005 and only became available in Portugal in 2006. Prior to being available on DVD it had been aired on a satellite television channel. A questionnaire on TV viewing habits and preferences was distributed to the students before the experiment and aimed at determining how many of them were familiar with the show. Out of 77 students only 6 had seen or heard of it. However, most students were familiar with the actor who played the main protagonist in the show, Will Smith, found him funny and were extremely motivated to watch the series. Student motivation was a decisive factor in the final choice of the materials. Harmer (2001:51) reminds us that:

> most researchers and methodologists have come to the view that intrinsic motivation is especially important for encouraging success. Even where the original reason for taking up a language course, for example, is extrinsic, the chances of success will be greatly enhanced if the students come to love the learning process.

The selection of the ten episodes was based on relevance of language and cultural content for the students' ninth grade curriculum and, simultaneously, it appeared relevant and of interest to the average student in this age group. On two occasions, the selection was also influenced by the approaching dates for the celebration of Hallowe'en and Thanksgiving. It was considered that the timely viewing of these episodes might encourage students' involvement in the topics. Throughout the episodes several key themes were addressed, such as teenagers and the generation gap, ethical values, family relations, racial discrimination and environmental issues. Being a US production with a

British character playing the role of the family butler, another constant feature throughout the series was the cultural and linguistic differences between the UK and the US. British English versus American English is, in turn, a feature in the students' English language curriculum. Table 2 shows what target lexical phrases were tested in each week's viewing:

Table 2: Summary of episodes and target words/phrases

Weeks	Episodes	Target expressions/ idioms/ lexical phrases
1	*The Fresh Prince of Bel-Air*	show up, nephew by marriage, get rid of someone, take a hint, turn down an invitation, make a big thing out of nothing, say grace, go off duty, take something hard, that's not killing anybody
2	*Mixed Identities*	for crying out loud, straighten things out, take care of someone, punch it man, to be heading for, to be glum, take chances, every other weekend, trade something, when in Rome do as the Romans do
3	*Kiss My Butler*	I'm so touched, to wait on someone, a spot of tea, he just lit up, don't talk down to me, this is highly irregular, matchmaker, he's some piece of work, a little rough around the edges, to be sober
4	*Homeboy, Sweet Homeboy*	quiet as a church-mouse, to be homesick, what a shame, a story we can all relate to, what does it entail?, to be held back, to carry one's weight, one's motto, propose a toast, to flip
5	*Someday Your Prince Will Be in Effect* (part 2)	put your money where your mouth is, take a hint, tough luck, count your blessings, it's on the house, to look a little down, law of nature, 5 o'clock sharp, a runway model, trick or treat
6	*Knowledge Is Power*	to break curfew, to be grounded, revenge is within my reach, that was a real scream, tuck someone in, it's too good to be true, let someone off the hook, to tell on someone, we're even, drop out of college
7	*Talking Turkey*	take a shot at someone, take after someone, clear the table, spoiled kids, to hurt someone's feelings, to miss something/someone, a free ride in a fancy car (idiomatic), to pass away, mow the lawn, to run the household
8	*Just Infatuation*	infatuated with someone, he is so deep, puppy love, I wish I was never born, let me walk you through this one, to get over something/someone, to have a crush on someone, she will be turning 11, to spank someone, to compliment someone
9	*The Banks' Shot*	to play for fun, wipe out the bet, to get along with someone, put two and two together, to be hard-headed, don't mess with my boy, I wouldn't talk if I were you, you

		can take him, they hustled me, you still stink (idiomatic)
10	*Working It Out*	you know the drill, to be mean to someone, that was the last straw, to get fired, you're walking a fine line, it doesn't bother me, they're so shallow, I don't like the sound of this, lip-synch, to be the envy of her friends

2.5. Piloting the questionnaire and the audiovisual material

Questionnaires with a number of items on idiomatic expressions and content questions were drawn up and tested on a group of 27 students from a nearby school, in the same town as the other two schools from which the sample subjects of the main study were drawn. The purpose was to determine if foreign language students at intermediate level were familiar with some of the idiomatic expressions occurring within the episodes of the *Fresh Prince of Bel-Air*. This group of respondents was in every way similar to the target population the instrument was designed for.

Based on the information gathered over three weeks, alterations to the questionnaire were made. We changed all open questions and sentence completion items to multiple choice items, as the former were too difficult for respondents and more time consuming. These intermediate level students clearly had a limited writing ability at this point in their study of the English language. Also, items containing slang or colloquial terms, used mostly by the leading actor in the series, did not work very well and were screened out in the final questionnaire.

A further remark on the choice of lexical items is that, although, for methodological reasons it was advisable to use lexical phrases that were entirely new to the participants, vocabulary acquisition could also include the learning of new meanings of well known words or combinations of well known words. Put differently, the meanings did not bear any relation to the already known isolated words. For example, students knew the meaning of 'puppy' and 'love' but not the combination of the two: 'puppy love'. So they learnt the meanings of compounds and idiomatic expressions and their appropriate use at the levels of pragmatics and discourse and grammar.

2.6. The methodology

The actual data collection process took place during the regularly scheduled class periods, but in an audiovisual room equipped with a DVD player, a projector and a screen. Before each viewing session the subjects received a handout with 20 items based on the content of the episode – 10 on general comprehension of events and 10 on lexical phrases used during the episode. The lexical phrases were graphically highlighted in boldface type print, so students were immediately aware of the emphasis and of their grammatical nature, as had been explained to them at the start of the study. These ten items were assumed to be unknown to most students and were designed as a measure of new vocabulary acquisition. Why ten items of each content area? There is general consensus among survey specialists that single items are fallible and that 4-10 items aimed at the same target, but drawing upon slightly different aspects of it, are desirable (Dornyei, 2003:34). Students were asked to mark the phrases they were familiar with before viewing the episode. This helped to confirm our ad-hoc assumption of the subjects' familiarity with the phrases and to indicate how much vocabulary learning took place during the experiment.

The multiple choice options were randomly supplied in English and Portuguese, for both groups. All options were grammatically correct with respect to the stem but the distracters (incorrect alternatives) were developed mostly on the basis of literal meanings in the multiword items. The item sequence was a significant factor, following the logical organisation of the events in the audiovisual material. This reassured respondents but did not mean that content based questions were grouped together. They were intermixed with lexical phrases, depending on their appearance in the episode.

Two pauses were made during the 15-minute viewing to allow students time to answer two sets of 7 and one of 6 questions at a time (7+7+6=20). This removed the anxiety students might have felt, resulting from the pressure involved in remembering everything until the end of the episode. It also eliminated the need for students to concentrate on answering the questions whilst viewing the episode, and thereby not following the picture, subtitles and audio text with undivided attention. Students viewed all the sessions in their school's small auditorium, equipped with a DVD player, beamer and screen, the room in which classes using audiovisual aids are normally held. They were seated in rows, with an empty seat in between each student.

The first consolidation test, C01, took place after 5 weeks. Consolidation test C02 took place after weeks 6-10 of viewing sessions had been completed and questions were based on the content of weeks 6-10 only. The final consolidation test C03 took place at the end of the 10 weeks of sessions and included questions from each of the 10 weeks. The scoring system for all questionnaires was one point for each correct item. These three post-tests were presented to the students without warning and without their having been able to revise the material. Consolidation test C03 was presented three weeks after the last viewing and after a two-week holiday period.

2.7. Results

Surprisingly, and contrary to our expectations, there was no marked difference in the results between the two groups of informants. Graph 1 reflects how both groups improved their performances over the course of the study and may give an idea of the effectiveness of the procedure that was followed for the learning of the new vocabulary.

Graph 1

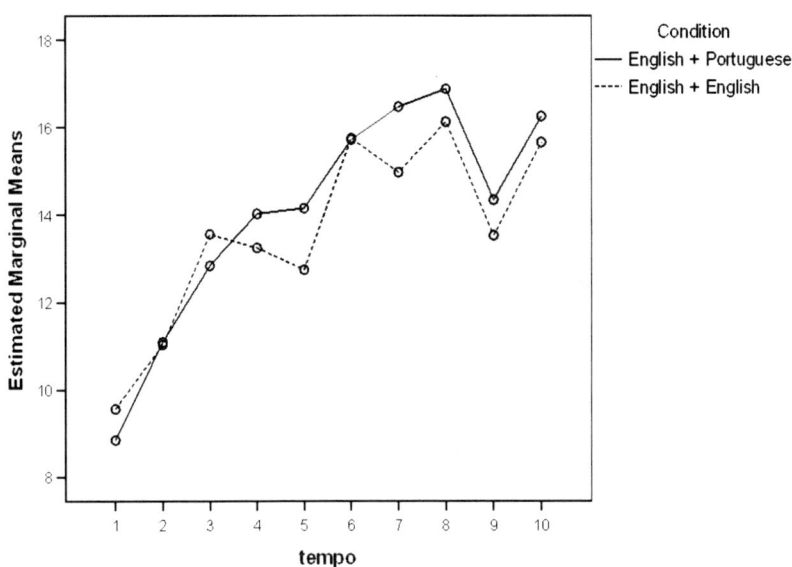

Estimated Marginal Means of MEASURE_1

From week 4 onwards there was a marked improvement in the overall performance, on the one hand, and consistently higher scores in group 1 (English audio with Portuguese subtitles), on the other hand – namely in weeks 4, 5, 7, 8 and 9. However, the truly significant differences in scores were in weeks 5 and 7, where group 1 had an advantage of 9.4% and 9.1%, respectively, over group 2. Apart from week 9, where the scores obtained by both groups dropped, group 1 revealed a steadily improving performance throughout the study.

The explanation offered by both teachers for the students' weaker performance in week 9 was that the viewing of *The Banks Shot* episode took place during the week prior to the end-of-term holidays and students had a number of tests for various other subjects during that week.

From beginning to end, students in class 1 moved from 36% to 80%; class 2 from 48% to 80%; class 3 had an initial performance of 36% and a final performance of 78%. Class 4 scored 53% at the beginning of the study and 76% at the end. The average of the 4 groups at the beginning was 43%, and almost doubled at the end with 79%. This indicates that students became familiar with, and started coping with, the viewing technique, but also, upon closer analysis, it was noticed that the initial discrepancies between groups were not significant at the end of the study. In the first week of the study, only class 4 managed to score above 50%, whereas at the end, in week 10, all 4 classes scored above 75%.

The other noteworthy factor was the Bulgarian student whose L1 was not Portuguese. Her performance in the post-tests over the 10 weeks scored the following: 5, 5, 10, 10, 16, 13, 17, 16, 13 and 15 (each score was out of 20). In the delayed consolidation tests her scores were 17 (out of 25) for C01, 16 (out of 25) for C02 and 31 (out of 50) for test C03. This student clearly experienced comprehension difficulties in the 1st and 2nd weeks but, following the tendency of all participants, overcame them after week 3 and marked an even greater improvement after week 5. The effort required by this student was much higher than for the rest as she had to rely more heavily on the English subtitles for possible explanations and content comprehension and grapple with two foreign languages when the multiple choice answers were provided in Portuguese. The processing effort needed for finding an equivalent translation in Bulgarian may have contributed to making the meaning more durable in the student's memory. Authors like Hummel (1995:451) have revealed that, in certain conditions, information which is more difficult to encode or that requires greater effort, is more memorable. The student's comments at the end of the study, in the questionnaire, were the following, translated from her sentences in Portuguese:

Advantages	*I loved watching 'The Fresh Prince of Bel-Air' and would like to watch more. Reading the subtitles helps to understand a few things that when I just hear them spoken, I don't understand.*
Disadvantages	*I don't like subtitles as I don't like reading and watching at the same time; I find subtitles distracting.*
	I will never use this technique as I normally watch films dubbed into my mother tongue (Bulgarian) or else with English audio only.

At the start of the experiment, this same student complained at not having subtitles available to her in Portuguese. It seems that she unconsciously relied on the subtitles but, when questioned, claimed to reject them.

In view of the results, the material proved to be relevant to these groups of teenagers, leading to their total engagement which, in turn, boosted their ability to learn. They were able to appreciate the humorous scripts and the recurring gags. Even though they were just required to answer questions after viewing an episode, it was not an abstract learning activity because their prior engagement had been stimulated. Part of the exercise was to provoke intellectual activity by helping them to be aware of equivalent expressions in their mother tongue and become aware of the meanings of new idioms.

3. Discussion and conclusions

In this experiment I have tried to assess whether different subtitling conditions had different effects upon the viewers' ability to perform in the post-viewing tasks, especially in understanding unknown idioms, and whether one viewing mode affected recall ability more than the other. The results revealed that the two types of subtitling did not have very different effects upon the students' capacity for performing in the post-viewing tasks. Both groups' overall performances did not differ significantly over the 10 weeks and students in both groups seemed to be unfamiliar with most of the lexical phrases in the tests. This is a likely indication that foreign language learning, at least at this level of schooling, does not focus much on such structures. Also, judging from some of the doubts students had, their age and level of schooling meant they had not yet mastered their own L1 comprehensively, with expressiveness and precision, which was a hindrance to the comprehension of the content in the foreign language.

To validate this assessment of their performance, a second set of consolidation tests was distributed to all subjects, three months after the end of the study. The tests contained 25 multiple choice items with options in L2 and 25 with options in L1 to assess whether good performance on recall was the outcome of exposure to the lexical phrases accompanied by L1 translations. The unexpected final results were very similar throughout the four classes, irrespective of their treatment condition in the experimental study. Interestingly, when the subjects were exposed to multiple choice answers in their L1, the scores were always higher than in the option of L2 answers, although the difference in scores was never higher than 5, i.e. 8%.

The multiple choice items involved more passive recognition skills and even possible guess work, as pointed out by Danan (1992). However, the results of the tests, except for consolidation test C01, reinforced the tendency to perfom better in terms of lexical phrases from week 4 onwards after exposure to standard subtitling. The score for the standard subtitling group in consolidation test C01 was a mere 0.75 of a point lower than the group with the English subtitles.

In terms of foreign language comprehension, both modes allowed for content comprehension but the standard subtitling mode – L2 audio + L1 subtitles – produced better results in all 13 tests, except in weeks 1, 3 and consolidation test C01. Consequently, hypothesis 1 holds true, that is, Portuguese students viewing English language audiovisual material with English subtitles reveal more difficulty in understanding content than those viewing audiovisual material with standard interlingual subtitles in their mother-tongue.

The multiple choice answers were randomly offered in English or Portuguese and it is not clear to what extent the translations were potentially transparent. In other words, the participants might have profited from information in the translations, even if they did not fully understand the lexical item or content in English. The results in the immediate post-tests clearly indicate that sufficient understanding and learning was taking place over the course of the study.

One of the aims at the outset seems to have been achieved, namely that of making learners aware of this resource for effective learning. As follow-up retrospective research, at the end of the study we asked the participants to complete a short questionnaire to find out their opinions regarding this experiment. The group of students who viewed the episodes with standard subtitling were naturally not asked questions about the difficulty of viewing television or films with foreign language audio and subtitles. These were some of the responses, *verbatim*, regarding the bimodal input condition:

Advantages	*Subtitles help us with our written English and also with speaking, which is a great help for when we have to read out loud in class*
	Helps in knowing how some words are written
	Learn new expressions; enrich vocabulary; learn to speak better
	Learn more vocabulary and new expressions; can also concentrate on pronunciation
	Being forced to read English makes us learn more
	Improves concentration at watching the episode/film
	Helps us to understand what we sometimes miss out on in the spoken text
	Helps us understand how sentences are constructed
	Helps you learn to wright (sic) English better
	We can pick up the pronunciation

Disadvantages	*The letters go by very quickly and there's no time to read, but maybe it's a matter of practice*
	Sometimes we don't have time to read everything; it's very fast
	Takes a bit longer to understand some things
	At the beginning of this technique it's puzzling and confusing
	We need to understand something already otherwise we miss out completely
	Difficult to read in English

The results also indicate how active viewing (i.e. the impact of images on comprehension) and student participation reflected on their performance in different vocabulary tests. Learner strategies are the key to learner autonomy, as outlined by Wenden (1985), who stresses the significance of identifying successful learning strategies in students of second languages.

However, the validity of the tests should be more convincingly supported by subsequently observed behaviour and with other communicative measures concerning the grammar point in question. For example, students should have been tested on their production skills of the said lexical phrases in delayed post-tests, both written and spoken.

The experiment also served our purposes in ascertaining that certain areas of language, such as lexical phrases, need standard subtitling, or translation, for clearer understanding and actual retention to take place. Also, one single encounter with a new lexical unit will seldom be sufficient to result in definitive learning (Schmitt and Meara, 1997).

Another aspect that is worth referring to is that the multiple choice format should have included the option of 'Don't know' or 'No response' because, although the respondent had the choice of leaving the question unanswered, the researcher is unaware if it was intentional or accidental. Having this option would avoid situations where guessing could occur. Also to be avoided are negative constructions in the items as they are deceptive and create difficulties for the respondents in understanding and answering.

This sample was truly representative of the target population in its most important general characteristics: age, nationality, educational background, EFL learning background, academic capability, and socioeconomic status. Our first question, at the outset of this study, has been answered. However, further research into the effects of subtitled audiovisual materials on Portuguese EFL learners should be carried out. At least, research should look into different age and ability groups and different aspects of the foreign language being learnt.

As the test scores in the studies are only an abstract representation of the test takers' language ability, the concept of test validity was considered from the initial stages of the test design. The multiple tests concerning the consolidation of idiomatic expressions, across time (a sub-test of all the tests after five weeks, after weeks 6 to 10, three weeks after the end of the study and again three months later), sought to ensure that the interpretations made of the test scores continued to be justified. Thus, after validating the test scores, by comparing the test takers' performances on different sub-tests, it can inferred that hypothesis 2 (i.e. recognising and retaining English idioms in the audiovisual material depends on having a translated version in L1) is only partially true. The performance scores in group 1 remained higher than those in group 2, from week 4 onwards, thereby allowing more solid grounds for generalisation and also for inferring that hypothesis 1 (i.e. students viewing English audiovisual material with English subtitles (L2+L2) reveal more difficulty in understanding content in general) was confirmed. Activating recognition rules of verbal utterances in a foreign language and reformulating the meaning in L1 takes time. Byram (2004:418) points out that the mother tongue is the language the speaker relies on for intuitive knowledge of the form, structure and meaning of language. However, the difference in performance between the L2+L2 group and the L2+L1 group was marginal and these preliminary results should not be interpreted as a conclusive answer to the most effective viewing mode for foreign language learning or improvement. Under other conditions, and over a longer period of time, with different linguistic and cultural aspects under observation, more significant test score differences might be seen. Perhaps this would lead to clearer evidence of the benefits of using the mother tongue. In addition, offering the learners the aural text in Portuguese and the subtitles in English (reversed subtitling mode) might also lead to different findings.

References

Byram, Michael (ed.) (2004) *Routledge Encyclopedia of Language Teaching and Learning.* London: Routledge.

Council of Europe (2001) *The Common European Framework of Reference for Languages: Learning, Teaching, Assessment.* Cambridge: Cambridge University Press.
www.culture2.coe.int/portfolio/documents_intro/common_framework.ht ml

Danan, Martine (1992) "Reversed subtitling and dual coding theory: new directions for foreign language instruction". *Language Learning* 42(4), 497-527.

Dornyei, Zoltan (2003) *Questionnaires in Second Language Research. Construction, Administration and Processing.* London: Lawrence Erlbaum Associates.

Harmer, Jeremy (2001) *The Practice of English Language Teaching* (3rd edition). Essex: Longman.

Hummel, Kirsten (1995) "Translation and second language learning". *The Canadian Modern Language Review* 51(3), 444-55.

Schmitt. Norbert and Paul Meara (1997) "Researching vocabulary through a word knowledge framework: word associations and verbal affixes". *Studies in Second Language Acquisition* 19 (1): 17-36.

Wenden, Anita (1985) "Facilitating learning competence: perspectives on an expanded role for second language teachers". *Canadian Modern Language Review* 41, 981-90.

Subtitling as a task and subtitles as support: pedagogical applications

Noa Talaván

Universidad de Educación a Distancia, Madrid, Spain

Abstract
This article analyses the role of both reading and producing subtitles as functional activities and didactic tools in foreign language education. Firstly, it examines the need for the educational use of both subtitles and subtitling in the classroom. Then, it provides a sample activity that exploits both tools with the aim of improving oral comprehension skills that is assessed through multi-methodological research. All in all, the didactic application of an activity based on the use of subtitles as learning support and of subtitling as the active production of subtitles by students in front of the computer, entails a series of benefits that are worth noting: it assists students in the development of oral comprehension skills, provides them with different types of support (visual, textual, and technological) for language development, encourages learners to face authentic input, and produces tangible output (the subtitles produced by students) that can be shared with their peers (or even on the web).

1. Introduction

Over the years, some foreign language teachers have criticised the use of subtitles for being a source of laziness. However, according to Rost (2002:151), "[a]lthough many teachers believe that the use of subtitles prevents students from 'really listening', judicious use of subtitles can be very effective at engaging learners in the content and motivating them to get as much as possible out of each video they use". Furthermore, it is important to realise that, no matter what, "automatic reading of subtitles does not prevent the processing of the soundtrack" (Danan, 2004:72). What is more, over time, viewers (more or less intentionally) develop strategies to process subtitles efficiently and increasingly derive more benefits from them.

Living in this modern society, where the visual component is becoming ever more powerful and the majority of the population moves between the computer and the TV and/or DVD on a daily basis, language learners may feel particularly comfortable with a foreign language activity that integrates all these familiar elements with which they interact in their private and professional lives. The fact that subtitling and subtitles bring together old and new technology may act as a motivating factor for students to face authentic foreign language exchanges from a much more stimulating perspective.

Subtitling as a task which entails the actual addition of subtitles to a clip by students, can have a notable impact on the improvement of their foreign language skills. It is, on the one hand, a functional and interactive exercise that allows students to share their work with their peers in a virtual learning environment. The use of subtitles as a support, on the other hand, presents a series of benefits for comprehension and vocabulary development. When they are used, different cues (audio, image and text) assist students in understanding a particular piece of information in the foreign language, particularly where authentic input is concerned. When both subtitling and subtitles are combined in a single task, their benefits are enhanced and they provide further paths for learning and understanding. Obviously, translation is always involved when subtitling and when using subtitles didactically, and this adds one more textual dimension to the picture: "once translation has linked the two verbal systems, viewers have established more paths for retrieval and may benefit from visual traces as well as from two distinct sets of verbal traces" (Danan, 2004:72).

The aim in these pages is to present a sample of possible pedagogical applications of subtitling and subtitles with the ultimate goal of enhancing oral comprehension skills. The potential of these activities has been scientifically assessed through a multi-methodological research design that is summarised below.

2. Subtitling and subtitles in foreign language learning

In Europe, the distinction between dubbing and subtitling countries in terms of foreign language acquisition has been discussed by authors like Dollerup (1974), d'Ydewalle and Pavakanun (1997), Díaz Cintas (2003), Gottlieb (1998), and Caimi (2008) among others. Spain, for example, is traditionally a dubbing country for different political, cultural and ideological reasons (Díaz Cintas, 2003), and this audiovisual translation choice seems to be one of the main reasons behind the poor level of proficiency in foreign languages which Spaniards appear to have. In this context, activities involving subtitling and subtitles in foreign language education are really worth the effort. A recent report by the European Commission (2005) shows significant differences as far as the acquisition of foreign language skills is concerned, based on the traditional division of European countries between dubbing and subtitling. This fact is clearly reflected in the Table 1 below (*ibid.*:3) where the responses of subtitling countries and dubbing ones are shown in sharp contrast:

Table 1

Respondents able to participate in a conversation in a language other than their mother tongue			
Subtitling Countries	Denmark 88%	Netherlands 91%	Sweden 88%
Dubbing Countries	Spain 36%	France 45%	Italy 36%

The need to promote subtitles and subtitling in foreign language learning has been acknowledged by the European Union itself, within its current agenda in defence of multilingualism: "Subtitling is a spectacular tool for helping people learn languages easily and enjoyably. A series of meetings will therefore take place in order to exploit this potential of the media with regard to language learning" (Europa, 2007:online). Unfortunately, research in this particular topic is scarce, especially when it comes to the use of subtitling as a language learning tool.

2.1. Review of previous research

A number of works have discussed the potential for using subtitles as a support for language learning. Firstly, the benefits of bimodal subtitles (intralingual, subtitles and audio in the same language) has been studied in connection with the following foreign language learning aspects: second language skills (Lambert *et al.*, 1981); overall comprehension (Holobow *et al.*, 1984); motivation (Vanderplank, 1988); phonetics and comprehension (Garza, 1991); vocabulary recognition and association (Borrás and Lafayette, 1994); listening comprehension (Huang and Eskey, 1999); implicit and explicit aspects of vocabulary learning (Bird and Williams, 2002); vocabulary building with listening and reading skills (Caimi, 2006); and listening and speaking for intermediate and advanced learners (Araújo, 2008).

Secondly, the role of standard subtitles (interlingual, mother tongue subtitles and foreign language audio) has been researched from the following perspectives: to improve linguistic balance in non-equivalent bilinguals (De Bot *et al.*, 1986); to encourage vocabulary acquisition thanks to mediation (Pavakanun and d'Ydewalle, 1992); to develop learner motivation (Ryan, 1998); to promote lexical acquisition in children (Koolstra and Beentjes, 1999); and to enhance listening and speaking in beginners (Araújo, 2008).

Thirdly, the advantages of reversed subtitles (foreign language subtitles and mother tongue audio) have been deemed to be useful when working on second language skills in general (Lambert *et al.*, 1981), comprehension in general (Holobow *et al.*, 1984), and vocabulary acquisition (d'Ydewalle and Pavakanun, 1997).

Fourthly, subtitles for the deaf and the hard-of-hearing (bimodal subtitles that provide relevant paralinguistic information contained in the soundtrack) have been discussed in relation to the following foreign language learning areas: reading fluency and metalinguistic knowledge (Parlato, 1986), the ability of immigrants to listen and read at the same time (National Captioning Institute, 1990), and motivation as well as oral comprehension improvement in intermediate students (Koskinen *et al.*, 1991; Huang and Eskey, 1999).

Finally, there are also other works that should be mentioned: several studies on the use of English subtitled materials in Japan (Kikuchi, 1998); reversed and bimodal subtitles used together to teach vocabulary (Danan, 1992); the applications of both bimodal and standard subtitles to teach lexical expressions and discourse markers (Davis, 1998); and the use of keyword captions (a summarised version of bimodal subtitles) for comprehension and language improvement (Guillory, 1998).

On the other hand, the use of subtitling software and techniques has been studied by a very small number of authors: Díaz Cintas (1995, 1997, 2008) has suggested the possible pedagogical benefits of subtitling, particularly in terms of lexical development and socio-cultural learning; Williams and Thorne (2000) undertook qualitative research on the benefits of standard and bimodal subtitling to enhance motivation and transferable skills; and Hadzilacos *et al.* (2004) developed specific software in order to use subtitling as a tool to enhance foreign language learning skills in general.

Most of the studies mentioned above make use of authentic videos. Authentic videos contextualise the learning process because they present complete communicative situations (Lonergan, 1989), including body language, socio-cultural and pragmatic aspects, among other things. Subtitles and subtitling within this setting turn into very efficient tools when used to enhance foreign language education in general and oral and reading comprehension in particular, since they allow students to monitor the input, making it truly comprehensible.

3. Pedagogical applications

After looking at this review of previous research, it follows that the production of subtitles for selected authentic video clips, combined with the use of subtitles as a support, is a fairly novel idea with promising benefits for foreign language students. Focussing on subtitling, it should be noted that the central characteristics of this professional practice, such as condensation, segmentation and synthesis (Botella Tejera, 2007), can help students to achieve a better comprehension of the oral input, since they need to understand the various communicative messages (not just the words or the grammar rules) in order to subtitle the scene. Besides, learners may also profit from the advantages of using translation as a pedagogical tool. Examples of these benefits include the fact that translation encourages students to think about meaning and form concurrently and that it helps them to notice non-equivalences in terms of form or use (Stoddart, 2000).

Subtitling can be performed in different ways, for instance, either into the students' mother tongue or into the foreign language, as a word for word transcription of the audio information, or as a summary of the main ideas. Obviously, using subtitling from a pedagogical perspective would require accompanying tasks focussed on the precise skill or issue that occupies the focal point of the lesson. In particular, subtitling as a pedagogical resource can efficiently enhance comprehension of idea units (Buck, 2001), that is, comprehension *per se*, (somehow free from grammar and lexical problems or interferences) as will be demonstrated in the experiment below.

In order to understand the potential usefulness of the pedagogical applications of subtitling and subtitles in language learning, a series of aspects needs to be defined: (1) software used, (2) subtitling mode, (3) type of subtitles, (4) video clip features, and (5) type of learning tasks. It should be noted that these parameters may vary according to the precise interests, resources and/or goals of the educational context in question:

1. The subtitling software used in this context is Subtitle Workshop (www.urusoft.net/download.php?lang=1&id=sw). Other subtitling programs can also be used. A particularly suitable alternative is LvS (Learning via Subtitling, http://levis.cti.gr/index.php?option=com_docman), a program specially developed in order to apply subtitling as a functional, didactic tool in the language class (Hadzilacos *et al.*, 2004). Both options are freeware and very user-friendly. The only difference between them is that LvS is designed to prepare the activities in advance as complete units, ready for use by the students, including clips, instructions, subtitles, comments, etc. If working with Subtitle Workshop, the in and out times for each subtitle should be selected in advance by the teacher, so that the students' work can focus just on understanding the main ideas of the scene. As noted before, the goal is not to turn foreign language students into subtitlers, but rather to use these audiovisual translation applications for didactic ends. This software is not designed to store the whole activity in advance and, therefore, it is the role of the teacher to monitor the activity progression and to provide the necessary guidelines for the students.

2. Once the software has been chosen, the subtitling mode must be selected: students can be asked to create either standard, bimodal, reversed subtitles, or even subtitles for the deaf and the hard-of-hearing. Given the inherent benefits of traditional interlingual translation as a pedagogical tool, standard subtitling has been chosen for the present activity. In fact, translation has recently been revitalised in the context of foreign language education thanks to its relevant role as far as mediation (among people, languages, cultures, etc.) is concerned (Cook, 1998; Council of Europe, 2001; Sokoli, 2006).

3. In terms of the type of subtitles that can be used as a support for comprehension, all varieties are possible, depending on the students' needs and/or goals. In the present case, bimodal subtitles have been selected since they are the most functional in general terms. They can be employed to assist oral comprehension, to develop general receptive skills, to learn about spelling, vocabulary and grammar, and also to promote writing skills.

4. As far as audiovisual material is concerned, the use of two short video clips of one to two minutes in length is a good option. These clips should be related in terms of content and vocabulary, so that students can notice their improvement in terms of comprehension from one clip to the next. The following selection criteria should be borne in mind too: it is preferable if the clips present useful, interesting, and self-contained situations, and the language exchanges suit the corresponding communicative and linguistic goals.

5. Finally, the students' tasks may take on a variety of foms depending on the didactic purpose of the lesson. In this case, the aim is the development of oral comprehension skills, and summarising and note-taking are the activities selected. These two tasks, in particular, do not guide the students' comprehension by means of fixed specific questions and answers as is usual with true/false or multiple choice activities. On the contrary, they provide them with enough freedom to select a particular comprehension path. Thus, learners just need to analyse and describe, with the help of notes, whatever they find relevant from the information received.

A sample activity outline is provided in Table 2 below, where the different stages involved are summarised and adapted to both a 60 and a 100 minute class:

Table 2

STAGE	ACTIVITIES
Pre-viewing 5/10 minutes	Oral discussions: on content, characters, opinions, vocabulary, etc.
Viewing I 10/15 minutes	First clip with bimodal subtitles and oral comprehension test or exercise
Central task 15/30 minutes	Subtitling (creating standard subtitles) plus final viewing of the resulting product (individual or collaborative)
Viewing II 10/15 minutes	Second clip with bimodal subtitles and oral comprehension test or exercise
Post-viewing 15/30 minutes	Oral discussions (on content, characters, opinions, vocabulary, etc.), lexical questions, language analysis, role-plays, etc.

The previous outline shows a general example of the stages involved in such an activity. As to the tasks that accompany the viewings, the aforementioned summary of the main ideas and messages received, during which students can take notes, has proved to be very useful in the improvement of oral comprehension skills. Nonetheless, other types of test or tasks could also fit within this framework.

As for the video clips, they should be played twice so as to counterbalance the difficulty of facing authentic input, making students' subsequent tasks relatively easier (Buck, 2001). As discussed above, the in and out timecodes necessary to create the subtitles, i.e. spotting, should be decided by the teacher in advance, so that students can just focus on subtitling the verbal input. This minimises the interference of non-linguistic technical issues, coupled with the fact that specific rules in terms of time and number of characters per subtitle do not need to be strictly followed as they might hinder the progress of the activity. What really matter are both the encouragement provided by the support given by subtitles, and the fact that subtitling a video clip encourages learners to play a very active role, offering them a functional and semi-professional result that can be immediately checked and shared with other students, teachers, and indeed almost anybody through the world wide web. This relates closely to fansubbing (Díaz Cintas and Muñoz Sánchez, 2006), whereby people create their own subtitles and upload them on the internet, so that they can be shown together with a particular video clip. YouTube, for example, frequently asks users for subtitles whenever a particular video has not yet been subtitled.

4. Undertaking multi-methodological research in the field: a sample

The previous activity was tested through a multi-methodological research design, making use of fifty subjects who undertook similar lessons in a computer room with their own individual PCs. The lessons were based on the activities described in Table 2 above, and the task accompanying the viewings took the form of an oral comprehension test. The test asked students to write a summary of the main ideas in the clip in their mother tongue, so as to make the research assessment as objective as possible. This choice avoids the interference of external factors (writing skills, grammar and vocabulary knowledge, etc.) that might obscure the results, when it comes to analysing oral comprehension individually.

4.1. Methodology

The subjects, adult students taking general English at B1 level (Council of Europe, 2001), were divided into two groups: a control group (that did not practise subtitling, but did rely on the support of subtitles) and an experimental group (that performed the whole activity). During the time in which the experimental group subtitled, students from the control group received an equivalent amount of foreign language information: they discussed the context and vocabulary in the clip in English, watching the clip three more times without subtitles. Thus, the only difference between both groups was the actual task of producing standard subtitles; that is, the remaining stages were performed by both groups in a similar way.

The goal of the study was to analyse whether oral comprehension skills improved thanks to the didactic use of subtitling and/or to the support of subtitles. Among the few studies that deal with the use of subtitling to enhance foreign language skills, Williams and Thorne (2002) highlight the fact that their students reported a considerable improvement in their listening skills. On the other hand, using bimodal subtitles as a support already involves one obvious receptive skill: reading comprehension. The close connection between listening and reading skills, i.e. the use of similar strategies for the comprehension and the decoding of language (Vandergrift, 2006), makes working on the development of oral comprehension particularly suitable when bimodal subtitles as a support are involved. Reading (subtitles in the foreign language) and listening (to foreign language oral output) make use of similar comprehension strategies which interact and assist one another in a single goal, that of improving general comprehension skills.

4.2. Results

In order to assess the validity of these audiovisual translation tools, the results of the two oral comprehension tests accompanying each of the viewings need to be compared. Apart from the tests, other assessment tools, such as observation and questionnaires, were used so as to confirm and expand the quantitative information provided by such data. Focussing on the tests, the grading was based on the number of idea units (Buck, 2001) that the students could extract from each clip.

The comparison between the results obtained by both groups in the two tests provides information as to the relevance of using subtitles as support. Figure 1 shows the general starting level of both groups and Figure 2 presents the level of progress in oral comprehension achieved by the whole group in the second viewing:

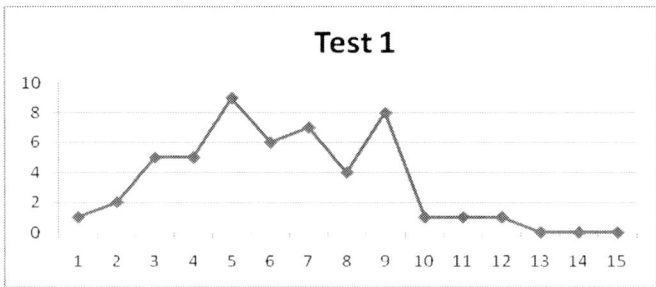

Figure 1: Test 1 – all subjects

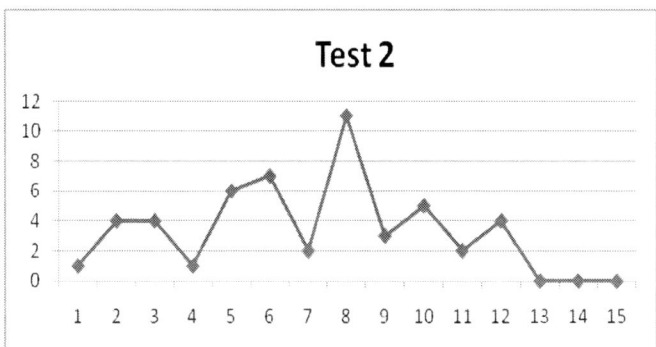

Figure 2: Test 2 – all subjects

In the first test the group average grade was 5.8 and the standard deviation 2.48, while in the second test the average was 6.6 and the standard deviation 2.98. Although the standard deviation increased in the second test, the average rose considerably and, statistically speaking, the distribution of results was much more natural. Therefore, it can tentatively be inferred that the use of subtitles as a support has a positive effect on the development of oral comprehension skills.

The second fact that needs to be highlighted concerns the results of test 2. On this occasion, the experimental and the control groups were treated separately as only the former made use of subtitling as a didactic tool. Figures 3 and 4 show this contrast:

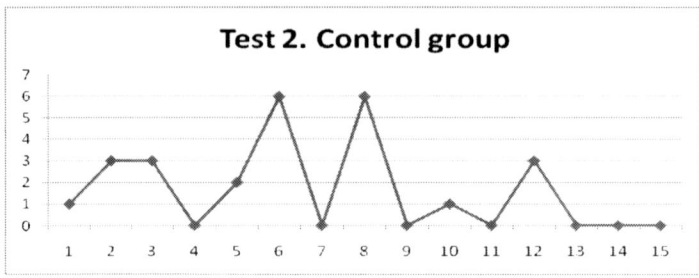

Figure 3

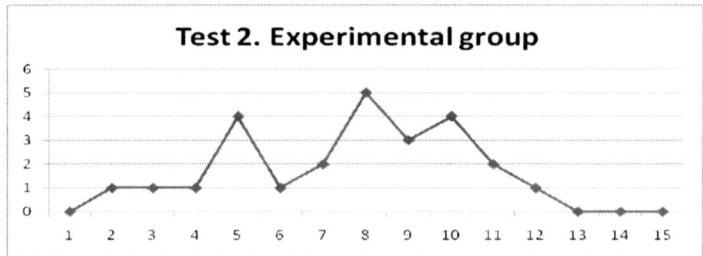

Figure 4

The control group obtained an average mark of 5.9 in the second test and the standard deviation was 3.2, while the experimental group got an average grade of 7.3 accompanied by a much lower standard deviation, 2.6, and showing a more natural distribution of results. This contrast lead to the assumption that a significant improvement in terms of oral comprehension occurs when subtitling is used as a pedagogical tool in foreign language education.

These preliminary results were subsequently confirmed through a hypothesis test that statistically proved the validity of both assumptions. The qualitative part of the research included a thorough analysis of observation and an exploitation of the results collected from the questionnaires and the oral comprehension tests. The data obtained provided the necessary triangulation to corroborate and expand the quantitative results. The following points can be said to be the main pedagogical implications derived from this research:

- The production of standard subtitles by students (subtitling as a task) helps to improve oral comprehension within a multimedia environment and following a task-based approach.
- The textual support of bimodal subtitles (subtitles as support) used when students watch authentic videos improves the comprehension of later similar viewings.
- This type of activity (that includes subtitling as a task and subtitles as a support) can foster the acquisition of a series of 'can dos' related to audiovisual comprehension, according to the *Common European Framework of Reference for Languages* (Council of Europe, 2001).
- The use of these tools encourages autonomous learning both inside and outside the classroom.
- From a didactic perspective, subtitling as a task and subtitles as support both strengthen the role of mediation in foreign language education.

5. Conclusion

All in all, the use of subtitling and subtitles combines a series of qualities that motivate, foster, and facilitate the development of oral comprehension: it is recreational, familiar and dynamic, utilises multiple codes, and makes the achievement of this receptive skill easier, both individually and collaboratively.

It is important to emphasise here Krashen's (1985) Input Hypothesis, whereby we acquire language by receiving comprehensible input or by understanding messages. Authentic videos can be challenging for the average foreign language student, but the language can be understood with the help of subtitles, either by having them already available on the screen or by creating them. In this sense, it can be stated that audiovisual translation allows students to improve foreign language acquisition. Another of Krashen's (*ibid.*) posits was that we should learn a foreign language in the same way we learn our first language. This would necessarily involve the use of authentic videos – once again accompanied by subtitling or subtitles for better understanding – as samples of authentic communication and as familiar manifestations of everyday life.

Nowadays, new technological resources such as digital and satellite TV, DVD or Blu-ray, allow the audience to choose the soundtrack and the subtitles that they want to watch. Likewise, the ever growing presence of computers nearly everywhere makes the production of subtitles by students a realistic task that can be performed both inside and outside the classroom context. Not using this type of technology to improve foreign languages in general, and English in particular, could be seen as a real waste of resources.

References

Araújo, Vera (2008) "The educational use of subtitled films in EFL teaching", in Jorge Díaz Cintas (ed.) *The Didactics of Audiovisual Translation*. Amsterdam and Philadelphia: John Benjamins, 227-38.

Bird, Stephen and John Williams (2002) "The effect of bimodal input on implicit and explicit memory: an investigation into the benefits of within-language subtitling". *Applied Psycholinguistics* 23(4): 509-33.

Borrás, Isabel and Robert Lafayette (1994) "Effects of multimedia courseware subtitling on the speaking performance of college students of French". *The Modern Language Journal* 78(1): 61-75.

Botella Tejera, Carla (2007) "Aproximación al estudio del doblaje y la subtitulación desde la perspectiva prescriptivista y la descriptivista: la traducción audiovisual". *Tonos digital: revista electrónica de estudios filológicos* 13.
www.um.es/tonosdigital/znum13/secciones/tritonos_A_doblaje.htm

Buck, Gary (2001) *Assessing Listening*. Cambridge: Cambridge University Press.

Caimi, Annamaria (2006) "Audiovisual translation and language learning: the promotion of intralingual subtitles". *The Journal of Specialised Translation* 6: 85-98.
www.jostrans.org/issue06/art_caimi.pdf

Caimi, Annamaria (2008) "Subtitling: language learners' needs vs. audiovisual market needs", in Jorge Díaz Cintas (ed.) *The Didactics of Audiovisual Translation*. Amsterdam and Philadelphia: John Benjamins, 240-53.

Cook, Guy (1998) "Use of translation in language teaching", in Mona Baker (ed,) *Routledge Encyclopaedia of Translation Studies*. London y New York: Routledge, 117-20.

Council of Europe (2001) *Common European Framework of Reference for Languages*. Cambridge: Cambridge University Press.

Danan, Martine (1992) "Reversed subtitling and dual coding theory: new directions for foreign language instruction". *Language Learning* 42(4): 497-527.

Danan, Martine (2004) "Captioning and subtitling: undervalued language learning strategies". *Meta* 49(1): 67-77.

Davis, Randall S. (1998). "Captioned video: making it work for you". *The Internet TESL Journal* 4(3).
http://iteslj.org/Techniques/Davis-CaptionedVideo

De Bot, Kees, John Jagt, Henk Janssen, Erik Kessels and Erik Schils (1986) "Foreign television and language maintenance". *Second Language Research* 2(1): 72-82.

Díaz Cintas, Jorge (1995) "El subtitulado como técnica docente". *Vida Hispánica* 12: 10-4.

Díaz Cintas, Jorge (1997) "Un ejemplo de explotación de los medios audiovisuales en la didáctica de lenguas extranjeras", in María del Carmen Cuéllar (ed.) *Las nuevas tecnologías integradas en la programación didáctica de lenguas extranjeras.* Valencia: Universidad de Valencia, 181-91.

Díaz Cintas, Jorge (2003) *Teoría y práctica de la subtitulación.* Barcelona: Ariel.

Díaz Cintas, Jorge (2008) "Teaching and learning to subtitle in an academic environment", in Jorge Díaz Cintas (ed.) *The Didactics of Audiovisual Translation.* Amsterdam and Philadelphia: John Benjamins, 89-103.

Díaz Cintas, Jorge and Pablo Muñoz Sánchez. 2006. "Fansubs: audiovisual translation in an amateur environment". *The Journal of Specialised Translation* 6: 37-52.
www.jostrans.org/issue06/art_diaz_munoz.pdf

d'Ydewalle, Géry and Ubolwanna Pavakanun (1997) "Could enjoying a movie lead to language acquisition?", in Peter Winterhoff-Spurk and Tom H.A. van der Voort (eds) *New Horizons in Media Psychology.* Opladen: Westdeutscher-Verlag, 145-55.

Dollerup, Cay (1974) "On subtitles in television programmes". *Babel* 20(4): 197-202.

Europa (2007) *A Political Agenda for Multilingualism.* Europa Rapid Press Releases.
http://europa.eu/rapid/pressReleasesAction.do?reference=MEMO/07/80&format=HTML&aged=1&language=EN&guiLanguage=fr

European Commission (2005) *Europeans and Languages.* Eurobarometer 237. http://ec.europa.eu/public_opinion/archives/ebs/ebs_237.en.pdf

Guillory, Helen G. (1998) "The effects of keyword captions to authentic French video on learner comprehension". *CALICO Journal* 15(1-3): 89-109.

Garza, Thomas (1991) "Evaluating the use of captioned video materials in advanced foreign language learning". *Foreign Language Annals* 24(3): 239-58.

Gottlieb, Henrik (1998) "Subtitling", in Mona Baker (ed.) *Routledge Encyclopedia of Translation Studies.* London and New York: Routledge, 244-8.

Hadzilacos, Thanasis, Spyros Papadakis and Stavroula Sokoli (2004) "Learner's version of a professional environment: film subtitling as an ICTE tool for foreign language learning". Proceedings *World Conference on E-Learning in Corporate, Government, Healthcare, and Higher Education 2004.* Wachington, DC., 680-5.

Holobow, N., W. Lambert and L. Sayegh (1984) "Pairing script and dialogue: combinations that show promise for second or foreign language learning". *Language Learning* 34(4): 59-76.

Huang, Hsin-Chuan and David E. Eskey (1999) "The effects of closed-captioned television on the listening comprehension of intermediate English as a Second Language (ESL) students". *Journal of Educational Technology Systems* 28(1): 75-96.

Kikuchi, Toshikazu (1998) "A review of research on the educational use of English captioned materials in Japan". *Memoirs of Numazu College of Technology* 32: 147-60.

Koolstra, Cees M. and Johannes Beentjes (1999) "Children's vocabulary acquisition in a foreign language through watching subtitled television programs at home". *Educational Technology Research and Development* 47: 51-60.

Koskinen, Patricia, Robert Wilson, Linda Gambrell and Carl Jensema (1991) "Captioned video technology and television-based reading instruction". *Literacy: Issues and Practice. Yearbook of the State of Maryland International Reading Association*. Maryland, Massachussets: Bethesda, 39-47.

Krashen, Stephen (1985) *The Input Hypothesis: Issues and Implications.* Essex: Longman.

Lambert, W., I. Boehler and N. Sidoti (1981) "Choosing the languages of subtitles and spoken dialogues for media presentations: implications for second language education". *Applied Psycholinguistics* 2(2): 133-48.

Lonergan, Jack (1989) *Video in Language Teaching*. Cambridge: Cambridge University Press.

National Captioning Institute (1990) *Using Captioned Television to Improve the Reading Proficiency of Language Minority Students*. Falls Church, Virginia: National Captioning Institute.

Parlato, Salvatore (1986) *Watch Your Language: Captioned Media for Literacy*. Silver Spring, Maryland: T. J. Publishers.

Pavakanun, Ubolwanna and Géry d'Ydewalle (1992) "Watching foreign television programs and language learning". *Cognitive Modelling and Interactive Environments in Language Learning* 1: 193-8.

Rost, Michael (2002) *Teaching and Researching Listening*. London: Longman.

Ryan, Stephen (1998) "Using films to develop learner motivation". *The Internet TESL Journal* 4(11).
http://iteslj.org/Articles/Ryan-Films.html

Sokoli, Stavroula (2006) "Learning via Subtitling (LvS): a tool for the creation of foreign language learning activities based on film subtitling", in Mary Carroll, Heidrun Gerzymisch-Arbogast and Sandra Nauert (eds)

Proceedings of the Marie Curie Euroconferences MuTra: Audiovisual Translation Scenarios.
www.euroconferences.info/proceedings/2006_Proceedings/2006_Sokoli_ Stravoula.pdf
Stoddart, Jonathan (2000) "Teaching through translation". *British Council Journal* 11: 6-13.
www.britishcouncil.org/portugal-inenglish-2000apr-teaching-through-translation.pdf
Vandergrift, Larry (2006) "Second language listening: listening ability or language proficiency?". *The Modern Language Journal* 90(1): 6-18.
Vanderplank, Robert (1988) "The value of teletext sub-titles in language learning". *ELT Journal* 42(4): 272-81.
Williams, Helen and David Thorne (2000) "The value of teletext subtitling as a medium for language learning". *System* 28(2): 217-28.

Notes on contributors

Conceição Bravo grew up in South Africa. Her interest in translation came as a necessary skill for foreign-language learning/teaching and stemmed from an upbringing in this culturally diversified and multilingual environment. She holds an MA in Postcolonial Studies and a PhD in "Translation and Intercultural Studies", from Universitat Rovira I Virgili, Spain. She teaches English Language and Culture in the Language Department at the University of the Algarve and Portuguese to foreign Erasmus students. She is particularly interested in audiovisual translation, in the form of subtitles, as an aid in FL learning/teaching and as a mediator between cultures.

Cristóbal Cabeza i Cáceres holds a BA in Translation Studies and is currently working on his PhD. He lectures in subtitling for the deaf and heard of hearing and audio description in the MA in Audiovisual Translation at Universitat Autònoma de Barcelona. He also works as a professional audiovisual translator and has participated in the Spanish audio description of films such as Woody Allen's *Match Point* and Isabel Coixet's *Elegy*. Since 2007 he has been audio describing operas in Catalan at Barcelona's Liceu Theatre.

Agnieszka Chmiel works as an Assistant Professor in the Department of Translation Studies at the School of English, Adam Mickiewicz University in Poznan, Poland, where she has trained conference interpreters since 2000. In her 2004 PhD thesis she focussed on the neurocognitive aspects of conference interpreting. Her research interests include conference interpreting, audio description, audiovisual translation, cognitive studies, memory and visual imagery in interpreting. She also works as an interpreter and translator.

Jorge Díaz Cintas is Senior Lecturer in Translation at Imperial College, London. He is the author of numerous articles and books on audiovisual translation, including *Audiovisual Translation: Subtitling* (with Aline Remael, 2007), *Media for All* (co-edited, 2007), *The Didactics of Audiovisual Translation* (edited, 2008), *Audiovisual Translation: Language Transfer on Screen* (co-edited, 2009) and *New Trends in Audiovisual Translation* (edited, 2009). Since 2002, he has been the president of the European Association for Studies in Screen Translation. He is a member of the international research group TransMedia.

Anna Foerster holds an MA in Applied Translation Studies from the University of Leeds and is writing her PhD on Aesthetics in Subtitling at Imperial College, London. She works as a guest lecturer at London Metropolitan University, where she teaches Translation Studies and Audiovisual Translation and has many years of working experience as a translator and subtitler for large TV stations, leading subtitling companies as well as film and theatre productions.

Adrián Fuentes Luque is Senior Lecturer at the Universidad de Cádiz and the Universidad Pablo Olavide in Seville, Spain. He is also a professional translator, having served as Senior Translator at the Australian Embassy in Spain. His research areas include audiovisual translation, the translation of humour, and the translation of advertising and tourist texts. He is the editor of *La traducción en el sector turístico* (Atrio, 2005), the first monograph on translation in the tourist sector.

Elena Zagar Galvão is currently working towards a PhD in Translation Studies at the University of Porto, Portugal. She has an MA in English Studies from the University of Tennessee at Knoxville, a postgraduate diploma in Translation and Terminology from the University of Porto, and a degree in translation from the University of Trieste, Italy. Since 1998 she has been teaching general and specialised translation at the University of Porto. She also works as a freelance interpreter and is a member of AIIC.

Anna Matamala is a member of the TransMedia international research group, and a full-time lecturer at the Universitat Autònoma de Barcelona, where she is the director of the MA in Audiovisual Translation and teaches audiovisual translation. She has been working as an audiovisual translator for the Catalan television (TVC) for more than ten years and holds a PhD in Applied Linguistics from the Universitat Pompeu Fabra. Her main interests are audiovisual translation, media accessibility and applied linguistics. She has taken part in many regional, national and international funded research projects on audiovisual translation and media accessibility, and has published in international refereed journals such as *The Translator*, *Catalan Journal of Linguistics* and *Perspectives*.

Jenny Mattsson received her PhD in English linguistics in 2009 from the University of Gothenburg, Sweden. Her main academic interests are translation studies and pragmatics, and she combined them both in her PhD thesis entitled *The Subtitling of Discourse Particles*. She has presented her research at several international conferences and has published several articles on the subject. She is a member of the European Association for Studies in Screen Translation (ESIST).

Josélia Neves holds a degree in Modern Languages and Literature, a Masters in English Studies and a PhD in Translation Studies with a thesis on Subtitling for the Deaf and Hard of Hearing. She has worked as a subtitler for over 10 years and has been teaching Audiovisual Translation since 1997. She has carried out a number of projects with television broadcasters, DVD producers, museums and education providers for the provision of inclusive communication solutions for sensory impaired people. She has considerable experience teaching AVT at postgraduate level and has been guest lecturer in postgraduate programmes throughout Europe. She is in charge of audiovisual translation on a PhD programme at the University of Coimbra, Portugal. She is presently working on a postdoctoral research project at Imperial College, London.

Kristijan Nikolić is a freelance subtitler, a university lecturer of translation at the Department of English, Faculty of Philosophy, University of Zagreb, and a PhD student of translation at the University of Vienna. He has been doing research in translation and subtitling.

Alicia Palomo López holds a BA in Translation and Interpreting from the University of Malaga (Spain) and an MA in Audiovisual Translation from Roehampton University where she completed her dissertation on audio description for children. She currently works as a visiting lecturer at Roehampton University and is writing her PhD thesis on audio description at Universitat Jaume I, Castellón, Spain. Alicia has delivered papers on AD at various international conferences and has published several articles on the topic.

Jan Pedersen was educated at the Universities of Stockholm, Copenhagen and Uppsala. He received a PhD from Stockholm University in 2007 with a dissertation entitled *Scandinavian Subtitles, a Comparative Study of TV Subtitling in the Scandinavian Countries*. He is vice president of the European Association for Studies in Screen Translation (ESIST), and constituting member of TraNor. He also worked as a translator for many years, subtitling shows like *Late Show with David Letterman*, *The Simpsons* and *Nikolaj og Julie*. Jan teaches courses in linguistics and translation theory at the English Department at Stockholm University, where he is Director of Studies.

Irene Ranzato is a translator and a visiting lecturer at Sapienza University of Rome, where she teaches English language, audiovisual translation and intersemiotic translation. She has written several articles on translation and a book on Tom Stoppard. She is currently translating and editing the letters between Evelyn Waugh and Nancy Mitford. She is researching for a PhD in Translation at Imperial College, London, focussing on forms of manipulation and censorship in dubbing translation.

Isabel Galhano Rodrigues studied Linguistics, Germanic and Romance Philology at Christian-Albrechts-University in Kiel, Germany. She holds two MAs with a thesis on contrastive linguistics and on turn-taking in conversational signals. Her PhD on speech and body movements in face-to-face interaction was published in 2007. She is Associate Professor at the Faculty of Arts of the University of Porto, Portugal. Her research interests include multimodality in face-to-face interaction and other specific contexts, gesture choreography, and gesture space in Portuguese spoken in different cultures.

Gala Rodríguez Posadas graduated in 2005 from the University of Granada, Spain, with a degree in Translation and Interpreting and a final-year dissertation on cohesion in audio description. In 2006 she completed a postgraduate course in SDH and AD and has since worked as a freelance audio describer for ONCE, the Spanish National Organisation for Blind People. In 2007 she received her Diploma in Doctoral Studies. After four years of collaboration with the TRACCE project, financed by the Spanish Science and Technology Ministry, she received a placement in order to develop her PhD through a pre-doctoral grant with AMATRA in 2008, a project financed by the Andalusian Government.

Pablo Romero-Fresco is a Senior Lecturer in Audiovisual Translation at Roehampton University, where he teaches dubbing, subtitling and respeaking. He has also taught respeaking as part of the MA programmes on Audiovisual Translation at the Università di Bologna (Forlì) and Universitat Autònoma de Barcelona, both on-campus and online. He is a member of the research group Transmedia Catalonia, for which he co-ordinates the EU-funded research project D'Artagnan (DTV4ALL), which focusses on the optimisation of subtitling for the deaf and hard-of-hearing on digital TV.

Agnieszka Szarkowska holds a PhD in Audiovisual Translation from the Institute of English Studies at the University of Warsaw, Poland. Now an assistant professor at the Translation Studies Department in the Institute of Applied Linguistics at her alma mater, she teaches translation and works as a freelance translator. Her research interests include audiovisual translation, especially subtitling for the deaf and hard-of-hearing, interlingual subtitling, audio description as well as translator training and e-learning. She is a member of ESIST and takes part in the DTV4ALL project.

Noa Talaván holds a PhD in Audiovisual Translation from the Universidad Nacional de Education a Distancia, Spain, where she is a junior lecturer in the Foreign Languages Department. She specialises in audiovisual translation and foreign language education. She is a certified translator (English-Spanish) and currently holds a position as academic coordinator of English C1 at the Centro Universitario de Idiomas a Distancia, Spain.

Maria José Veiga is a researcher in the Departamento de Linguas e Culturas at the University of Aveiro, Portugal. Her research interests are in linguistics and literature. She wrote her PhD on the subtitling of audiovisual humour. Her publications include foreign language methodology, Portuguese and Anglo-American literature, and audiovisual translation.

Patrick Zabalbeascoa works at Pompeu Fabra University in Barcelona, Spain. He lectures in translation theory, humour translation, and audiovisual translation, mostly from English into Spanish and Catalan. His research is focussed on translation studies, with special attention to audiovisual texts. He has also dealt with translation theory, developed a model of priorities and restrictions, and proposed alternative approaches to traditional views on translation techniques, or shifts. His research interests, and much of his teaching, also embrace aspects in the translation of humour and metaphor. Some of his most recent thinking and publications have to do with developing the idea of mapping translation solutions through a system of binary branching, and also mapping audiovisual text components on coordinates defined by an audio/visual axis, and a verbal/non-verbal axis.

Soledad Zárate completed a Master's degree in Audiovisual Translation at Roehampton University, London, and wrote a thesis on *Subtitling for Deaf Children on British Television*. She has contributed articles to *The NDCS Magazine* and *The Sign Language Translator and Interpreter* and given papers at international conferences in Antwerp (Belgium), Łódź (Poland), Leiria (Portugal), Montpellier (France) and Berlin (Germany). Since April 2008 she has been conducting doctoral research at Imperial College, London on *Subtitling for Deaf Children*, with a particular focus on the incidental learning that takes place in the process of reading subtitles.

Index

Lightning Source UK Ltd.
Milton Keynes UK
UKOW04f1857100215

246043UK00001B/76/P